I am blessed to know Leo. His passion for sharing the Gospel and seeing people transformed by Christ is refreshing and challenging. The encounters shared here will bless you and keep you mindful that the Great Commission is the mission.

Dr. Lee Brand Jr., senior pastor of Faith Baptist Church in Bartlett, Tennessee

If there is a man who exemplifies living on mission, fulfilling the Great Commission, and teaching others to do the same, it's Leo Lytle. This book is filled with fascinating accounts of the extraordinary things God can do through willing vessels.

The Rev. Jeremiah Walpert, pastor of Twin Rivers Church in Springfield, Oregon

I've known Bro. Leo Lytle for more than 40 years. One thing that he has been consistent in is sharing the Gospel and seeing many folks come to know Jesus Christ as their personal Lord and Savior. I'm excited for this book as he and Valerie take us on this Cross journey.

Dr. Richard Kaufman, pastor of Martin Baptist Church in Martin, Louisiana

Leo Lytle has a heart for reaching people for Jesus, and Valerie has proven to be a true supporter and ministry partner. The people they've met and the stories they tell are sure to inspire all who read this book!

Dr. Kent and Donna Lenard, Good Exchange Baptist Church in McLeod, Texas

"Therefore go," (Matt. 28:19). In 1988, Leo Lytle became my pastor/brother. From then to now, Leo has been outside the walls of the church building with evangelism, reaching souls for Christ! Even now, with wife Valerie, they are crisscrossing America, fulfilling the "going" with the Cross Ministry. Now read and enjoy their journey.

The Rev. Lloyd Bye; Pineville, Louisiana

"Available!" It's the one word that describes the Lytles. They are available to listen and to share with everyone the Gospel of Jesus Christ wherever the Lord leads and they have opportunity. The experiences of how they have been used to carry out the Great Commission are amazing.

The Rev. Dan Flyger,
Pastor of Fellowship Baptist Church in Scotland, South Dakota

In 2024, Bro. Leo Lytle and I crossed paths along the Gospel trail. Our connection was immediate because we shared a common purpose as laborers together with God. I feel privileged to regard Leo and Valerie as my friends in Christ, having observed their unwavering dedication to sharing the Gospel message of Jesus Christ with a world in need. This burden unmistakably drives their ministry. Leo and Valerie exemplify devoted service to our Lord and Savior Jesus Christ.

The Rev. Jeffrey Johnson, pastor of Kennedy Baptist Church in Pavo, Georgia

CROSS-ing AMERICA

Sharing Jesus Around the Nation

Leo Bell Lytle III
and Valerie Lynne Culp-Lytle

CROSS-ing AMERICA

Sharing Jesus Around the Nation

Leo Bell Lytle III
and Valerie Lynne Culp-Lytle

NEBP
NORTHEASTERN BAPTIST PRESS
Bennington, VT

Published by Northeastern Baptist Press
      Post Office Box 4600
      Bennington, VT 05201

Cover design and typesetting by Leason "Tripper" Stiles

Softcover ISBN: 978-1-953331-74-8

For I am not ashamed of the gospel of Christ:
for it is the power of God unto salvation
to every one that believeth;
to the Jew first, and also to the Greek.

Romans 1:16

Table of Contents

Dedication

By Leo and Valerie Lytle
November 2024, Pine Valley, Texas

Just as the Cross Ministry involves many people all working together for the cause of Christ, we find that even the dedication of our book cannot be narrowed down to just one person. We are going to spotlight the late George Darren Watson for the dedication. But we first want to also dedicate our book to the following people:

Evangelist Joe Aulds and his wife, Donna Aulds. Joe was the pastor under whom Leo surrendered to preach. Leo says he learned from Joe the "importance and the power of preaching the inerrant word of God."

Dale and LaVera Frost, co-founders of the Cross Ministry

Lawrence (Buddy) and Susie Jordan, co-founders of the Cross Ministry

Vic Bass of Vic Bass Ministries and his wife, Sheila Bass

Steve Cowart, pastor of Trinity Baptist Church in Lufkin
and his wife, Donna Cowart

The Cross Men and the Cross Women

Our multi-generational families and our parents: the late
Nellie Mae Lytle and the late J. Fred Lytle and Ida Mae Culp and
the late David Merle Culp

George Darren Watson
(May 26, 1963 – September 21, 1998)

Friends from 1985 until Darren's death from a complication of leukemia in 1998, Leo credits George Darren Watson with teaching him to love street evangelism. On Bourbon Street in New Orleans, La., Leo learned from Darren how to stand strong for Jesus even in the face of derision. When somebody spit from a balcony onto Darren's back once, Leo had only a Gospel tract on hand with which to wipe the large glob of spittle off Darren's coat. But Darren stopped him.

"Don't waste a tract on it," Darren said.

Leo says his street evangelism experiences with Darren Watson laid the groundwork for our ministry across America today.

"I admired his courage, his commitment and his love for those who were lost," Leo said. "I fondly remember those times with Darren."

On another occasion, Darren was standing alone in the French Quarter holding a large wooden cross and passing out Gospel tracts when a woman came up to him and took him to task.

"You should be ashamed of yourself," the woman said to him, as Darren later told Leo. "I'm a Christian. You're embarrassing Christ by being out here in the French Quarter with a cross."

Darren's response was one that Leo often repeats:

"Ma'am," Darren said to the woman politely. "I like my way of doing it a lot better than your way of not doing it."

From Darren, Leo learned to ignore the criticism of the world, most of whom are not doing anything for the cause of Christ anyway. He learned to stand for the Savior however He leads.

"George Darren Watson was the real deal," Leo says. "He loved Jesus! He loved people! His example of sharing Jesus 'outside the walls' of the church has played a foundational role in our ministry! I miss him --- but I know where he is!"

For I am not ashamed of the gospel of Christ: for it is the power of God unto salvation to every one that believeth; to the Jew first, and also to the Greek.
Romans 1:16 KJV

An Overview:
Border To Border, Coast To Coast

By Valerie Culp-Lytle
August 2025, Pine Valley, Texas

"I will praise thee, O Lord, with my whole heart;
I will shew forth all thy marvelous works."
Psalm 9:1 KJV

———————

Once we get started testifying about the wonders God has done, it's hard to stop. We have seen His hand at work so many times. Our ministry takes us border to border, coast to coast around the United States and even to other countries. Everywhere we go, we see the faithfulness of God. This book is us sharing some of what we've seen and experienced as we have done our best to share the Good News of the Gospel of Jesus Christ with a lost world.

Here's a little sample of the type of stories you'll find here. It's better than taking us to lunch. At least with the book you can take a break when needed (she wrote, with a smile.) These are some of our favorites that didn't get included in the main body of the book, which is based on our first seven years in evangelism. Truly, we can just go on and on — and on — about the goodness of God.

———————

San Luis, Arizona

The young man seemed a bit dazed. He sounded like a soldier reporting to his next duty station with orders that he didn't fully understand.

CROSS-ing AMERICA
Sharing Jesus Around The Nation

Leo and I were set up in San Luis, Arizona with the United States/Mexico border just out of sight. It was late September 2023, still very hot. We had our usual set up of wooden crosses arrayed around us, but we were making heavy weather of the Spanish language. Virtually everyone who passed by us was speaking Spanish and definitely did not have anywhere near the comfort with English that we had thought they would have.

Now, I did study some Spanish in college in the early 1980s. I also did take care of a number of Spanish-speaking women in my nearly 20 years as a fulltime labor and delivery nurse. But this background lends itself to my inclination to begin most conversations by telling people to take off all their clothes, put on a gown – open to the back – and leave a urine sample in the little cup. Press the call bell-button if they feel the urge to push. That only takes one so far in general conversation and not very far at all in evangelism!

There in San Luis, with Mexico about a block away, the stark border wall brusquely divided the arid landscape in two. Passersby were speaking some other version of Spanish besides my careful, present-tense, textbook Castilian Spanish. As for Leo, he can order quesadillas and tamales in a Mexican restaurant, but that's the extent of his Spanish skill. The situation made it very difficult to engage with people. Leo and I bowed our heads in that parking lot and prayed, something to the effect: "Lord, we are here. Please use us to tell people about You. But You know we are having a language issue."

In what seemed like less than five minutes, Raul stood in front of us.

Did he want a free cross, we asked. Sure, he would take one, he told us. But that's not why he was there. He said he was supposed to help us. He went on to tell us that he had been driving with his mother when he spotted us and felt such a strong conviction in his heart to get involved that he took his mother home and came right back. He just knew that he was supposed to help us, he repeated. Did we need an interpreter?

God is good! He always supplies any need we have. For the next couple of hours, Raul stayed with us, faithfully translating. We saw several people pray to be saved. The young man shared that he was a Believer, active in his church, and had been feeling led for the past two years or so to start sharing his faith. But, he told us, he did not really know how to share his faith or how to even get started.

Wow, God! We saw what You did there. What took place in those couple of hours that Raul stood with us on the street in San Luis, Arizona was a compressed sort of Paul and Timothy interaction. Leo gave Raul a crash course in evangelism, and Raul soaked it up. When we parted company, we felt led to leave Raul with some evangelism tools. We gave him about 25 "Jesus Is Lord" crosses as well as some Gospel tracts, Bibles in Spanish and Bible study workbooks for new Believers in Spanish. We prayed for him as we left. As it turned out, we had to pass by the same spot a little while later as we were finding our way out of town. Raul was still in that parking lot. He seemed to be earnestly engaged in a Gospel conversation. Raul is definitely one of the many people we hope to see again in Heaven. We want to hear how God kept working in his life.

As earlier expressed, the stories in this book are quick snapshots of a few of the myriad times that God has worked in our lives. We stand amazed. We want to make sure to give God all the glory. As the beloved hymn says, "Great things He hath done!"

Most of the time, the tools that God has allowed us to use are wooden crosses made out of a fence picket. They have the words "Jesus Is Lord" stenciled on them. Leo shares the background story of the "Jesus Is Lord" crosses early in the book. The recurrent theme in the story of the crosses is God raising up one person after another to do His will and accomplish His purpose. A whole book could certainly be written about the actual making of the crosses and all the people and all the provision of God involved in that process. But where Leo and I come in is in the distribution of those crosses. We do NOT just give them away. Instead, we do our best to use them to talk to people about Jesus. Leo shares in the book how he came to realize what powerful tools for evangelism the crosses could be.

"When Brother Leo came on board, it changed the whole dynamic," Lawrence "Buddy" Jordan said in a June 2023 meeting of cross ministry leaders. Mr. Jordan is one of the founders of the cross ministry in East Texas, along with his brother-in-law, Dale Frost.

Vic Bass, leader of Vic Bass Ministries, agreed. Vic Bass had come alongside Mr. Jordan and Mr. Frost to help lead the cross ministry for several years before eventually passing that torch to Trinity Baptist Church in Lufkin, Texas. Longtime brothers in the faith, Leo said he vividly remembers Bro. Vic saying to him that there had to be a way they could work together. Leo took a load of crosses on one of his preaching trips across the country, and the Holy Spirit revealed to him how the crosses could be active soul-winning tools.

"When we put a cross in Leo's hands, it changed everything," Vic Bass said in that June 2023 meeting of cross ministry leaders.

Steve Cowart, pastor of Trinity Baptist Church in Lufkin, Texas, which currently administers the cross ministry, shared in that June 2023 meeting how much more effective this type of street ministry is for reaching lost people as compared to traditional church. For all a church's expenditures, programs and preaching, many churches these days see relatively few people saved, Pastor Cowart said. He said he and the members of his church are so happy to be a vital part of a ministry that is actively reaching the lost and seeing many, many people come to Jesus.

The subject of reaching souls for Jesus makes me want to offer clarification. We tell the people we meet that establishing a personal relationship with Jesus Christ is between Him and them. Just repeating religious words does not save a person.

We tell a lost person that Jesus is reading his or her heart when he or she prays to be saved. He is looking for genuine belief that He is the son of God, that He willingly died on the cross to pay for sin, and that He arose from the dead. Jesus is looking for genuine repentance and desire to be forgiven of sin, a genuine desire for Him to be one's Lord and Savior, and a genuine desire to accept the free gift He alone offers of eternal life. Our role is to point people to Jesus and help them establish a relationship with Him if they want to be guided in that direction. The Holy Spirit takes it from there.

We do also tell them to find a Bible-preaching church and to follow the Lord in Believer's baptism as an outward symbol of an inward change. We give them a Bible, a Gospel tract, a Bible study book aimed at new Believers, a pen and Leo's cell phone number in case they have questions. When we are working in conjunction with a local church, we love to be able to introduce the new Believer to church leaders who can invite them to join their local church body. Again, the Holy Spirit takes it from there.

California; across the border from Tecate, Mexico

The Holy Spirit has a lot of work to do when Leo and I are on the road. It was during that same trip in September 2023 along the United States/ Mexico border, when God raised up another interpreter. In this case, Ramon "Ray" Garcia called Leo's cell phone while we were driving in California. He said a friend of his had seen Leo's number on our van while we slept at a rest stop for truckers. Ray, who holds international chaplain credentials, also offered to interpret. We gratefully accepted, and called him when we decided where to set up the next day. Ray drove to join us and stayed with us translating until we left the area. We remain social media friends to this day. Ray is a faithful encourager to us.

Imperial Beach, California

Before we met Ray, we had met one person after another in Imperial Beach, California who the Holy Spirit sent to us. On that day, also in September 2023, we saw God supply one need after another, within minutes of each need arising. Imperial Beach, California is famous as the most southwesterly city in the continental United States. But where to set up in the most southwesterly city in the continental United States was not immediately apparent to us. The Holy Spirit brought us Robert "Bob" Truxall right away to lead us to a good spot to share. We hadn't been there very long when we met somebody who said he worked with incarcerated young people and saw a huge need for some kind of Christian ministry in that facility. Almost immediately, here came someone who did jail and prison ministry, so that we could try to get those two people in contact with one another.

Just a little while later in the same spot, I was able to lead a young man to the Lord. He listened attentively to everything I had to say and prayed to be saved. Afterwards, he shared that he had just been released from either jail or prison. Again, almost immediately, here came someone who worked at a nearby church who had himself been incarcerated and was now living for Jesus. He invited the young man to that next Sunday's church service and told him to plan on sitting with him. The young man accepted the invitation eagerly. The young man's mother was standing with him. Tears of joy were shining in her eyes as she saw these events unfold and her son start down the right track for a change. In real time, she was seeing one prayer for her son after another being answered. Answered prayer, after answered prayer... I had tears of joy in my eyes, too.

So often Leo and I are, in fact, privileged to harvest seeds that were planted much earlier by somebody else and watered by the prayers and tears of somebody else. It is not unusual for a man or woman to pray to be saved and then tell us that their parents or their grandmother or their wife has been praying for them for years. We love to be able to have the blessing of the harvest. But we also rejoice in being able to plant a seed or water one. When someone allows us to share, but declines to make a decision for Jesus, we often say "Seed well-planted and well-watered." Then we just have to pray that somebody else comes along someday for the harvest, or that the person learned enough to seek out additional spiritual counsel on their own. The Holy Spirit can certainly keep working on a person's heart long after their fleeting encounter with us.

Hall Summit, Louisiana

It was in Hall Summit, Louisiana in 2022 where Leo was able to harvest a seed planted years earlier and watered by so many tears and prayers of Godly parents. Leo was sharing crosses at an outdoor event. Evangelist Sam Moore from Arkansas was scheduled to speak later in the day. A young woman would turn out to be the only person who prayed to be saved that day with Leo. She would also turn out to be the daughter of a pastor and wife whom Leo had met in the past.

We found out about the "rest of the story," as the late radio broadcaster Paul Harvey used to say, at a Bible conference we attended later that same year in Louisiana. Some mention had been made of our ministry in the general assembly, and a pastor's wife stood up and said she had something to share. We have since become better-acquainted friends. She and her husband have given us permission to share their daughter's story.

As the mother told the assembled group of church leaders, their daughter had fallen into a bad crowd while still in high school. She got involved with a gang, started doing drugs and rejected the Christian teaching of her parents. Her life was on a downward spiral.

"We could not reach her," her mother told the audience. "But Leo could." The Holy Spirit used whatever words Leo spoke to the prodigal daughter that day to soften her heart, convict her of her sin and call her to Himself. She prayed to be forgiven and to be saved. According to her parents, she has lived for Jesus ever since. All glory to God!

Leo Bell Lytle III
and Valerie Lynne Culp-Lytle

Vista, California

One more "rest of the story" for now. On that same trip along the U.S./ Mexico border in September 2023, we got a call from a man who was behind us on an overpass in Vista, California. Leo shares this man's story in the chapter entitled "This and That." It culminates with the man, who said he had been an atheist for most of his life, praying to be saved. But it was about a year and a half later that we learned the follow-up. Bro. Vic's phone number was on the back of the large cross Leo gave the man in Vista. The man texted to say thank you and to share more of his story. Here is his exact text message:

"Hello so sorry but long ago like year and a half or year you were in cali in vista on the freeway and you were giving away crosses which I got a big one and small one and wanted to say thank you so much for being Gods worker cause that day was a day I was planning a suicide so I prayed asking God for a sign and literally you are giving away crosses."

It is SUCH a privilege to be "God's worker." We hope you enjoy reading these testimonies of God's goodness as much as we enjoyed living them. We know you'll join us in saying, "All glory to God!"

Preface

By Valerie Culp-Lytle
October 2024, Pine Valley, Texas

*"But watch thou in all things, endure afflictions,
do the work of an evangelist, make full proof of thy ministry."*
2 Timothy 4:5 KJV

This book was basically finished when our oldest daughter asked us why we had written it.

She was editing it for us and raised a good point. She said if a non-Believer finds our book lying on a bench in a bus station someday and starts reading it, the non-Believer will probably wonder why we bother doing what we do. What is the point?

That is an excellent question to answer first. We had not really thought about people not understanding the urgency we feel to share the Gospel of Jesus Christ. Certainly we encounter non-Believers out in the world. We even count a scant handful of non-Believers among our friends and family. But the overwhelming majority of our friends and family believe as we do.

So, here's the answer for why we do what we do:

Leo and I believe that God, Jesus and the Holy Spirit are real and true. God, Jesus and the Holy Spirit are the Holy Trinity, God in three persons. We believe Jesus Christ is the resurrected Son of God and that belief in Jesus and acceptance of the forgiveness and salvation He alone can provide is the only way to be saved and to gain Eternal Life. We believe each person must make the decision to accept or reject Jesus Christ as Savior and Lord for himself or herself.

This decision must be made while the person is still alive. We absolutely do not believe that another person can pray a person out of Hell into Heaven after that person has already died. Nor can anybody donate enough money to move a person who has already died from Hell to Heaven. Nobody knows how long he or she will live. Death is certain. Heaven and Hell are real. Therein lies our feeling of urgency to reach lost people while we can, whenever we can.

2 Corinthians 6:2, KJV, says in part: *"... now is the accepted time; behold, now is the day of salvation."*

For those who are exposed to the Gospel message and yet choose to reject it, we believe that an eternity in Hell awaits. We believe Hell is a literal place of physical, emotional, mental and spiritual anguish and pain, and forever separation from God. So, when we lead a person to the Lord, we believe we are literally rescuing that individual from unending torment in Hell after they die.

A photograph I saw once illustrates the concept beautifully. In the picture, a sheep labeled "Lost Person" is being swept away by raging flood water. Holding onto the sheep in peril with all the strength he can spare and not be swept away himself is another man labeled "The Evangelist." Standing on dry ground and helping both to secure the Evangelist's footing and provide more pulling strength to rescue the flood victim is a second man labeled "The Church." The photograph is one of those clever illustrations that floats around the Internet. It didn't come with any credit or attribution. But my hat is off to whomever dreamed up the illustration, because it is so apt.

Of course, nobody can be saved without first being drawn by the Holy Spirit. The Bible says it like this:

"No man can come to me, except the Father which hath sent me draw him: and I will raise him up at the last day." - John 6:44 KJV

The role of an evangelist is to work with the Holy Spirit to explain God's plan of salvation when the Holy Spirit begins to draw a lost person to Himself. The Holy Spirit softens the lost person's heart and opens his eyes to his sin and his need for repentance and a Savior. Then the evangelist, standing at the edge of the floodwaters, so to speak, is ready with a Scriptural explanation to illuminate the way. Leo does this by explaining to the person at risk that the only spiritual safety is found in the Lord Jesus Christ. The church --- in our case, several churches and numerous fellow Believers --- have our backs and provide prayer and financial support. As Leo's wife and fellow follower of Jesus, I do what I can to help.

Leo Bell Lytle III
and Valerie Lynne Culp-Lytle

One more illustration that also beautifully depicts how Leo and I think of our efforts to share the Gospel of Jesus Christ can be found in the famous starfish story. The starfish story is one of those often-quoted bits of writing that illustrate a truth. Its actual name is "The Star Thrower." It is part of a 16-page essay by the same name written by Loren Eiseley, published in 1969, according to Wikipedia.

In "The Star Thrower," -- paraphrasing: *A young boy is walking along a beach where he sees that hundreds of starfish have been washed up onto the shore and left behind by the receding tide. He is picking them up one by one and flinging them back into the water so that they do not die on the sand. A man comes along and asks why he is bothering to make the effort.*

"You can't possibly save all these starfish," the man says to the boy. "What difference do you think you can really make?"

Without pausing, the young boy walks to the next starfish, picks it up and tosses it into the water.

"Just made a difference to that one," he replies.

That's how Leo and I feel about what we do, coming behind the Holy Spirit. We can only make a difference to a limited number of people. But to those people, the difference is Eternity spent rejoicing with Jesus. Like the boy on the beach, Leo and I are going to keep on doing what we can to make a difference.

How To Go
To Heaven

Heaven clearly sounds like the best place to spend Eternity. But how does a person **get** to Heaven? How can an unworthy human being approach a holy and righteous God? The answer is found in the person of Jesus Christ. Jesus' finished work on the cross created a bridge for Believers to cross from Earth into Heaven, with the cross serving to span the chasm of sin that would otherwise always separate us from God.

Jesus said it like this:

"Jesus saith unto him, I am the way, the truth, and the life: no man cometh unto the Father, but by me." John 14:6 KJV

The Gospel is beautifully summarized in this one Scripture, found in John 3:16:

"For God so loved the world, that he gave his only begotten Son, that whosoever believeth in him should not perish, but have everlasting life." John 3:16 KJV

Many Christians use a collection of Scriptures taken from the Bible's New Testament book of Romans to show how to be saved. It is called "The Romans Road," and it includes the following verses. The boldface subheads listed here were provided by an Internet site called "Bible Study Tools":

The Human Problem: Sin
"For all have sinned, and come short of the glory of God;" – Romans 3:23 KJV

The Consequence of Sin:
"For the wages of sin is death; but the gift of God is eternal life through Jesus Christ our Lord." – Romans 6:23 KJV

The Solution: Christ's Sacrifice

"But God commendeth his love toward us, in that, while we were yet sinners, Christ died for us." – Romans 5:8 KJV

The Response: Faith

"That if thou shalt confess with thy mouth the Lord Jesus, and shalt believe in thine heart that God hath raised him from the dead, thou shalt be saved." – Romans 10:9 KJV

The Assurance of Salvation

"For whosoever shall call upon the name of the Lord shall be saved." – Romans 10:13 KJV

The Result of Salvation: Peace with God

"Therefore being justified by faith, we have peace with God through our Lord Jesus Christ." – Romans 5:1 KJV

Living In The Spirit

"There is therefore now no condemnation to them which are in Christ Jesus, who walk not after the flesh but after the Spirit." – Romans 8:1 KJV

Those are some of the Bible verses that deal with the topic of salvation. When a person accepts the truth of these verses for himself, admits his sin, repents and asks for forgiveness of his sin and wants to be saved, that person prays to Jesus with a spirit of repentance and faith. The late, great evangelist Billy Graham recommended the following version of the sinner's prayer:

"Dear Lord Jesus, I know that I am a sinner, and I ask for Your forgiveness. I believe You died for my sins and rose from the dead. I turn from my sins and invite You to come into my heart and life. I want to trust and follow You as my Lord and Savior. In Your Name, Amen."

Jesus reads each person's heart as he prays to Him to be saved. Jesus alone can judge genuine repentance and genuine faith. Jesus wants everybody to come to Him by faith. We cannot earn or deserve the forgiveness and eternal life that comes with salvation. We are saved by grace.

"He is not willing that any should perish, but that all should come to repentance." – 2 Peter 3:9 KJV

Leo Bell Lytle III
and Valerie Lynne Culp-Lytle

"For by grace are ye saved through faith; and that not of yourselves: it is the gift of God: not of works, lest any man should boast." – Ephesians 2: 8-9

One more look at what the Bible says about salvation:

"Believe on the Lord Jesus Christ, and thou shalt be saved." Acts 16:31 KJV

In summary, the Gospel of Jesus Christ tells us that God sent His only son, Jesus, to die on the cross to pay for our sins. If we are truly sorry for our sins, we can ask Jesus to wash us clean with His blood that He shed on the cross and forgive us of our sins. We can ask Him to come into our heart and life and save our soul by asking Him to save us and become our personal Lord and Savior. We accept His free gift of salvation and eternal life. We then ask Him to help us to follow Him all the days of our lives and thank Him for saving us. Some Believers like to sum up the response to the Gospel with an ABC format:

A: ADMIT that you're a sinner.

B: BELIEVE that Jesus is God's Son and that Jesus died on the cross to save us from our sins. Believe He rose from the dead on the third day and is alive today.

C: CONFESS your faith in Christ.

Once a person has prayed to be saved, the Bible is full of instructions for Believers about how best to live their lives in a way that will be pleasing to God. A new Believer can start with baptism, which does not save a person, but is instead a way to publicly identify with Jesus Christ and symbolize dying to one's old, sinful way of life to be raised in newness of life with Him. It is important to begin attending a Bible-preaching church and having fellowship with other Christians. Regular Bible study and prayer are also vital building blocks in the Christian life.

If you have asked Jesus to save you and want to reach out to us, we would be happy to research your area and help you locate a Bible-preaching church. Our mailing address is Leo Lytle Ministries, P.O. Box 158, Diboll, TX 75941. Leo's phone number for texting is 936-225-1660. We can also receive messages or posted comments on our Facebook page entitled "Leo Lytle Ministries."

Welcome to God's family!

Foreword by Leo

September 2024, Pine Valley, Texas

"For I am not ashamed of the gospel of Christ: for it is the power of God unto salvation to everyone that believeth; to the Jew first, and also to the Greek." Romans 1:16 KJV

Thank you for taking the time to read our book. It is a small sampling of some of our experiences over the past seven years as we've traveled to every state in America sharing Jesus Christ and free crosses. We have also been privileged to share the Gospel in Mexico, Canada and Nicaragua. We sometimes sing Willie Nelson's hit song, "On the Road Again" as we start a new trip. Certainly, I am grateful to still be having new adventures with the Lord (for context, I am 71 years old on the eve of this book being published).

It is always exciting to begin each journey with a trailer loaded with 2,000-plus "Jesus Is Lord" crosses graciously provided by Trinity Baptist Church in Lufkin, Texas and a team of volunteers from local churches. They are called the "Cross Men" and "Cross Women," and they faithfully cut, paint, and assemble multiple thousands of these crosses every year. Their efforts enable us to share them with folks in towns and cities across the nation. Only Heaven knows the impact their efforts are having across the country!

In addition, Bro. Vic Bass has assembled a prayer team that undergirds this effort every mile of the way. On each trip, we text him where we plan to go and update the day's happenings every evening. Bro. Vic passes the information along to his prayer team as soon as we update him. He likes to say, "we are riding with you."

CROSS-ing AMERICA
Sharing Jesus Around The Nation

The sign on the back of our trailer reads:

FREE CROSSES
936-225-1660
CALL: I'LL PULL OVER

Usually before we even leave East Texas somebody calls, and the first soul is won to Christ.

Normally, we have an invitation or several invitations for me to preach that provide the skeleton of the trip. But we are never quite sure where the LORD will lead us to stop along the way. The one thing we have learned is this: when we stop at a vacant parking lot or an abandoned business, put out the FREE CROSSES signs and scatter crosses around our trailer, people are going to stop to get one. It happens in Vermont, it happens in California, it happens in Michigan, it happens in South Carolina – it happens all over America!

This opens an opportunity to ask them the all-important question I learned many years ago from Evangelism Explosion, developed by the late Dr. D. James Kennedy: *"Have you come to the place in your life where you know for certain that if you were to die today you would go to Heaven?"* It's a thought-provoking and powerful question that cuts to the chase – to what is really important – where will you spend eternity?

What I love about this method of sharing Christ is two-fold. First, we're not out knocking on doors. They are coming to us. That's hard to beat! Secondly, we are able to begin an almost immediate spiritual conversation with those who stop. After all, they're stopping to get a free cross on which these words are clearly painted: "Jesus Is Lord." So, we're not going to waste too much time talking about the weather.

This has proven to be a very effective method to share the unchanging Gospel message. In my 50 years so far of sharing Jesus, I've never seen a more efficient and productive way of reaching the lost and hurting "outside the walls" of our churches. We urge pastors and church leaders to give it a try in their communities.

We trust that as you read this book, God will not only encourage you, but challenge you to do what you can to "go and tell." Friends, our world is hurting like never before and the only hope is Jesus. With a heart full of His unchanging love, reach out with the blessed Gospel and tell somebody!

Foreword by Valerie

September 2024, Pine Valley, Texas

"Praise ye the Lord. Praise the Lord, O my soul.
While I live will I praise the Lord:
I will sing praises unto my God while I have any being."
Psalm 146:1-2 KJV

We have not been wandering in the wilderness these past seven years. But we have zig-zagged around the nation, again and again. If one drew lines on a map that traced our routes, those lines would look like we were wandering. Up and down, back and forth and all around in the United States of America, we have traveled. We have stood on countless patches of cracked concrete holding up crosses and leading people to the Lord.

We have not been **wandering**, though. We have been **following**. We have been following the leading of the Holy Spirit and responding to every opportunity that came our way. If a church, for example, invited Leo to preach or to present "The Door," we accepted the invitation. Along the way, there and back, we would do street ministry in the towns on our route. We would also try to find other churches that might want him to preach while we were in the neighborhood.

God has honored that approach. More than 5,000 people have prayed to be saved after we shared the Gospel with them during the first seven years of this ministry. These conversions have taken place outside the walls of a church for the most part, occurring mostly on the side of the road or in abandoned parking lots. All glory to God!

CROSS-ing AMERICA
Sharing Jesus Around The Nation

We've given away "Jesus Is Lord" crosses and shared the good news of the Gospel of Jesus Christ in all 50 states and in two provinces in Canada during our first seven years in evangelism. Leo shared crosses and preached in Mexico in 2024. We also traveled to Nicaragua in 2024, albeit without the wooden crosses. Leo preached in Nicaragua, led many people to the Lord there, and we both spoke to youth. As Leo said in his foreword, I am also grateful to still be having new adventures with the Lord. (UP-DATE: I am 65 years old on the eve of this book being published.)

Seven is a number of completion in the Bible. So, as we approach the completion of seven years in evangelism, it seemed to us the appropriate time to stop and stack stones, so to speak. We are offering this book as a monument to testify as to God's provision, protection, leading and blessing. Our intention is that this book gives thanks and praise to God and testifies to His sovereign majesty.

Our prayerful hope is that this book will also inspire other people to both take a stand for Jesus and to step out for Him. A brave stand. A bold step. And then another step and another and another.

We also prayerfully hope that should this book be read by anybody still lost, that it would point them to Jesus and encourage them to seek the salvation that is only found in Him.

As we look forward to whatever new horizons the Lord has in store for us in evangelism, we thank Him for the fact that our seventh year in evangelism will be complete on March 31, 2025, if He is willing. It has been a rollicking ride on a winding road. To somewhat simulate that rollicking ride on a winding road, the chapters in this book represent destinations that weave in and among one another, rather like the actual travel did at the time. We went wherever we were asked to go.

The exception to the flexible presentation is the group of stories from the year 2020. That year will forever be important in world history because of the COVID-19 pandemic. Those stories we have presented in chronological order as our contribution to the historical record of that tumultuous year.

Leo and I are just two members of the vast team of people who make up the Cross Ministry. There are other people who share the "Jesus Is Lord" crosses and lead people to the Lord. Many of them are friends of ours. For any of us to have crosses to share, they must first be built. That task is accomplished by a team of dedicated volunteers called the Cross Men and the Cross Women. They start with cedar fence pickets and then cut the wood, assemble the pieces, paint the words, stack the crosses and deliver the crosses.

Vic Bass of Vic Bass Ministries heads up dedicated prayer teams who bathe the whole effort in prayer. Bro. Vic's supportive wife and soldier for the Lord is Sheila Bass. Steve Cowart is pastor of Trinity Baptist Church in Lufkin, which now oversees the making of the crosses. Pastor Steve's supportive wife and soldier for the Lord is Donna Cowart.

Vic Bass Ministries turned over the management of the Cross Ministry to Trinity Baptist Church in Lufkin in December 2023 after leading it for years. Prior to Bro. Vic taking the helm of the Cross outreach effort, the Cross Ministry was headed by Lawrence "Buddy" Jordan of Lufkin, Texas and Dale Frost of Nacogdoches, Texas. These two men, who are brothers-in-law, are married to supportive wives and soldiers for the Lord as well. They are Susie Jordan and LaVera Frost.

The Cross Ministry requires financial, administrative and organizational efforts to keep it afloat. The Cross Ministry also requires generous donors who supply the money to buy the wood that become the crosses that attract the people to stop. The people then listen to the Gospel message, are wooed by the Holy Spirit and end up praying to be saved. The Lord has raised up volunteers in all these areas who help accomplish His kingdom work.

So many more people are involved in this great work. We have 12 supporting churches. We have friends and family and social media followers who also pray for our evangelism outreach and some who donate Bibles to be given away. Cecilia Vann, a sweet volunteer from Trinity Baptist Church in Lufkin, makes our handmade signs.

Leo and I are simply two more soldiers in this large volunteer army for the Lord. But we are two people who have seen firsthand the goodness of God. We are two people who are raising a "Hallelujah." We are two people who are saying, "Look at the great thing God did here --- and here and here and there." We are two people who want to leave a monument so that God's goodness is remembered. For that purpose, we thank you very much for reading this book.

All glory to God!

Stories From The Road

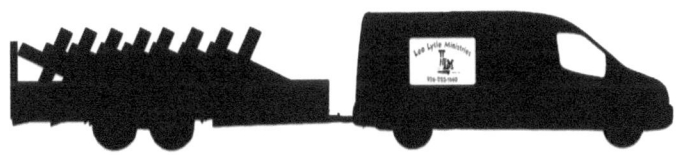

1

The Perfect Picture

By Valerie Culp-Lytle
September 2022, Cambridge, New York

"Therefore be ye also ready:
for in such an hour as ye think not the Son of man cometh..."
Matthew 24:44 KJV

R ain was looming. The weather forecast said so, and we could all see it in the massing clouds.

Whatever we were going to do, we had to do it right away. There was no time to waste.

Leo was preaching in Cambridge, New York at Open Bible Baptist Church, pastored at that time by Dr. Mark Ballard, president of Northeastern Baptist College in Bennington, Vermont. It was September 2022. Several students from Northeastern Baptist College were in attendance at the morning church service. The plan was for them to join us in sharing "Jesus Is Lord" crosses on the sidewalk right outside the church in downtown Cambridge. Our hope was to be able to lead some people to Jesus.

With the sky about to open any minute, we all sprang into action the moment the final "Amen" was uttered. We ran out of the front door of the church. Everybody picked up a cross and found a place on the sidewalk. There was a smile on every face. We were excited to be together and about the Lord's business. Very soon we were interacting with passersby. The rain did start, but it fell softly. So, we just stayed where we were, doing our best to share Jesus in the rain.

It struck me as I stood there with those earnest young people: this is how Christians should live every day. Truly, there is no time to waste. The day is approaching for the Lord's return. The Bible says so, and we can all see it in fulfilled prophecies and world events. The best thing to do is for each of us to joyfully take up our cross and run to share Jesus with the world.

2

Stack Stones: Always Remember

By Valerie Culp-Lytle
September 2024, Pine Valley, Texas

"And he spake unto the children of Israel, saying, When your children shall ask their fathers in time to come, saying, What mean these stones? Then ye shall let your children know, saying, Israel came over this Jordan on dry land."
Joshua 4: 21-22 KJV

———

Rocks in the wilderness. The chapters in this book are our rocks in the wilderness.

The Bible has numerous accounts of the Israelites setting up altars to commemorate a blessing that God granted them in a particular place. Special days, annual feasts and observances were also ordained to glorify

and thank God for an act of supernatural provision and protection. The altars, special days, feasts and observances would also serve as a tool for helping future generations know what God had done.

Sometimes the memory aids were rocks. They were stones set into place to mark a miracle of God. The stones would serve as a site for gratitude and praise as well as serve as a tangible and enduring reminder. Generations to follow would be taught what mighty work of God happened there.

It is important to note that these memorials were set into place and a period of reflection and thanksgiving observed BEFORE God's children kept pressing forward. God's people were not supposed to just keep going and going. Certainly, they were never to take for granted any favor of God. Instead, God's children were to stop right then and mark the miracle. They were to reflect and offer thanks and praise. They were to commit to teaching their children and their children's children and beyond what God had done for them. Furthermore, they were to earnestly seek God's favor anew each time a need would arise.

This is exactly what we are doing with the chapters in this book. Before we keep going, we want to stop to give glory and praise to God for what

He has already done in our ministry. We never want to take for granted the favor of God. Instead, we thank Him afresh for each instance of His provision and protection. We will seek His direction and blessing for each new undertaking before we embark on it. And always, we want to remember the goodness of God. It is our sincere hope that these chapters will serve as tangible and enduring reminders of the mighty works of God for years to come and generations to follow.

The Bible cites several times that stones were used to mark sacred spots. The first rocks of remembrance were those that Jacob slept on during the night when he dreamed of a ladder going from Earth to Heaven. Genesis 28:14,18-19 tells how the next morning, Jacob made a pillar of those stones and poured oil atop the pillar. These rocks were to mark the spot where God told Jacob in that dream that his seed would spread over all the earth and that in him and in his seed all the families of the earth would be blessed. Jacob called that place Bethel. (Genesis 28:14, 18-19)

Leo Bell Lytle III
and Valerie Lynne Culp-Lytle

Rocks in the wilderness show up again in the Old Testament as the Israelites were at long last about to enter the Promised Land. Joshua 3 gives an account of the Israelites coming up against the Jordan River in full flood stage. The floodwaters were yet another obstacle before they could finally set foot in the Promised Land. But the flooding river did not stop them. God told Joshua to tell the priests carrying the ark of the covenant to step into the Jordan River, and He would stop the flow of the water. That is exactly what happened. In a miracle reminiscent of

how God had held back the waters of the Red Sea decades earlier when the Israelites were in flight from Egypt, God heaped up the waters of the Jordan River until every single Israelite passed over on dry land. God held back the water at both the beginning and the end of His children's long journey to the Promised Land.

As soon as the last Israelite was safely out of the Jordan's riverbed, God had new instructions for Joshua. God told Joshua to select one man from each of the 12 tribes of Israel. Each man was to shoulder a large stone from the spot in the river where the priests had stood on dry land. They were to carry the stones to their lodging place for the night. Joshua placed 12 stones in the river itself on the spots where the priests had stood. But then Joshua also stacked 12 stones in Gilgal, which was the first place the Israelites camped after crossing the Jordan River and entering the Promised Land.

The King James Version of Joshua 4:20-24 describes it this way:

Joshua 4:20: "And those 12 stones, which they took out of Jordan, did Joshua pitch in Gilgal.

Joshua 4:21: "And he spake unto the children of Israel, saying, When your children shall ask their fathers in time to come, saying, What mean these stones?"

Joshua 4:22: "Then ye shall let your children know, saying, Israel came over this Jordan on dry land.

Joshua 4:23: "For the Lord your God dried up the waters of Jordan from before you, until ye were passed over, as the Lord your God did to the Red sea, which he dried up from before us, until we were gone over:

Joshua 4:24: "That all the people of the earth might know the hand of the Lord, that it is mighty: that ye might fear the Lord your God for ever."

A third time we see a rock in the wilderness used to mark a miracle of God is after God gives victory in battle to the Israelites over the Philistines. The Israelites had been in fear for their lives, but God granted them a decisive and long-lasting victory instead. Scripture in 1 Samuel tells what happened immediately after God delivered His people:

"Then Samuel took a stone, and set it between Mizpeh and Shen, and called the name of it Ebenezer, saying, Hitherto hath the Lord helped us." (1 Samuel 7:12 KJV)

We are in our seventh year of evangelism at this writing. For seven years so far -- and counting – we have watched with amazement and gratitude as God has provided for and protected us again and again. Human beings are incapable of ever adequately expressing the full glory of God. But with these words we do attempt to record at least some of God's loving kindness to us so far. We want those who come after us to know what God has done to allow Leo Lytle Ministries to accomplish Kingdom work.

Our book is like the stone the prophet Samuel called Ebenezer. Samuel said of the stone Ebenezer -- and we echo – "Hitherto hath the Lord helped us." All glory to God.

3

The Story of the "Jesus Is Lord" Crosses

By Leo Lytle

2024, Lufkin, Texas

"For the preaching of the cross is to them that perish, foolishness;
but unto us which are saved, it is the power of God."
I Corinthians 1:18 KJV

———————

More than a million "Jesus Is Lord" crosses built at this writing and thousands of people who have prayed to be saved can all be traced back to backlash against the actions of one man and his fight against the cross. Instead of stamping out a handful of the symbols of Christianity in his town, the actions of this man instead led to more than a million crosses being spread to all 50 states and even other countries. The cross numbers continue to grow, being made and distributed all year.

God has a way of bringing about eventual good from a difficult situation. The story of Joseph and his brothers in Genesis, for example, shows Joseph revealing himself to his brothers years after they sold him into slavery and telling them that God had used their actions for good, as a way to save them from famine gripping the land.

"But as for you, ye thought evil against me; but God meant it unto good, to bring to pass, as it is this day, to save much people alive." Genesis 50:20 KJV.

CROSS-ing AMERICA
Sharing Jesus Around The Nation

It is often said that God works in mysterious ways. Certainly, that is true in the story of the "Jesus Is Lord" crosses. The cross-making effort local to Lufkin, Texas traces its origins back to the actions of that one aforementioned man in Michigan, who self-identified as an atheist, and a subsequent sermon preached by one evangelist at a church in Lufkin, Texas. The cross-making effort local to Lufkin, Texas has seen, since 2015, a group of mostly senior adult volunteers making the "Jesus Is Lord" yard crosses that have been freely distributed across the United States. They have made well more than a million crosses at the time of this writing.

(Update on the eve of this book's publication, September 2025: An additional 100,000 crosses have been made.)

My wife, Valerie, and I have been blessed to be part of this unique ministry since 2018 by using these crosses to share the Gospel throughout America. What follows is the story of how it all got started. The two sources used for this background came from an article in Villages-News [The Villages, Florida] published January 30, 2017 and from a story in The Saginaw News published May 12, 2008.

These news accounts detail a civic turmoil in a small town in Michigan named Frankenmuth. The city was founded in the 1840s by a group of Bavarian immigrants who came to the area as missionaries. It has a rich Christian heritage. Many years later, with private donations, the city approved the erection of a 55-foot cross in a local park in 1976. It was done in recognition of their Christian heritage and America's bicentennial. In fact, the Frankenmuth city crest displays a Luther Rose and includes a heart, flower and cross in honor of the city's Lutheran origins.

In 2008, a resident of Frankenmuth who said he identified as an atheist took exception to two wooden crosses prominently displayed on a bridge in Frankenmuth that spans the Cass River. With the help of the Washington D.C.-based organization Americans United for the Separation of Church and State, he was successful in having the city of Frankenmuth remove those crosses from the bridge. Then the atheist decided to take it a step further and have the tiny white cross removed from the city's crest. This would prove to be a step too far for the city's residents who were exceptionally proud of their Christian heritage.

The residents acted. Led by the local associate pastor of the St. Lorenz Evangelical Lutheran Church, the Rev. Mark Brandt, they made close to 1,000 three-foot crosses. Hundreds of the residents of Frankenmuth displayed them in their yards all over the community. After seeing this

Leo Bell Lytle III
and Valerie Lynne Culp-Lytle

quiet but effective display of their pride in the town's Christian heritage, the atheist removed his complaint. He commented on his decision saying, "They're good people, and I don't want to feel unwelcome. I didn't mean for it to be disruptive."

We later learned he moved to a different town in Michigan.

But the reverberations were just beginning to be felt.

In January 2015, some 1,221 miles from Frankenmuth and seven years after the atheist's lawsuit, revival services took place at Denman Avenue Baptist Church in Lufkin, Texas. In one of his messages that week, the guest evangelist, Bro. Bob Pitman of Muscle Shoals, Alabama, challenged those in attendance to consider what they could do to make a difference for Christ. He challenged them to find something each of them could do and then do it! Two men who attended that service were especially moved by the message – brothers-in-law Lawrence "Buddy" Jordan of Lufkin, Texas and Dale Frost of Nacogdoches, Texas.

In the following days, they met together with their wives, Susie Jordan and LaVera Frost, and prayerfully considered what they could do. Dale shared a newspaper article with the group about the church in Frankenmuth that he had received in an email. After much discussion and prayer, they decided to start making crosses in East Texas. They carefully designed a cross using a wooden fence picket on which they painted the simple but powerful message, "Jesus Is Lord."

In February 2015 both men separately sent a letter to Bro. Pitman, the evangelist who preached the revival at Denman Avenue Baptist Church, thanking him for the challenging message and informing him of their plans. Lawrence "Buddy" Jordan wrote in part:

"I searched my soul for what I might be doing as just one person to help bring our nation back to Christ! I have partnered with my brother-in-law, Dale Frost, to put crosses in every yard in our cities (Lufkin and Nacogdoches, Texas)."

CROSS-ing AMERICA
Sharing Jesus Around The Nation

Dale Frost wrote in part:

"I heard your message that evening, and the Holy Spirit spoke to me. My brother-in-law and I formed a plan that evening to start building crosses and give them away free of charge."

Dale began to make crosses in Nacogdoches, Texas and "Buddy" started making them in Lufkin. Soon they were distributing thousands of them in both of their communities and other nearby towns. However, they couldn't keep up with the demand. In God's perfect and impeccable timing, He raised up Bro. Vic Bass to join the two brothers-in-laws to help meet that demand.

Bro. Vic Bass, who lived in nearby Diboll, Texas, was intrigued when he first saw the crosses. He started making them and began organizing volunteers to help. Soon Bro. Vic joined forces with Dale Frost and Lawrence "Buddy" Jordan and consolidated this effort into a very productive operation. The "Jesus Is Lord" crosses were being produced by the thou-

sands. Volunteers organized by Bro. Vic, soon to be known as the "Cross Men" and "Cross Women," followed the same design that the Jordans and the Frosts were using. Like mushrooms popping up after a rain, "Jesus Is Lord" crosses begin to appear in front yards, in front of businesses,on roadsides and in all sorts of places across East Texas.

As time went by, some of the original volunteers who had been working with Bro. Vic turned their attention to other priorities. It grew more difficult for the remaining volunteers to keep up with the demand for crosses. Bro. Vic is fond of sharing the story of how he was fighting discouragement, driving one day while praying tearfully for the Lord to please send him some help. He felt led to stop in at Trinity Baptist Church in Lufkin to talk to the pastor about it. But he didn't know how his request would be received, as he was not acquainted with the pastor there, nor the members.

Trinity Baptist Pastor Steve Cowart listened attentively. He promised to find at least four volunteer men who would help Bro. Vic the next morning. Sure enough, the promised volunteers were ready to go the next day. It turned out to be a match made in Heaven. Members of Trinity Baptist Church embraced making the crosses with gusto and, in fact, began enthusiastically supporting all aspects of the Cross Ministry.

At the time of this writing, more than one million "Jesus Is Lord" crosses have been distributed across America from border to border and coast to coast. Most importantly, many of the crosses have been used as a tool to lead recipients to a relationship with Jesus Christ as their Savior and Lord. All Glory to God!

The cross ministry continues, but some of the details of day-to-day operations have changed over time. At the end of 2023, Bro. Vic Bass and

his wife, Shelia, moved to Marble Falls, Texas to be closer to their son and their grandchildren. Bro. Vic continues to lead his prayer team of faithful prayer warriors who are absolutely essential to the ministry. Bro. Vic turned over the production of these amazing crosses into the very capable hands of Pastor Steve Cowart of Trinity Baptist Church in Lufkin, Texas. Many of the Cross Men and Cross Women are also members there. They have not missed a beat as they continue this wonderful ministry.

(UPDATE: On the eve of this book's publication, September 2025, Trinity Baptist Church in Lufkin has made 100,000 of the crosses since assuming administration of the Cross Ministry. That's a great start toward a second million!)

Who would have ever guessed that God would use the actions of an atheist to help spread the Gospel. As the "Jesus Is Lord" crosses continue to be spread around the nation, only God knows what the eventual impact of these quiet witnesses for Him will be. To God Be the Glory!

ADDITIONAL UPDATE

On the eve of this book's publication, August 2025,
we had the privilege of going to Frankenmuth, Michigan

By Valerie Culp-Lytle

Eddie Beyerlein is the man who made the very first wooden cross that led directly to the current, vibrant Cross Ministry headquartered in Lufkin, Texas at Trinity Baptist Church. Mr. Beyerlein is 93 years old now, still a faithful member of St. Lorenz Evangelical Lutheran Church in Frankenmuth. Leo and I were privileged to spend about two hours with Mr. Beyerlein and his wife, Jane, on Friday (August 29, 2025) at their home in Frankenmuth, Michigan.

The Holy Spirit worked everything out so beautifully. We were all given the gift of seeing a perfect full-circle unfold before our eyes.

Had Leo and I arrived at St. Lorenz Evangelical Lutheran Church two minutes earlier or two minutes later, we would likely not have encountered Mike Block, who was leaving his brother-in-law's funeral. We had driven to Frankenmuth from Flint, Michigan, where we had led several people to the Lord in front of an abandoned building. God's perfect timing was very much in evidence.

Leo had started trying to make contact with the folks at St. Lorenz Evangelical Lutheran Church weeks earlier. He had followed up with more calls before we left. But he had not been able to reach anybody who knew much about the 2008-2009 stand that the church had taken in response to two lawsuits. The actions taken by the church members and townspeople were the direct inspiration for the current Cross Ministry headquartered at Trinity Baptist Church in Lufkin, Texas.

Leo Bell Lytle III
and Valerie Lynne Culp-Lytle

But despite Leo's repeated efforts in the weeks before our trip, we were approaching the Frankenmuth church on Friday without a contact person to meet or interview. We decided that, if nothing else, we would take a few pictures of the church, say a prayer and leave them a couple of crosses with a note.

What we got instead was exponentially better, praise God. Before the day was over, we would get to talk to FOUR people who were very much involved in the 2008-2009 stand for Jesus.

Leo and I walked into the part of the church complex where we could see activity. We met Mr. Block, who had his hands full with an arrangement of white roses. He told us that the church office was about a block away, with the school, and offered to lead us there. He took us there, but the office had closed at noon. Mr. Block then offered to take us to the home of the man who had made the first cross during Frankenmuth's historic stand against two lawsuits in 2008 to 2009.

Mr. Block led us to the home of Eddie and Jane Beyerlein. Mr. Beyerlein actually had a cross in his hands when we first laid eyes on him. He had just made it: "It's still warm," he said.

The Beyerleins welcomed Leo and I open-heartedly. They were amazed and joyful to hear about how their cross effort had inspired a Cross Ministry in East Texas that just keeps getting larger and adding more ministries. Most importantly, they were amazed and grateful to God to learn that thousands of people have prayed to be saved, directly impacted by the Cross Ministry in its various forms.

Ultimately, Mr. Beyerlein told us, he made somewhere between 1,500 to 1,800 of the 36-inch by 18-inch by 9-inch crosses. Most of them were painted white. Church members and town residents placed the crosses all over Frankenmuth in their front yards and at their businesses.

"We would have people come to town and want to know who died," Mrs. Beyerlein said. Mr. Beyerlein agreed: "Everybody asked, 'What are all the crosses doing here in town?'"

What the crosses were doing was standing as silent witnesses. Standing for Jesus. Showing that the citizens were standing their ground.

Mr. Beyerlein said he was kept busy.

"Any spare minute I had (during that time), I was making crosses," Mr. Beyerlein said. "I enjoyed every minute of it."

The beautiful full-circle part of the experience came as we were preparing to wrap up our visit. A neighbor across the street had seen Leo's cell phone number on our cross trailer and called for a free cross. Leo and Mr. Beyerlein walked across the street to take a cross to her. Mr. Beyerlein said those neighbors had lived there about a year and a half, but he had not met them.

Leo led the woman and her two sons to the Lord with Mr. Beyerlein standing beside him. Afterwards, Mr. Beyerlein sang a hymn. He has been active in the music ministry of his church for more than half a century.

As Mr. Block and I watched Leo and Mr. Beyerlein walk back across the street to our trailer filled with wooden crosses, we thanked God for letting us all experience that full-circle moment. From the first wooden cross Mr. Beyerlein had made, to the trailer full of crosses we had parked in front of his home, it had led to this moment of three of his neighbors praying to be saved.

The best work is Kingdom work. What a privilege it is to live for Jesus. That is, in fact, pretty close to the words inscribed on a sign in front of St. Lorenz Evangelical Lutheran Church:

"St. Lorenz Lutheran Church was founded in 1845 by German immigrants who came to the Saginaw Valley with the desire to 'show others by word and deed how beautiful it is to live with Jesus.'

"That continues to be the mission of this congregation and its members."

Eddie and Jane Beyerlein had no idea of what they and their church members in Frankenmuth had inspired. When we told them all of it during our visit in August 2025, they were amazed and filled with joy.

"Just a little spark will make a big fire," Mr. Beyerlein said.

"My heart is blazing," he said several times during our time together. "This is one of the best days of my life."

All glory to God!

4

Faces in the Crowd

By Valerie Culp-Lytle
August 2021 and February 2023,
Fairbanks, Alaska and Lexington, Kentucky

"Are not two sparrows sold for a farthing? And one of them shall not fall on the ground without your Father. But the very hairs of your head are all numbered. Fear ye not therefore, ye are of more value than many sparrows."
Matthew 10: 29-31 KJV

───────────

In the approximately three years of Jesus' public ministry, Jesus was very often surrounded by crowds. But He focused on individuals in those crowds from time to time, and a few of those individuals made it into the pages of the Bible: Zacchaeus in the sycamore tree. The rich young ruler. The woman with an issue of blood who touched His garment. The little boy with loaves and fishes. And others.

In our ministry, we have met thousands of people. Many of them blend and melt together in the river of memory that flows through the years. But a few people stand out in our ministry memories. A few of our encounters with these people are making it into this book.

Two memorable people we met on the same afternoon in Fairbanks, Alaska. We were there in late August 2021. We had flown into Anchorage, Alaska and had a truck rental that would start a couple of days later. Community Bible Fellowship in Gonzalez, Louisiana (now known as Wisdom's Call) helped ship the crosses to Alaska. Pastored at that time by Leo's longtime friend and former missionary to China, Mike Robertson, Community Bible Fellowship volunteered to pay close to half of the cost to ship 250 large, unassembled crosses to Alaska.

Grand View Baptist Church in Anchorage had generously agreed to store the cross pieces in their basement until we arrived. Grand View Baptist also supplied us with two electric drills and allowed us to use their fellowship hall to assemble the crosses. The first two people who prayed to be saved in Alaska did so in the parking lot of Grand View Baptist Church.

But, anyway, we were in Fairbanks. It was raining softly. We were there in late August, so it was a little chilly. I had on a long-sleeved shirt covered by a rain jacket with its hood on my head. Underneath the hood, I wore a hat that kept the rain out of my face.

The first memorable person I met we'll call Ron. He walked with an alarming lurch. He also had a rigid bulge in the right pocket of his jack-

et. It clearly seemed to be a weapon of some kind, probably some sort of hand tool. I tried to engage him in a Gospel conversation but did not get very far with him. However, we did talk some about addiction. It was a subject on which he could speak with authority. He said that despite his physical challenges and substance addiction, he was able to work enough to pay for his own needs and compulsions.

"I don't believe in robbing people," he told me. "I worked hard for this high."

"Well, that is a relief to hear," I said to him, as I kept an eye on his right-hand pocket.

Then a second man walked up to join Ron and me on the sidewalk. This second man was also obviously under the influence of some type of chemical. This second man was not nearly as affable as Ron. He wasn't interested in a Gospel conversation, either. He seemed angry from the jump and grew increasingly belligerent. "I'm hungry," the second man said at one point. I gave him an orange, a protein bar, and a bottle of water. I told him we do not give people money, but he was not assuaged. His voice got a little louder, and he moved menacingly closer.

Leo Bell Lytle III
and Valerie Lynne Culp-Lytle

Surely Leo was keeping an eye on me, I thought to myself. I cast a quick glance over my shoulder toward Leo's side of our rented truck to see if he had me in his sights. He did not. Not even a little bit. Leo was deep in an actual Gospel conversation on the other side. I could hear fragments of their words. No way would I interrupt them and possibly quench the Spirit. There would be no smooth defusing of the escalating situation coming from Leo.

Surprisingly, though, the defusing was provided by Ron. He stepped closer, too, putting himself between me and Belligerent Man. Ron told the man he had something or other, some type of drink, I think. "Come on," Ron said to him, "I'll share it with you." And he put his arm around Belligerent Man's shoulders and led him away from me. It is not every day that I get help from a friendly man high on something with a lurching gait and a makeshift weapon in his pocket. But it IS every day that the Lord provides protection. I was grateful.

A young woman I'll call Janet was my next memorable person to encounter on the street in Fairbanks. She had very short hair, wore a jacket zipped up against the wet chill of the day and was carrying a large cup from a fast-food chain filled with ice and a clear liquid. Unlike Ron and Belligerent Man, Janet did want to have a Gospel conversation. I went over the plan of salvation, step by step. She assured me that she had already asked Jesus to forgive her sins and save her. But she wanted to stay and talk. Finally, I asked her if she wanted a free cross or not.

"I don't know what I would do with it," Janet answered, "I'm homeless."

As her story emerged, I learned that she lost her home sometime after her mother had died. Her mother had been a hopelessly ensnared alcoholic who could not stop drinking. One day, Janet told me, her mother went to sleep and never woke up. Things went quickly downhill. Janet said she lived with an uncle for a while, but he beat her so badly he broke some of her ribs. She felt safer on the streets. Her bigger problem now, she said, was that she was afraid to go to sleep for fear that she might not wake up like her mother did.

I told her that Jesus can help with fears, phobias or any bad situation, if only she would turn it over to Him and ask for His help. I prayed for her. I offered her food and warm clothes and a Bible. She accepted a couple of small food items, a bottle of water and a small Bible. Finally, I tried to convince her to allow Leo and I to locate a shelter for her and take her there. We would look one up, talk to them to be sure they would accept her and then drive her there.

"No," she said. "I'm not ready to stop drinking. I am drinking now." She half-lifted her cup.

"I know," I said. "I can smell it."

Nothing I said would sway her. She declined any offer of additional help but I was loathe to leave her. Wasn't there something else we could do, I asked.

"How about a hug?" was her response.

I opened my arms, pulled her in for a tight hug and held on for a long time. I think that hug did us both a lot of good. Maybe it will warm her heart when she thinks back on it. Maybe someday the thought of it will give her a little spark of hope that will encourage her to eventually seek and accept help for her addiction.

That hug warms my heart when I think of it. It also informs how I interact with people experiencing homelessness now. When Janet asked for a hug, it opened my eyes to how desperate some people may be for simple human touch or any scrap of affection, even if it comes from a stranger.

I have learned to look further than physical needs and even spiritual needs. With eyes opened by meeting Janet, I now clearly see how fervently so many people yearn to be acknowledged, to be heard. Some of them simply long for human touch.

Janet came clearly back into my mind on another chilly day. This was in February 2023, in Lexington, Kentucky. A young man with a backpack came up to where we were set up with the crosses in an abandoned parking lot. Leo talked to him first, and the young man assured him that he had already been saved. Then Leo asked him if he was hungry.

"Oh, yes sir!" the young man answered.

Leo sent me to the doughnut place next door with the young man, who I will call Ryan. Leo told me to buy enough food to fill Ryan up now and have some leftovers. It had been our intention to pay for this food. But a very nice young woman behind the counter at the doughnut place said she wanted to pay for his food. I left Ryan sitting in the fragrant warmth of the doughnut shop, poised to eat his fill.

A little later, Ryan emerged and walked back over to us. He walked up to thank me for feeding him. His nose was already reddening from being back out in the chill.

"Are you cold?" I asked him.

"Yes, ma'am!" he answered.

I slipped off the blanket I had draped around myself and placed it over his shoulders. Remembering Janet, I asked Ryan if he would like a hug and a prayer.

"Oh, yes, ma'am," he said. "Please."

Ryan stepped into my embrace. I hugged him tightly over his new blanket and began to pray. He was taller than me. After a moment he rested his forehead on top of my shoulder. The weight of his head resting against me was oddly moving. It was exactly like a child accepting comfort from a parent. As I have so often thought and felt out on the road, this young man was around the same age of some of our own sons and daughters. Please God, I would hope that somebody, somewhere would offer them similar comfort if ever their world turns sideways. Or if ever any of them find themselves adrift in desperate straits.

As I prayed for Ryan, I told the Lord that I didn't know what had taken place in Ryan's life to land him in his present circumstances. But I asked the Lord to please bless Ryan and strengthen his walk with Him so that he would be open to the direction of the Holy Spirit about what next steps to take. I asked the Lord to intervene in Ryan's life in such a way that he could draw no conclusion other than it was the Lord working in his life. I prayed that Ryan would resolve to stay ever focused on Jesus, with the help of the Holy Spirit.

Ryan sniffed from time to time during the prayer. Maybe his nose was running from the cold and from the downward position of his head. Certainly, both of us had shiny wet eyes when we at last lifted our heads and stepped apart. There's something about talking to God on behalf of somebody else ---- and certainly something about being the recipient of somebody talking to God on your behalf --- that summons tears. There is a sweet generosity, poignancy and vulnerability built into the act of one person praying for another. It touches the heart and wets the eyes.

There's something else that praying for a person does. It lets the recipient of prayer know that in the vast, heaving sea of humanity, eye contact has been made. Somebody has noted his or her individual needs and issues in the roiling landscape of needs and issues in the world at large. Someone has made the effort to lay those needs and issues out as petitions before the throne of God. Their faces have shone out of the crowd. They have been seen. And they will be remembered.

5

God Had
A Better Plan

By Leo Lytle
November 2018, Wagner, South Dakota

"Now faith is the substance of things hoped for,
the evidence of things not seen."
Hebrews 11:1 KJV

Daylight was fading fast.

The fleeting hours before dark reminded me of the urgency we should all feel to reach people for Christ in what are likely the last days before He returns. The air was cold on this late afternoon in November 2018 because Novembers in South Dakota are certainly colder than our Novembers in the Piney Woods of East Texas. Cold or not, I had a burning desire to share the Good News of the Gospel.

I had been blessed to share "The Door" message at The Lighthouse Church in Wagner, South Dakota on Sunday morning, November 4, 2018 at the invitation of Pastor Scott Alderink. I'd met Scott earlier in the week while I was sharing Christ and crosses in Wagner beside a restaurant he man-aged. Even though I had already preached on this autumn Sun-day, I wanted to try to do something else for the Lord in the couple of hours of daylight re-

maining. I decided to spend some time in a Yankton Sioux neighborhood that was close to my motel.

My plan was to take as many crosses as I could carry and go door to door, hoping for the opportunity to share Christ. But God gave me a better plan.

I saw a well-built building with a sign that said "BIA Corrections Yankton Agency." It was the local prison in Wagner, operated by the Bureau of Indian Affairs under the Department of the Interior. Instantly, I

felt led to see if I could get in there and share Jesus. I hastily picked up a stack of our "Good News for You" Bible study booklets and some New Testaments and made a beeline toward the entrance.

I saw a button for the intercom system and pressed it, unaware of what the LORD was going to do with this button-push of faith. In less than a minute, a voice asked who I was and what I wanted. I said, "I'm an evangelist from Texas. I have some Bible study booklets for your inmates." It hit me right then that this was a request that would probably be denied. I had no credentials to flash and no prior appointment.

The voice asked a few more questions of me and then asked me to wait. In a few minutes the locked door opened, and a female guard invited me to come inside. Boy, was I ever surprised! As I walked in, I looked around like a cow staring at a new gate. It was starting to get exciting.

She asked if there was a particular prisoner I wanted to see. I said "No," adding that I'd like to give the booklets to anyone who would like one. By this point I was amazed that God's plan had gotten this far. She said, "Take a seat. I'll go see if anyone is interested." When she returned, she had more good news. She said there was one man and three women who wanted to talk with me. I would need to wait until the conference room was empty as there was a visit underway at the moment. Wow! Sitting there waiting for this completely unexpected opportunity, I was really starting to like God's plan! It was all I could do to keep from jumping up and shouting "GLORY!"

As I awaited my opportunity to speak with these prisoners, I recalled how God had in the past miraculously opened prison doors. Paul, Silas and Peter were all well-acquainted with the inside of a prison. They also saw how God, in His perfect timing and miraculous power, opened those prison doors for them to be released. He was doing just the opposite here for me --- enabling me to get inside the prison. I love watching God work.

When the conference room was clear, the guard ushered me to a table with chairs on both sides. She would bring the man in first, she said, and then bring all three women together.

Jason (not his real name) arrived. We chatted for a few minutes. I told him who I was and why I was here. Then we began to talk about him, his family and how he came to be incarcerated. He had made some unfortunate choices. Haven't we all?

His choices had included robbery, which had earned him several years in prison. After we'd talked for a while, I steered the conversation to spiritual matters. I shared a long and very thorough Gospel presentation with Jason. At the conclusion, he said he wanted to give his life to Christ. We prayed together in that visitation room, and he did just that. Praise God! He left with a New Testament and two of the Bible study booklets I had I brought with me, one for a friend back in the cellblock.

In a few minutes the guard brought in three women. One was very young, around 17 or 18 years old. Another appeared to be in her late 30s or early 40s, and the other woman seemed to be in her 50's. As with Jason, we talked about their families. The young woman teared up immediately. She said she really missed her mom and family. It's difficult to be so young and be separated from family and friends. Alcohol and drugs had been the vehicle that brought all of them to this place.

Again, I steered the conversation to spiritual matters. After many tears and another careful Gospel presentation, one by one they each said they wanted to be saved and to begin a new direction in their lives. Each one placed her trust in Jesus Christ alone for her salvation. It was a special moment. They also left with New Testaments and the Bible study booklets. They took a few extra ones for friends. They are certainly not the first to begin their journey with Christ in a prison. Valerie and I regularly meet people on our travels who tell us they were saved in prison. May God bless the many men and women who volunteer their time to reach the prison population for Jesus.

The guard came back for me and ushered me to the entrance. I thanked her and left the remaining Bible study booklets and New Testaments with her to give to anyone who might want one. She then unlocked the front door. It closed loudly behind me. I felt like I was walking on air as I made my way back to my truck and trailer. My heart was so warmed that I didn't even notice the cold South Dakota winds swirling in the night. With tears in my eyes, I took one last look, overwhelmed that God had opened the doors of that prison to let me inside.

Yes, I had made my original plan for how I would try to reach people with the Gospel in Wagner, South Dakota. But God had a better plan. His plan is always better.

6

Sharing His Love on Bourbon Street

By Leo Lytle
June 2023, New Orleans, Louisiana

"By this shall all men know that ye are my disciples,
if ye have love one to another."
John 13:35 KJV

———————

Nestled tightly in the crook of a big crescent in the mighty Mississippi River a few miles before it empties into the Gulf of America lies the historic, famous city of New Orleans. Often called the "Big Easy," it's known for nightlife, live music and spicy cuisine along with many more unique features. It is a cosmopolitan city and melting pot of French, African and American cultures. New Orleans is a city like no other.

New Orleans will always hold a special place in my heart. During my days as a student at New Orleans Baptist Theological Seminary, I worked as a "sash and door" man for more than two years to pay my way through school. Short visits to the Big Easy still appeal. I'm thankful that I got to play a small role in the restoration of some of the architectural beauty of this unique city from the French Quarter to Uptown and from St. Charles Avenue to Canal Street. I love to see some of the doors and windows I made back then still being used nearly 40 years later.

I've taken youth groups and others there to minister on many occasions and have enjoyed introducing them to "N'awlins." A number of times I have stood on Bourbon Street holding up a large cross and sharing Gospel tracts with people passing by. My most recent Bourbon Street evangelism outreach took place on June 12, 2023.

CROSS-ing AMERICA
Sharing Jesus Around The Nation

New Orleans was named "Murder Capital of America" in 2023. It was not the city's first time to earn the title, either. Any outreach undertaken in New Orleans needs to be seasoned with a bit of caution. We would be reminded on this night that the seasoning needs to also include a large measure of one other particular ingredient.

On Sunday, June 11, 2023, I had the privilege of preaching at Wisdom's Call Fellowship in Gonzales, Louisiana where Brother Gene Gale

serves as pastor. It is only 56 miles from New Orleans. Wisdom's Call is one of our supporting churches. Members have faithfully prayed for and financially supported our evangelism ministry since its beginning. Their former pastor, Brother Mike Robertson, served as a missionary to China before leading their church. Filling the pulpit after Mike Robertson's retirement, Brother Gene has continued the legacy of enthusiastically supporting mission work. We always enjoy being with our friends there.

Since we were going to be so close to New Orleans, we decided to share Christ and free "Jesus Is Lord" crosses, graciously provided by Vic Bass Ministries, on the streets in the Crescent City. Our good friends, neighbors and fellow soldiers for Jesus, Monty and Roni Nettles, joined us to help.

On Monday morning, June 12, 2023, we saw eight people pray to receive God's free Gift of Eternal Life Jesus Christ in the Gentilly area of New Orleans. We were only a block from the New Orleans Baptist Theological Seminary, where I had graduated in 1985. Afterward, we made plans to carry our big rolling cross to Bourbon Street that evening. Monty volunteered to carry the cross and then hold it upright on Bourbon Street. That night, Roni, Valerie and I carried Bibles, Gospel tracts and follow-up materials as we made our way to the French Quarter. Also joining us were our friends from Northeastern Baptist College in Bennington, Vermont: Tyler and Mykayla Ballard. (Tyler and Mykayla were in New Orleans to attend the annual Southern Baptist Convention. We also attended a few sessions of the convention. Mykayla was expecting their firstborn at the time. Micah John Ballard would be welcomed into the world in September.)

It turned out to be a great night on Bourbon Street. Here is just one of the stories:

Not long after finding our spot and getting organized, a young man who worked at the restaurant near us was on the street with some menus trying to draw in diners. As we were close to each other, I struck up a conversation with him. He explained that when they were having a slow night the manager had the waiters take menus out on the street to help generate business. After a little small talk, he asked what we were doing. I explained rather nonchalantly our effort, as we were both paying attention to the passersby. But I was hoping his interest might lead to a Gospel conversation. Eventually, I turned to face him and politely asked:

"Have you come to the place where you know for certain that if you were to die tonight you would go to Heaven?"

"No," he said.

"I know you're busy," I said. "But if you would like to hear how I found out and how you, too, can know for sure, I would be happy to share that with you when and if you have the time. It takes about three or four minutes. We'll be here for a couple of hours. I'd love to talk with you when you have the time."

Then we both went back to what we were doing – him trying to drum up business and me trying to encourage folks to come to Christ!

About 10 minutes later he came back to me and said, "I have a few minutes and would like to hear about how to go to Heaven." We engaged in a friendly Gospel conversation. In short order, that young man bowed his head in prayer and accepted Jesus as his personal LORD and Savior right there on Bourbon Street in front of the restaurant where he worked. All Glory to God!

I gave him a Bible marked at the Gospel of John and our follow-up material to help him get started on his journey with Christ. In all my many times sharing Christ on Bourbon Street through the years, this young man was the very first person willing to give himself to Jesus in that setting. It was exciting for sure. Before we left that evening, eight more names were written in the "Lamb's Book of Life." The field called "Bourbon Street" was ripe unto harvest that evening. Hallelujah!

The young man and I had one last conversation. He told me that what attracted him to us was the way we were doing what we were doing. He had a front row seat from his restaurant watching many others attempt to share the Gospel. He said that most Christian preachers he sees in the French Quarter are harsh, loud and threatening. It sounded like he was describing the "Turn or Burn" approach. But he said he could see that we seemed to genuinely love and care for people. That is what drew him to Christ. It reminds me of that song we used to sing, "And they'll know we are Christians by our love, by our love. Yes, they'll know we are Christians by our love."[1]

God used Paul to write, *"But the fruit of the Spirit is love, joy, peace, long-suffering, gentleness, faith, meekness, temperance; against such there is no law."* (Galatians 5:22-23 KJV)

A lost and hurting world is watching us as we pass through this life. Do they see Jesus in us? Do they see His love in action? They should!

---

1. According to Wikipedia, the song "They'll Know We Are Christians" (also known as "They'll Know We Are Christians By Our Love" or "We Are One in the Spirit") is a Christian hymn written in the 1960s by Catholic priest Peter Scholtes.

7

Light in the Darkness

By Valerie Culp-Lytle
August 2023, Kolin, Louisiana

"Then spake Jesus again unto them, saying, I am the light of the world:
he that followeth me shall not walk in darkness, but shall have the light of life."
John 8:12 KJV

The Holy Spirit teaches us His gentle lessons anytime, anywhere, when we keep our hearts, minds and souls open to His guidance. Even in a restroom.

It was a sunny Sunday morning in August 2023 near Kolin, Louisiana. Leo and I had provided witness training to a good-sized group gathered at Pine Grove Baptist Church on Saturday. We distributed crosses provided by Vic Bass Ministries. Where needed, we shared the Gospel. We extended invitations to Pine Grove Baptist Church. In fact, we told people, this visiting evangelist, Leo Lytle, would be preaching there the next day. On top of that, there was Pine Grove's preacher right over there, we said, if they wanted to meet him and ask any questions. The high temperature hit 107 degrees that day in Kolin. God blessed our efforts, sweat-soaked as they were. Five people prayed to be saved during that outreach.

On Sunday mornings when Leo is preaching somewhere, our custom is for Leo to have me say a few words before he brings the message. Often, I share about the cross ministry. I explain how God put together our ministry with Vic Bass Ministries and the Cross Men and Cross Women, Trinity Baptist Church in Lufkin and our other supporting churches, as well as some benefactors who insist on anonymity. Working together for the cause of Christ, we have been blessed to see several thousand people pray to be forgiven of their sins and saved by grace.

It is also my custom to stop by the restroom shortly before the worship service is set to begin. This one in Kolin was an interior restroom, with no windows. It had a wooden partition that separated the commode stalls from the sink counter. It was also pitch-black dark inside when the lights were turned off.

This realization hit me when a woman exiting the restroom casually flipped off the light switch, unaware that another person was in one

of the other stalls. Complete darkness engulfed me. Not one glimmer of light came from anywhere. I literally could not see my hand in front of my face. I checked.

Engaged as I was in a familiar task, I completed that task in the stall with no problem and pushed open the stall door. I knew I needed to turn left. But as I turned left, I had to chuckle at how completely blind I was. I started taking baby steps toward the left. I might as well shut my eyes, because they were unable to help. I stretched my arms out in front of me so that I would not run into the wooden partition.

Shuffling with mincing little steps, inching along with my arms outstretched, I made progress in the direction of where I remembered the door to be. Very shortly, someone in the hallway bumped against the door, and a crack of light appeared for a split-second. It confirmed the direction and gave me confidence to close the gap in the space and feel for the light switch. As I was washing my hands, it occurred to me what a beautiful illustration I had just been given.

Here I was, moments away from standing before a congregation and encouraging the members to get outside the walls of the church and share the good news of the Gospel. Yes, I would acknowledge as I spoke, witnessing can seem scary and daunting. Many, if not most, Christians do NOT share their faith on any kind of a regular basis. They feel uncomfortable and unqualified. So, they stay silent. Plenty of Believers say they don't know the Bible as well as they should, or have enough Scripture memorized or have answers to potentially tricky theological questions.

But what my little moment in the darkness of that windowless, partitioned restroom had just beautifully pictured is that those fears need not hold us back. Yes, absolutely, we should all study the Bible more, memorize more Scripture and study to show ourselves approved as workmen rightly dividing the word of truth, as directed in 2 Timothy 2:15.

But we don't have to have lots of verses memorized, or have all the answers. The only answers we must know are that we are all sinners heading for Hell unless we seek Jesus' forgiveness, and that faith and trust in Jesus alone as personal Savior is the only means of salvation.

We live in a world made very dark by sin. Lost people blunder along blindly. Some are seeking direction and hope. Some aren't even looking. Many don't know there is a better way or a bright eternity waiting for those who put their faith and trust in Jesus Christ as Savior. What they all need is for somebody to shed some light and show the Way. All it may take for them is a brief glimmer of light to shine in the darkness to lead them into a new day.

When whoever it was bumped against that restroom door and allowed a sliver of light to show for an instant, that was all I needed to know where to head. I didn't need that person to come in and tell me what year the building was built or the capacity of the water heater serving the sinks. I didn't need them to come in and tell me who cleans the stalls and keeps the place stocked with soap. All I needed was a flash of light to show me the way.

Be a Believer who reaches out to those lost in darkness. No matter how lacking nor how flawed, be one who at least flashes the light that signals, "Over here! Come this way!"

"Then spake Jesus again unto them, saying, I am the light of the world: he that followeth me shall not walk in darkness, but shall have the light of life."
John 8:12 KJV

"Study to shew thyself approved unto God, a workman that needeth not to be ashamed, rightly dividing the word of truth."
2 Timothy 2:15 KJV

8

Two Sons of South Carolina

By Leo Lytle
September 2018, Saluda, South Carolina

*"Therefore if any man be in Christ, he is a new creature:
old things are passed away; behold all things are become new."*
I Corinthians 5:17 KJV

On the afternoon of September 11, 2018, I arrived in Saluda, South Carolina under threatening skies as I searched for a good location to share Christ and crosses. I'd been in South Carolina for the better part of a week and had many meaningful and encouraging conversations with people from several other towns and cities. I was thankful and excited that several people had asked Jesus to forgive their sins and had accepted Him as their LORD and Savior.

A thunderstorm soon swept into the small South Carolina town. I was glad to be able to park under the awning at an abandoned convenience store to wait it out. As the rain drummed on the awning, my thoughts turned to the history of Saluda County that I had read on the "Welcome" sign at the edge of town: "Welcome To Saluda County – Birthplace Of – Alamo Heroes – William Barret Travis – And – James Butler Bonham."

35

Most people with even a little knowledge of Texas history know who William Travis was. Travis, along with two other legendary heroes of The Alamo, James "Jim" Bowie and David "Davy" Crockett, were three of the 189 Texan defenders who fought to their deaths for Texas independence at the religious outpost turned fortress. This epic battle lasted for 13 days, ending on March 6,1836. The bodies of these 189 brave warriors of The Alamo were burned on orders from Mexican General Santa Anna. The site on which the siege took place is in the heart of San Antonio. It is the most visited historical site in all of Texas.

While Travis, Bowie and Crockett are the most famous of the many heroic defenders of The Alamo, and deservedly so, I want to draw your attention to another great hero. His name is proudly displayed on that welcome sign for Saluda County, South Carolina: James Butler Bonham.

I love history, especially American history. I'm particularly drawn to study lesser-known people involved in great historical events. This is why James Bonham's story inspires and encourages me. When a 29-year-old man willingly chooses to face certain death when he could have avoided doing so, I want to know why.

Bonham was born and raised in Saluda County, South Carolina. He and fellow Alamo hero William Travis were, in fact, second cousins. It's believed that he arrived at The Alamo in January 1836 along with James Bowie.

Mexican General Santa Anna and his army of more than 4,000 men began to lay siege to The Alamo in early March of 1836. This prompted Travis to ask his trusted second cousin to undertake a dangerous mission. He asked Bonham to take a message to Colonel James Fannin at Goliad. The message was a desperate request for aid.

Unfortunately, Fannin was not able to provide assistance. With no help coming, the fate of the defenders at The Alamo was sealed. Historians tell us that Bonham mounted his horse to return. Before leaving, according to historical accounts, Bonham was told it was useless to throw his life away by returning to face certain death. Bonham's response was that Travis deserved to know the answer to his appeal for aid. In his book "Lone Star: A History of Texas and Texans" T.R Fehrenbach writes that Bonham, "...*spat upon the ground, and galloped west into his own immortality.*"

As Bonham approached The Alamo on March 3,1836, he galloped in holding tightly to the side of his horse to avoid enemy fire. He delivered the news to his cousin and thereafter took his place behind one of the cannons. The historical legend of the Alamo says that 29-year-old James Butler Bonham died in battle three days later. He fought to the end at the Alamo along with his 26-year-old second cousin, William Barrett Travis, and the other 187 valiant, but doomed defenders.

Soon after the storm passed in Saluda, a grandmother with her 10-year-old granddaughter stopped by for a free cross. Both listened attentively as I shared why I was in Saluda with the crosses and as I shared the Gospel message. When I asked them, "Does this make sense to you?" Grandmother and granddaughter responded, "Yes!" So, I asked, "Would you like to receive God's free Gift of Eternal Life Jesus Christ?" They responded, "Yes!" again. Praise God, both prayed and asked forgiveness of their sins and to accept Jesus as their LORD and Savior!

Then the grandmother told me that she'd been thinking about becoming a Christian, and it was because of her brother. He had spent time in prison but had been out now for about a year. Her brother told her that he had given his life to Christ while in prison. She said she noticed a real difference in him she believed was genuine. He had been actively involved in a local church as well, she said. In

fact, she had been seriously considering becoming a Christian because of the change she'd seen in her brother. The Gospel "seed" had already been planted and watered in her life by her brother. I was blessed to be there for the "harvest!"

So why this story from Saluda, South Carolina? It's not about history, even though I loved learning about James Bonham. His bravery is inspiring. Bonham's story is a sterling example of selfless patriotism, courage and devotion to family.

This story is also not about the grandmother and granddaughter I met while waiting out the stormy weather in Saluda, either. Although it was certainly a blessing to see them both come to Christ. I love to see people saved.

As I see it, the main story here is the grandmother's account of her brother's victory in Jesus. His conversion to Christ and then his "followship" of Christ is a story to be celebrated. I don't know the cause of his incarceration. I don't know how he came to be saved in prison. I don't even know his name. But here is what I do know: somehow God in His perfect timing and amazing grace reached inside the walls of that prison and changed the heart of this man. I don't know who He may have used, nor exactly how it all came down, but it happened – praise God it happened!

This grandmother's brother became a new creation in Christ. Although he was in prison, he was no longer a prisoner to sin. Like God's Word says, *"Therefore if any man be in Christ, he is a new creature: old things are passed away; behold, all things are become new."* (II Corinthians 5:17 KJV)

Alamo hero James Butler Bonham's raw courage inspires me. This grandmother's brother, who gave up his old life and found a new life in Christ while in prison, inspires me, too. Your life will also leave a legacy. What kind of legacy will it be? Who will you inspire?

9

Hello, Hitchhiker

By Valerie Culp-Lytle
April 2019, Oglala, South Dakota

"Withhold not good from them to whom it is due,
When it is in the power of thine hand to do it."
Proverbs 3:27 KJV

———————

"As far as the eye can see" is no idle phrase in large parts of South Dakota. On some highways, the road and the open horizon sweep off into whatever the limit of vision is for the human eye. U.S. 18 from Oglala to Pine Ridge is one such road. It is straight for miles, with open plains on either side. Just sky and grass. There is nowhere to hide.

It was April 13, 2019. Leo and I had left Oglala, and were headed for thr Pine Ridge Reservation that the highway sign said was 15 miles away. Spring had not quite reached that far north. Snow still lay on the ground in many places, although short brown grass was visible in small patches. The sun was shining, but the wind was cold. Just that morning, I

had asked Leo to stop at a dollar store so that I could buy two pairs of warmer socks and another pair of knit gloves. The heater was out in our red 1998 Dodge Ram truck. But at least we were out of the wind inside the cab. With blankets tucked around us, we were warm enough. The truck cab seemed a safe sanctuary in a grandly sweeping, but

somewhat desolate landscape. I certainly would not want to be on foot in such a vast and lonely place.

But somebody was on foot. Up ahead, we could see a lone figure walking along the right side of the road, our side, from what seemed like miles away. It was a person in dark clothing, moving steadily onward.

"Do NOT pick up that person!" I said to Leo. "No hitchhikers! It's too dangerous. A hitchhiker could just kill us and steal the truck."

We continued driving, slowly gaining on the person walking.

"Seriously," I said to Leo. "Don't even think about it. Please don't pick up a hitchhiker."

As we drove, the walker grew larger in our sight. We could see it was a slender person, walking with the energy of youth. Even more menacing, to my way of thinking.

And then the moment of truth was upon us. We drew even with the walker.

"Do NOT stop!" I implored again.

We passed the walker without slowing down. I sighed with relief.

"I didn't look," I said, relaxing against the seat back.

"I looked," Leo said. "It was a young girl."

"Oh, no," I said. "Please turn around." Leo instantly hit the brakes and pulled our truck and 12-foot trailer bristling with wooden crosses into a U-turn. We drove back to her, passed her, made another U-turn and then came up beside her. She got in without hesitation when we offered her a ride, joining us on the truck's one seat.

The 15 miles the highway sign promised are a very long way in the cold when one is moving forward one footstep at a time, acutely aware of one's extreme vulnerability on the open road through the open prairie. She would have been at the mercy of anybody who pulled up alongside her. Truly, there was nowhere to hide, nowhere to run, except across miles of windswept acres.

Leo Bell Lytle III
and Valerie Lynne Culp-Lytle

She was about 16 years old. In one hand she clutched a plastic grocery bag filled with her few possessions. She said the wife of her father's "second family," with whom she had been living, had that morning accused her of stealing. She did not steal anything, she told us. But she wasn't going to stay there any longer. She packed her things in the flimsy sack and set off to walk to Pine Ridge. She had friends in Pine Ridge, she told us. They would let her stay with them.

She was calm and civil, but clearly in no mood for chit-chat. She sat very still, staring straight ahead and answered our few questions with scant words. We tried to be casually friendly and supportive without being heavy-handed. I gave her my new pair of gloves and one of the pairs of warm socks I had just bought. She accepted a few protein bars and a bottle of water. We must have given her a Gospel tract, although I am not certain of it. I know I wrote down both our cell phone numbers for her and told her she could call us anytime.

A distance that must have seemed a perilous ordeal as a walk was completed all too quickly when accomplished in a vehicle. We neared Pine Ridge. We had not yet been able to share the Gospel with her. She did not seem open to conversation of any kind, Leo and I agreed later.

But maybe we should have pushed a bit. Maybe we should have tried to lead her into a discussion about eternity. But right then she was focused on the next hour or two, on finding her friends and seeking sanctuary. At the time, neither of us felt that circumstances were right in those moments. Instead, we pinned our hopes on the invitation we gave her. At noon, we told her, at the community center in Pine Ridge --- the very location where we would be taking her --- we would be feeding people free pizza, followed by a brief presentation of the Gospel. It would be just an hour and a half for her to wait. She could join us for hot pizza and important news about how much God loves us all. Please join us, we urged her.

Leo and I both felt sure she would be at the pizza lunch. But she was not.

We never saw her again.

Somewhere around 20 people prayed with Leo that afternoon in Pine Ridge when he gave the invitation for those who wanted to ask forgiveness of their sins and ask Jesus Christ to be their Savior. But the young hitchhiker was not among them.

Fishermen ruefully talk about "the one that got away." As the years pass since our encounter, I still think of her from time to time. She is one who "got away." As Leo says, one reason fishermen lose a fish is that they do not "set the hook." We didn't "set the hook" for reasons that seemed valid at the time. We leave it to God to judge. I pray that she is still alive and that she has been saved by now. Maybe, just maybe, in what remained of the 15 miles between Oglala and Pine Ridge that day, we were able to at least show her a seed packet, if not actually plant a seed that might cause her to seek out salvation.

Maybe, just maybe what God intended for us to accomplish in her life is what we did. We gave her a ride. She reached Pine Ridge alive.

Because what we did not know then, but do know now, is that Indigenous women and girls are at great risk for experiencing violence. In fact, the National Indigenous Women's Resource Center says the murder rate of Native women is more than 10 times the national average on some reservations.

According to the Association on American Indian Affairs, American Indians and Alaska Natives are 2.5 times more likely to experience violent crimes and at least two times more likely to experience rape or sexual assault compared to all other races. More than four in five American Indian and Alaska Native women, or 84.3 percent, have experienced violence in their lifetime. Homicide is the third leading cause of death among American Indian and Alaska Native women between 10 and 24 years of age. Also, according to the Association on American Indian Affairs, in the U.S. and Canada, an average of 40 percent of the women who were victims of sex trafficking identified as American Indian or Alaska Native.

The website for the Association on American Indian Affairs said that the epidemic of Missing and Murdered Indigenous Peoples is silent genocide.

Going forward, Leo and I plan to increase our awareness of the problem of missing and murdered Indigenous people. In our yearly visits to Indigenous people's homelands, we will keep our eyes and hearts open for ways we might be able to help, even if only on an individual basis. We will also be ever more mindful of the need to get salvation literature into the hands of everyone we meet, however brief the encounter.

But we still aren't going to start picking up hitchhikers.

RESOURCES

The following are some helpful telephone numbers
that deal with these issues:

9-1-1, of course, but also:

StrongHearts Native Helpline: a 24/7 helpline that offers culturally-appropriate support and advocacy for America Indians and Alaska Natives who are victims of domestic and sexual violence. Phone or text: 1-844-7NATIVE.

National Runaway Safeline: 1-800-RUNAWAY (1-800-786-2929)

National Domestic Violence Hotline: 1-800-799-SAFE.

National Sexual Assault Hotline: 1-800-656-HOPE.

National Suicide Prevention Hotline: 1-800-273-TALK.

10

South Dakota, Still Special

By Valerie Culp-Lytle,
as told by Leo Lytle
South Dakota, 2018 to present

"Remember ye not the former things, neither consider the things of old.
Behold, I will do a new thing; now it shall spring forth; shall ye not know it?
I will even make a way in the wilderness, and rivers in the desert."
Isaiah 43:18-19 KJV

It took 23 years, but Leo finally made it to South Dakota.

Occasionally, someone will look over our evangelism travels and note that we seem to return again and again to South Dakota. It's a windswept state far from our home in East Texas, not as populated as many other states. Why South Dakota? people ask.

South Dakota represents an opportunity that Leo had that is rarely available in life. South Dakota had represented a road **not** taken in Leo's life. But when Leo answered the call to evangelism, he was at last able to make occasional visits **to** and make occasional forays **on** the road not taken.

With his 1915 poem "The Road Not Taken," American poet Robert Frost famously put into words the experience of having to choose between divergent paths. The poem acknowledges that the path we choose alters our trajectory in life. The last three lines of the third stanza state:

"Oh, I kept the first for another day!
Yet knowing how way leads on to way,
I doubted if I should ever come back."

But Leo got a chance to come back in a way. He was blessed with a second chance to explore a path not taken in the past, but whose unknown promise or perhaps undone work had always beckoned.

In this case, the road led to South Dakota. Leo says that he was a young pastor when he got a call from a representative of the Southern Baptist work in the Dakotas at the time, a man named Dewey Hickey. Bro. Dewey was acquainted with Leo's pastor friend and mentor, evangelist Joe Aulds (married to the sweet and supportive Donna Aulds).

Joe had given Leo's name to Bro. Dewey.

"I got a call from Dewey Hickey in 1995 when I was living in Shreveport, Louisiana," Leo said. "He asked me to consider pastoring in South Dakota. He said the churches were small, and that I might have to pastor two of them. I felt like I wanted to do it. But family concerns and financial circumstances led me to call him back and say that I didn't think it was the right time.

"I felt like it was one of those times in my life where I didn't have enough faith to step out," Leo said.

Fast forward 23 years.

"I felt led to go into evangelism after pastoring for 33 years," Leo said. "One of the first places I felt led to go, as far as any considerable distance from home, was South Dakota. I was able to track down Dewey Hickey, who was by then living in northwest Arkansas. He had long since retired from his position in the Dakotas. I told him of our previous conversation 23 years earlier.

"He did not remember it," Leo said. "I said to him, 'You might not remember it, but I do. I am planning to go to South Dakota, and I want your advice about it.'

"Within a few months, I was in South Dakota," Leo said. "I was carrying a load of crosses provided by Vic Bass Ministries and planning to preach at two churches. On my first day in South Dakota, I met a pastor and his wife in a small town where I was first sharing Christ and crosses," Leo said. "There was very little traffic in the small town, but I had just thought that it would be best to set up in the middle of a small town. I patiently stayed there, hoping to see someone come to Christ.

"The pastor who stopped to talk to me that day was Dan Flyger. Dan asked me what I was doing. I told him. He suggested that I go to a main highway, and he suggested two towns. He said I would see more people, have more people driving by and therefore have more opportunities. It was a lightbulb moment.

"Soon thereafter, I went to those two towns," Leo continued. "The next day, in the town of Winner, South Dakota, on the side of the road, a couple of ladies stopped who wanted a cross. I discovered that they did not know for sure that if they died, they would go to Heaven. After a Gospel conversation, both prayed to receive Christ."

"As I was leaving," Leo continued, "I stopped at a nearby convenience store where a number of people came up and asked for a free cross. That was the day that the realization hit me that this was going to work. I saw clearly that this would be an effective way to use these crosses to reach people for Christ."

So, South Dakota was the place where Leo did not go earlier in his ministry. Yet, Leo remembered the call to South Dakota from 23 years earlier. In the fullness of time, he made his way to South Dakota. It was there that the Holy Spirit used the effectiveness of the crosses to show Leo direction for the new chapter in his ministry.

"The next day, I drove to Pine Ridge Indian Reservation," Leo said. "As Bro. Dewey had shared, Pine Ridge was an economically depressed area. I pulled into a parking lot behind a community center. A man walked up to the truck. He asked me what I was doing there. I told him I was there to share Jesus and free crosses in the community, and I was looking for a place to do it."

The man in the parking lot turned out to be George Dreamerr, who managed the community center and has since become a friend.

"George told me that he was a Christian," Leo said. "He said there were nine other Believers who join him every Saturday to go out into the community sharing Christ with the locals. Then he told me that I was in the right place at the right time. He said in an hour, the parking lot would be full of people selling goods like a flea market. He suggested a spot on the parking lot that would be great for me and the trailer. I began to take out crosses and put the signs up. Immediately, people began to come.

"So many were coming that I started to be afraid I would run out of crosses," Leo said. "So, I put up a sign that said, 'Come back at noon for a free cross and a short message.'"

George Dreamerr loaned Leo a table so that Leo could use it to preach "The Door" message. By noon there was a good-size crowd gath-

ered. Leo preached an abbreviated version of "The Door" and then gave an invitation.

"That day there were around 25 people who gave their hearts to Christ either after 'The Door' message or when they came for a cross," Leo said. "I have no doubt that it was a Divine Appointment that day with George Dreamerr. In God's perfect timing, He put me with the right person at the right place at the right time. George and I are still friends. We've worked with him and with his father, George Dreamerr, Sr., several times now."

Since Leo's first visit to South Dakota, we have returned at least eight times for evangelism trips.

"Every time we go, we see a harvest of souls," Leo said. "That's why South Dakota."

11

A Call to Come Home

By Leo Lytle
September 2023, South Central (Los Angeles, California)

"And he arose, and came to his father.
But when he was yet a great way off, his father saw him,
and had compassion, and ran, and fell on his neck, and kissed him."
Luke 15:20 KJV

Fear was riding shotgun. It was an unwelcome passenger.

On the morning of September 18, 2023, I pulled out of a paid parking lot near Los Angeles International Airport after not sleeping well in our van. I had been thinking and praying about this day for many weeks. I had only shared what my plan was with one person: Susie Jordan of Lufkin. Susie, along with her husband, Lawrence "Buddy" Jordan, her brother, Dale Frost, and Dale's wife, LaVera Frost, are the ones who started this amazing "Cross Ministry" in February 2015 in Lufkin and Nacogdoches, Texas. Susie prays faithfully for us on every trip.

As I was leaving the Cross Barn prior to our trip to Arizona, Nevada, California and Hawaii, I had seen Susie there, and she asked about our itinerary. I told her that I planned to witness in the South Central neighborhood when I got to Los Angeles. Valerie

would be joining me later. I had said nothing to Valerie about it. I didn't want her to worry.

South Central is a large region of Los Angeles, California made up of the neighborhoods south of downtown Los Angeles. "This is a relatively impoverished area of the city," Wikipedia says, "infamous for gang violence and for being the epicenter of major race riots in the 1960s and 1990s."

The reason for my restless night's sleep was fear. I've faced fear before over these last few years as I've shared Christ in towns and cities

rocked by riots and violent protests. A nagging fear touched me as I shared Jesus on the streets in Minneapolis/St. Paul, Milwaukee, Kenosha, Chicago, Detroit, Portland, Seattle and others. But the fear I felt on heading for South Central went much deeper.

Fear is not my usual companion, but it seemed to be riding in the van with me as I drove toward South Central. We've all seen reports about the lawlessness in our nation's big cities on the news. As I drove, I prayed and gave my fear to God. I knew from many personal experiences the truth of what the Scripture says:

"Ye are of God, little children, and have overcome them: because greater is he that is in you, than he that is in the world." I John 4:4 KJV

On April 29, 1992, South Central experienced a six-day period that was the most destructive event of civil unrest in United States history at that time. There would be 63 people killed, 2,383 people reported injured, more than 12,000 people arrested, thousands of fires set, 1,100 buildings damaged and over one billion dollars in property damage over six days of riots, looting, arson and violence, according to Internet information. A Los Angeles County jury's decision to acquit four policemen accused of beating Rodney King the year before had triggered the turmoil that many of us watched on live television. The epicenter of the violence was the intersection of Florence and Normandie Avenues in South Central. I headed there.

As I drove, I could see again in my memory those televised images of bricks and rocks being thrown through the windshields of passing motorists and of people being dragged from their cars and beaten. The most iconic incident took place at the intersection of Florence and Normandie Avenues. Construction worker Reginald Oliver Denny was dragged from his dump truck and beaten nearly to death while the nation watched. He was one year older than me. A hovering news helicopter captured it all on tape. The footage of Denny being savagely assaulted was shown relentlessly on the nightly news. Eventually, he lay unconscious on the pavement in a pool of his blood.

Four L.A. residents came to Denny's rescue, put him back in his truck and drove him to a nearby hospital, which saved his life. Denny had suffered extensive injuries, including a skull fracture. He underwent years of rehabilitative therapy. All these thoughts swirled through my head as I followed GPS to the infamous intersection.

As I drove, I considered going somewhere else in Los Angeles. After all, nobody except Susie Jordan knew I might go to this neighborhood with a troubled and violent past. Maybe somewhere else in Los Angeles would be just as good. Maybe I could just set up in some shopping center along the way. They need Jesus there, too, I thought. True though that is, I knew in my heart that on this day God wanted me in South Central. So, I kept on following my GPS. I've learned that when I try to change or avoid God's plan or purpose it never turns out well. Even when we are afraid, He will always bless our obedience. We may not know His reason or purpose, but His plan is always our best choice.

As I entered South Central, I finally located Florence Avenue. Florence is a busy thoroughfare with lots of small shops and businesses serving an economically depressed community. My thinking was to drive down Florence toward Normandie and see if there were going to be any problems. After all, I was pulling a 16-foot trailer full of "Jesus Is Lord" crosses through this neighborhood. I figured that would be a good test of the waters. As God would have it, at the very moment I stopped for the traffic lights at the intersection of Florence and Normandie Avenues, my phone rang. Here I was in the exact location where societal strife had produced conditions that led to Reginald Denny and others being dragged from their vehicles and beaten, and someone sees my cell number on the back of the trailer and wants a free cross. So, when the light turned green, I drove on through the intersection and pulled over to the curb.

The man who had called was on foot. His face, neck and arms were covered with tattoos. He asked for two crosses. After we talked for a few moments, I asked him the question that I ask everyone: "Have you come to the place in your life where you know for certain if you died today you would go to Heaven?" He answered with a confident, "Yes!" He then shared his story of finding Christ in prison. Drugs, alcohol and a life of crime had been the reason for his incarceration, but Christ had saved him there, and he'd been out for a couple of years and was living for Jesus. Glory to God! I love to hear people share how they came to Christ. As I got back into the van, I felt reassured that I was right where God wanted me at that moment.

Emboldened, I began to look carefully for a possible location where I could park the trailer and put out the signs for "Free Crosses." I drove up and down Florence and finally located an abandoned car wash a few blocks from Normandie that would work. I spent about three and a half hours sharing Christ and free "Jesus Is Lord" crosses. I met and spoke with many people and gave away many crosses. Four people decided to accept God's free gift of Eternal Life Jesus Christ. Praise God! Yet, I was about to learn another reason why the LORD wanted me in South Central on that day.

Many of the people who stopped to talk with me were either on foot or on bicycles. Toward the end of the afternoon, I saw a young man riding in my direction on his bicycle. When he reached me, he stopped and stared at the crosses and at me. I asked him: "How about a free cross?" He just looked at me and seemed to be trying to speak, but the words wouldn't come. So, I asked a second question: "Have you come to the place in your life where you know for certain that if you died today you would go to Heaven?" His lips were quivering, and his eyes were suddenly swimming with tears. Then he finally spoke and said, "Yes!" The tears were now flowing freely down his cheeks as he told me his story.

"When I saw those crosses," he said, tears streaming, "I knew it was a sign from God for me to come home. I'm a Christian and even served as an assistant pastor until five years ago. Then some money came up missing at the church. Because I lived in a room there, they accused me of stealing it and fired me. I didn't take that money. But they wouldn't believe me. I couldn't understand why God let this happen to me."

Wiping his tears, he continued, "I've been mad at God now for a long time, blaming Him even though in my heart I know it's not His fault. He's not to blame for what happened. Then, today, I saw these crosses from down the road. It was as if God spoke to my heart to come home! So, I rode my bike to come to the crosses."

The Holy Spirit put the lines from an old hymn into my mind that fit the moment. I quoted them to him:

"Come home, come home. Ye who are weary, come home. Earnestly, tenderly, Jesus is calling; Calling, O sinner, come home!"[1]

I encouraged him and prayed for him. He picked up his cross and rode away on his bicycle down Florence Avenue. Praise God, this discouraged pastor had listened to the Holy Spirit speak to his heart and decided to "Come Home!"

As I watched him ride out of sight, I thanked God for leading me to this place. Where once there were riots, there was now restoration. If you have been on the run from God because of something that has happened in your life, please "come home." No matter what, it's never too late to "Come Home!"

---

1   The classic invitation hymn "Softly and Tenderly," which was originally known as "Softly and Tenderly Jesus Is Calling" was written in the 19th century by Will Lamartine Thompson (1847-1909.) According to Internet background information, Thompson was inspired to write gospel music after attending a meeting by evangelist Dwight L. Moody (1837-1899).

12

F'weet Ones

By Valerie Culp-Lytle
August 2021, Tillamook, Oregon

"For God hath not given us the spirit of fear;
but of power and of love, and of a sound mind."
2 Timothy 1:7 KJV

L eo felt led by the Holy Spirit to leave me alone on the street in Tillamook, Oregon.

That sounds bad. It sounds like Leo just walked away from me without looking back. It sounds like he left me standing there all by my lone-
some in a city of strangers. In a sketchy part of town. Not knowing how
long he would be gone. Not knowing who I would encounter. Alone.

That does sound bad.

But, yeah, it went down just like that.

And it turned out to be good.

It was August 2021. I had been with Leo for about a week, having
flown into Billings, Montana to join him. I was still working as a labor
and delivery nurse full-time. I could not be away from work for anywhere
near as long as Leo was planning to be gone. But I was going to be able to
be with him for 12 glorious days.

We had slept overnight in our van. The air was cool, and we slept
comfortably. In the morning, we drove to the Pacific Ocean at Oceanside
Beach State Recreation Site. We marveled at the fog-kissed beauty and
immense power of the water. We stood on the cool, smooth sand and let
the ice-cold water surge over our feet and ankles. We took a bit of time to

read some Scripture and pray. Now we were in a busy, but slightly grubby, part of the city of Tillamook. We were set up with our usual array of crosses and signs in a run-down but roomy parking lot.

We were set up, but the citizens of Tillamook who were passing by were responding with a figurative shrug. Nobody was stopping.

Leo felt led to get out the big gun, or, in this case, the big cross. Shortly before Easter 2020, our dear friend Vic Bass had asked Leo to build a large rolling cross with a wheel on the bottom that he could shoulder and walk around the entire loop in Lufkin, Texas. Leo built the big cross using some weathered wood that Bro. Vic provided. The result was a

nine-foot long, impressive cross that is lightweight. Bro. Vic did walk that large cross around the loop in Lufkin, with Leo taking turns with him, until they circled the whole loop. The total distance was about 15 miles. Remarkably, Bro. Vic accomplished this at a time when the neuropathy in his feet made even everyday walking painful. The power of the Holy Spirit sustained him in completing the task that he felt the Lord had laid on his heart. One man, also named Leo, prayed to be saved as a result of their loop walk with the cross. "The Lufkin Daily News" did a short, front-page story on their walk and included a nice picture.

Most of the time, the big rolling cross is strapped to the side of our trailer full of crosses. It is an eye-catching, silent witness for Jesus as we travel the roads of America. Every now and then, Leo unstraps it and walks with it. It was especially useful during COVID-19 lockdowns. Sometimes Leo would just walk with it on city streets and point silently up to the sky. It does draw attention. That was Leo's hope this day in Tillamook. He hoped the unusual sight of the big cross being carried down the sidewalk would pique interest and pierce hearts.

Once Leo feels sure of a direction, he is not one to waste time. He took the big cross off the trailer, prayed with me for the Lord to please use us both to accomplish His will, shouldered the cross and walked away. Very soon I couldn't see him anymore.

It was broad daylight on a busy street. I should be fine, I told myself. But I was a little scared. Abductions are a thing, even for adults. Human-trafficking is real. Kidnappings for ransom are real. Evil and violence are real. I should be fine, I told myself. I trust the Lord. But, yes, I was a little nervous.

Leo was barely out of sight when a white van pulled up beside me. It was a classic white van that I think of as a Kidnapper Special. True, we have a white van ourselves, but this one didn't have any reassuring cross and open Bible emblazoned on the side. This van was unmarked and mostly windowless.

"Seriously?" I thought to myself. "Here we go."

"Lord," I prayed. "Please let this not be anything bad."

It seemed to get worse. Three people emerged. They looked rough. They clearly had some miles on them. One was a tall, bearded man wearing a brown ball cap and dark sunglasses. The second member of the trio was a big, beefy man in a sleeveless T-shirt. His left hand had scarred knuckles. He looked strong enough to clap a huge hand over one's mouth while he picked one up and shoved one into an unmarked white van that would then speed away and blend anonymously into traffic. While one's husband was who-knows-where. The final member of the threesome made me even more uneasy. She was a diminutive woman. Lots of times bad guys have a woman in cahoots with them.

"Oh, Lord," I prayed silently. "Be with me, please."

The Lord WAS with me, of course. Very quickly I learned that all three of the people were Believers. They had a ministry themselves. The focus of their ministry was to help people trying to overcome drug addictions. I realized that I should not allow appearances and circumstances to bring me to a place of fear, suspicion or judgment about others.

We talked about living for Jesus in today's world. I said that Leo and I try to spread the Gospel of Jesus Christ and push back against the darkness threatening to overshadow our nation.

The big, beefy guy said he felt led to share a word with me. He let me videotape him and agreed that I could share this word with others. His name was Scott. Here's what he said:

"It is so important when you come up against principalities of darkness that are putting stumbling blocks in your life in any way or your loved ones that you need to first humble yourself before the Lord and ask for forgiveness of all your sins and shortcomings and for Jesus to wipe your slate clean. And once you've done that, you are in a position to wield the sword of Christ against these principalities of darkness by going to Ephesians and praying, "Jesus, please Lord, under the authority of the blood of my Lord Jesus Christ, I ask that you remove these principalities of darkness from my life. Cut them off at the knees and remove them for evermore and send them back to where they belong, under your authority. In Jesus' mighty name. Amen."

So, instead of being abducted, I was uplifted by the people in the white van. I love how the Lord can turn our fears into joy when we stand firm in faith.

The interlude put me in mind of a sweet memory of my now deceased father, David Merle Culp. Daddy was a masterful storyteller. He filled the childhoods of my three children with wonderful yarns that he would make up on the spot. Most of the stories would involve my children and Granddaddy as they had all kinds of fantastic adventures. A recurring theme would be the children being followed by some menacing predator such as a hungry-looking wolf. The kids would try to escape, to no avail, and then the wolf would be upon them. The kids would be pressed against a rock face, and the wolf would be so close they could see saliva dripping from his sharp teeth, and then the wolf would open his mouth wider and --

"It was a sweet one!" Daddy would say, slapping his knee.

Turns out, the wolf/bear/scary creature du jour just wanted to taste the chocolate pudding it knew they had in their backpacks. We were a camping and hiking family. My son, David Isaac Wilkerson, initially could not correctly pronounce the word "sweet." He would say, "f'weet." Our family still uses that phrase to this day. One of our husbands will do something especially thoughtful, and the rest of us will say, "He's a F'weet One!"

The people in the white van that day in Tillamook, Oregon were F'weet Ones. Praise God.

But they were not the only memorable visitors I had while I was alone. Next up was a well-dressed man who started our conversation with a question.

Leo Bell Lytle III
and Valerie Lynne Culp-Lytle

"Is that man I saw walking down the road with a cross your husband?" he asked.

"Yes," I said.

"I knew when I saw him and then saw you, that you had to be together," the man said.

He continued, "This is your vacation, isn't it?"

"Yes," I said.

"Why would anybody do this on their vacation?" he asked, and went on, "Why would anybody walk down a sidewalk carrying a giant cross? You know, I asked myself that, and I am thinking the only reason anybody would do that is that they genuinely believe it."

"That's right," I said. "We do genuinely believe it."

The man said he was a high school teacher. He said he had friends who had been born again, but that it had never happened to him. He said he was interested in it, though.

"I would love to tell you about it," I said.

Right away it was apparent that this was not going to be a short and simple witnessing episode of the A-B-C variety. This man wanted to hear the long version. We went over a blood sacrifice being necessary for forgiveness of sins, and how Jesus gave Himself to be the ultimate sacrifice. Right around then, Leo finally saw fit to rejoin me. I was glad. Thanks to the work of the Holy Spirit, I had the fish on the line and was reeling him in, but I sure was happy when Leo showed up in time to handle the dip net. The teacher talked with Leo awhile longer, and then he prayed to be saved. He would be the first of four who made decisions for Christ in that location.

Leo's sidewalk journey with the big cross had indeed served to pique interest and pierce hearts. Alone, each of us had done what we could to advance the cause of Christ that day. But I was glad when the Lord let us reunite. With Leo, my favorite place to be is together.

13

Afternoon Parking Lot Revival

By Leo Lytle
January 2024. Brewton, Alabama

"Trust in the LORD with all thine heart:
And lean not unto thine own Understanding.
In all thy ways acknowledge Him and He shall direct thy paths."
Proverbs 3:5-6 KJV

Goldilocks would have been proud.

It was Monday, January 15, 2024, and I was earnestly seeking God's direction for where to set up for some street evangelism. A spot here and there looked like they might work in a pinch. But like the heroine in the fairy tale, I was in search of somewhere "just right."

I was on the third day of a 20-day evangelism trip to Alabama, Georgia, South Carolina and Florida as I drove through southeast Alabama with a trailer full of "Jesus Is Lord" crosses. When I passed through Bay Minette, Alabama, I didn't find a location that seemed to be "the spot" in which to share Christ and crosses. Then it was on to Atmore, Alabama, where again, I didn't feel led to stop. Although I was heading east, making progress toward Georgia, I really wanted to spend some time in Alabama.

On Interstate 65 I saw a sign for an exit toward Brewton, Alabama. I quickly looked at my map and saw it was about 17 miles south of the interstate. It was a little out of the direction I was headed, but even so, I felt strongly led to take the exit south to Brewton. Could this be the place God had in His plan for me today?

Like most places we stop to share Christ and crosses, I'd never heard of Brewton, Alabama. As I entered the town, I began looking for any possible locations and was surprised to find several possibilities. Before long the LORD led me to a perfect spot. It was the large parking lot of a long-closed grocery store. It wasn't far from a creek.

Brewton has two large creeks that flow through town. One is Burnt Corn Creek, named so nearly 200 years ago after early settlers discovered "burnt corn" left behind by Native Americans. The other is Murder Creek that separates Brewton from East Brewton. I was curious how that creek got its name.

A Wikipedia search turned up the following information: Most believe that Murder Creek was named after a massacre that occurred there in 1788. Colonel Joseph Kirkland and his companions were heading for the Louisiana Territory with sacks of silver. As they traveled down the creek, they encountered a group of people pretending to be traders but who were, in fact, outlaws. As the Colonel and his men bedded down for the night, these outlaws attacked them, killed them all and stole the silver. In time, the leader of the outlaws, who went by the name of "Cat," was captured and taken back to the creek in a specially constructed cage under heavy guard. He was hung from a tree by the spot on the creek where he and his outlaws had massacred Colonel Kirkland and his companions. Hence the name "Murder Creek."

After crossing over Murder Creek from East Brewton, I soon pulled into the large parking lot and intended to put up "FREE CROSSES" signs and scatter crosses around the trailer. However, before I even got the first sign up, folks began to pull in the parking lot. For the next six hours, there was a steady stream of people. Most of them were interested in hearing who I was and why I was giving away free crosses.

Leo Bell Lytle III
and Valerie Lynne Culp-Lytle

It was an exciting and interesting day. In my experiences over the past seven years, I've only seen a few days like this one where the Holy Spirit moved in such a mighty way. One was on my first trip to Kenosha, Wisconsin a few weeks after the riots there in the aftermath of George Floyd's death. Another was in Raymondville, Texas where Valerie and I shared the Gospel nearly non-stop for more than six hours with scores of people giving their lives to Christ. Also, a couple of times in Pine Ridge, South Dakota we've seen big responses to the invitation to pray to be saved.

Three times in Uvalde, Texas the LORD drew in scores of people who were saved. The most recent time at this writing was in January 2023, just a week after our Raymondville, Texas experience. We were already running out of crosses, Bibles and our follow-up material, so we called Bro. Vic Bass for a resupply. We needed the fresh supply to continue our trip to Del Rio, Presidio, Van Horn and El Paso. Bro. Vic, Joe Horton and our good friend and music evangelist Wayne Reynolds drove about 380 miles one-way to get to us in Uvalde. They joined us in sharing Jesus and crosses that afternoon and the next morning. Many people prayed to receive God's free Gift of Eternal Life Jesus Christ!

Before I left Brewton, at least 36 people had placed their trust in Jesus Christ for their salvation. It was a glorious experience. God alone deserves all the glory and praise for what happened there that Monday afternoon.

What was also interesting about the Brewton experience was the role that social media played. As I drove on to Andalusia, Alabama that evening and for the next couple of days, I received many calls from folks who had seen it on a local Facebook page. My Facebook page was tagged by someone, so I was able to see some of the comments from that day as it progressed. The following quotes are just a few of the more than 160 comments that day from Brewton:

"God is never wrong. Thank you, sir for being obedient and stopping in our town that needs Jesus." *Angelia*

"Thank you so much for coming to Brewton today!!! You truly touched my heart and several others. It is people like you who reminded me of how a little love of God goes a long way!!! God Bless you and safe travels my friend in Christ!!! *Jenny*

"So thankful you stopped in Brewton, Alabama! Praying for your ministry." *Kim*

"Praise God for each person who gave their life to Jesus! *Elton and Kathy*

"Thank y'all! We got one (free cross) and y'all made a great impact on my family and friends. God bless y'all on your travels!" *Shaun*

"... as far as I know he is still there because he drew a big crowd of people and was sharing God's Word with them." *Angelia*

"Wow!!! This is incredible! As of 2:52 he's still there! There were about four people who gave their lives to Jesus as I was getting there." *Tiffany*

"Look at God! He said he was called to stop in Brewton and these four souls just might have been the reason why!" *Lisa*

"As of 3:08, he is still there. Five people gave their lives to the Lord!" *Courtney*

"He is still at the old Pic N Save, I just took the boys." *Tracey*

"He is heading to Maxwell's on 29." *Tonya*

"My mom got a hold of him. He drove past Ridge Road for 15 miles, and he came right back just to give us some crosses!" *Amelia*

"It is amazing to see these posts about the impact this ministry has had at each place it stops! The Lord Himself is well pleased, I am sure!" *Jimmie*

I'm so thankful that I followed the Holy Spirit's leading and saw Him working in Brewton that day. It was like a one-day revival as many were saved and others rededicated their lives to Jesus Christ. Thank you, Jesus!

14

All About The One

By Valerie Culp-Lytle
June 2022, Deerfield, Kansas

"A man's heart deviseth his way, but the Lord directeth his steps."
Proverbs 16:9, KJV

Unknown to us, we were physically lost. Lost, AND in a broken-down vehicle. But our mechanic was spiritually Lost. Before the sun would set, the Lord had set all our feet onto the way we should go.

Day Three of our 2022 Midwest Ministry Trip was all about one special Divine Appointment. We got up on Friday, June 17, 2022 in Liberal, Kansas full of big hopes for the day. The night before, I had texted Bro. Vic one of our periodic updates that he shares with the prayer support team.

"It's funny," I had chattily texted Bro. Vic at the close of Thursday, "We had about two and a half hours of sleep in the van in a church parking lot, ate a few cheese crackers for lunch and have been out in 100-degree heat. Leo had loaded and installed a trailer-full of kitchen cabinets before the dedication service on Wednesday night at Trinity (Trinity Baptist Church in Lufkin). And then Leo drove for more than seven hours

after the service. But we don't even feel that tired. Seeing people saved is so exhilarating, as you know! God gives the increase and supplies the energy. A great day, all glory to God! Thank you all for your prayers!"

All that was true, except I realized later that while I DID only get about two and a half hours of sleep while the van was PARKED, I had ACTUALLY slept the vast majority of the more than seven hours that Leo drove. I just woke up at the gas stations: "Didn't we JUST fill up with gas a little bit ago?," I would groggily ask Leo. Like the prudent man he is, he mostly let my queries pass without comment. I even quoted a beloved bit of Scripture for good measure:

"But they that wait upon the Lord shall renew their strength; they shall mount up with wings as eagles; they shall run, and not be weary; and they shall walk, and not faint." --- Isaiah 40:31 KJV.

Bro. Vic, being the wise man he is, had simply replied, "Amen. He is our energy." That's true, too. But what is also true is that by the time we checked into a cheap motel in Liberal around 11:30 p.m., the exhilaration we were feeling from seeing 17 people saved on Thursday had ebbed. I was suddenly so tired that by the time I climbed the stairs to the second floor (with Leo carrying all the heavy stuff), I sprawled sideways on top of my side of the bed. I did not move until morning. I did not undress, did not brush my teeth, did not get under the bedspread. I just lay there, fully clothed, uncovered and sideways, until daybreak.

But after breakfast and a shower, we were ready to go again. We thanked the Lord for the 17 souls saved on Thursday and eagerly anticipated what great things He would do on Friday.

Leo's plan was that we would stick with U.S. Highway 83 into Ne-

braska and eventually veer off to go to Chadron. From there we would be in position to make it to Pine Ridge, South Dakota, where Leo hoped to preach on Saturday. At about 11 a.m. on Friday, Leo noticed our van's air conditioner was suddenly blowing hot air. The van was overheating. Leo made an immediate U-turn, went back to a convenience store in Garden City and bought two gallons of water and some coolant. He added what the radiator would take when he could do so safely. We thought at the time that maybe the very hot weather combined with hours and hours of relentless highway miles had caused the van to run low on water.

Everything seemed fine after that. The air conditioner was blowing cold air again. We went on our way. About 17 miles later, we saw that everything was NOT fine. The temperature defiantly headed right back to hot. The van's engine started missing violently, almost shuddering. We pulled over, cooled down, added more water and started backtracking toward Garden City. We figured it was a large enough town to have mechanics.

But after about three miles, we came upon the tiny town of Deerfield. We stopped at a convenience store. Leo opened the radiator carefully to see if it needed MORE water. What water there was, was bubbling a good three inches high out of the top of the radiator. I am no auto mechanic. But it seemed to me that was not a good sign. A man inside the store told Leo about a tire and auto repair place right there in Deerfield called Willy's. The man in the store gave us directions to Willy's, and we headed that way. My quick Internet search brought up H&W Tire and Auto Repair. I called the number and explained our dilemma to a man who I'll call Henry. He said the shop didn't do auto repair anymore, but he was willing to help us if it was an emergency.

We went to where we understood the shop was, but could see no sign proclaiming H&W Tire and Auto Repair. What we DID see was the van's temperature gauge moving inexorably back to "H." I called the number back to ask where, exactly, they were located, and Henry said, "I can see you." Praise God for that, because the van had gone on "Hot" again.

Henry, who turned out to be a co-owner of the business, diagnosed a cracked radiator. He ordered a new radiator and dispatched his wife to go pick it up. He loaned us their shop truck so we could drive to the only 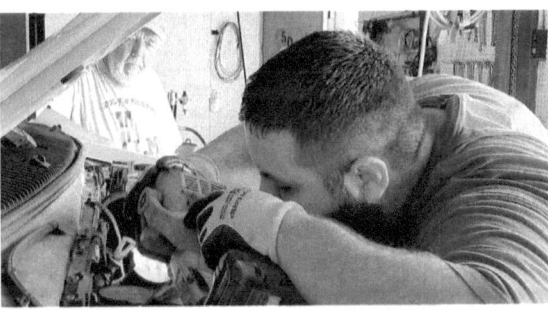 restaurant in town. He made sure the truck had enough gas in it. We enjoyed a delicious and leisurely lunch of Mexican food. We prayed for the Lord to show us what He wanted us to do in Deerfield.

Once the new radiator was installed, Henry test-drove the van, looked everything over again and topped off fluids. Then Leo gave Henry a free "Jesus Is Lord" cross and secured Henry's permission to ask him a question...

Henry prayed to be saved. Heaven rejoiced as his name was entered into the Lamb's Book of Life. We bade him a warm goodbye with our profuse thanks. Our goodbye was of the "See you in Heaven" variety. Although, if we ever go through Deerfield, again, we would love to stop in and see Henry. He sure is a nice man. And now he is a saved man.

After we left Deerfield in mid-afternoon and made it to Lakin, Kansas, we made an interesting discovery. I mentioned to Leo that the sign on the side of the road said "50" and weren't we supposed to be on "83"? Leo assured me that we were, in fact, on "83." No question about it. "Well, then," I asked him, "why do the signs keep saying "50?" We realized we had accidentally been on the wrong road since we had gone through Garden City earlier in the day, before our radiator cracked. Instead of heading north, we had been going west. But even lost on the road, the Lord was still able to use us for His purposes.

Henry would turn out to be the only person saved on Friday. We gave away crosses in Liota later that afternoon and met some special Believers, but nobody else was saved. Our day had unfolded differently than we had imagined, but consistently with how the Lord sometimes works. Friday was a day all about not the 99, but the one.

---

3 *"And He spake this parable unto them, saying,*

4 *What man of you, having an hundred sheep, if he lose one of them, doth not leave the ninety and nine in the wilderness, and go after that which is lost, until he find it?*

5 *"And when he hath found it, he layeth it on his shoulders, rejoicing.*

6 *"And when he cometh home, he calleth together his friends and neighbors, saying unto them, Rejoice with me; for I have found my sheep which was lost.*

7 *"I say unto you, that likewise joy shall be in heaven over one sinner that repenteth, more than over ninety and nine just persons, which need no repentance."*

Luke 15: 3-7, KJV

15

Life In The Time Of COVID-19

With a nod to Gabriel Garcia Marquez and his famous book
Love In The Time Of Cholera

By Valerie Culp-Lytle
September 2024, Pine Valley, Texas

*"For I am persuaded, that neither death, nor life, nor angels, nor principalities,
nor powers, nor things present, nor things to come, Nor height, nor depth,
nor any other creature, shall be able to separate us from the love of God,
which is in Christ Jesus our Lord."*
Romans 8: 39-39 KJV

———————

Jesus Christ divided time, for all time. The ages before His birth are known as B.C. (Before Christ.) But in some secular circles, the capital letters BC have taken on an additional meaning within the past few years: Before COVID.

The COVID-19 pandemic that began in Wuhan, China in December 2019 would go on to leave an indelible mark in world history. The reason for the capitalization of the word COVID is because it is an acronym for **CO**rona**VI**rus **D**isease. Viral in nature, COVID-19 is also called SARS-CoV-2, short for severe acute respiratory syndrome coronavirus. The World Health Organization declared the outbreak to be a global pandemic on March 11, 2020. Millions of people died worldwide. The statistics on those deaths are nuanced and so bewildering that literally only God knows how many people died because of COVID-19. Even at present, COVID-19 is still claiming some lives, but on a far smaller scale.

Right now, most adults in the world have their own version of weathering COVID-19. But as the decades roll by, the ranks of survivors will thin and eventually disappear. Best to capture first-hand accounts now. For that reason, to preserve a little slice of world history as it affected us, we are presenting chapters in this book that deal with the year 2020 in chronological order. Everywhere else in this book, we've mixed up dates and destinations in a random way that mimics the crisscross, up and down, all around way that Leo and I have traveled the United States of America during these first seven years of our evangelism ministry. But 2020 we are presenting as it unfolded for us. We praise God to have survived it.

In January of 2020, Leo and I took a personal trip to New England. It was not a ministry trip. We had just been meaning to visit some New England states to see a few historical sites and enjoy some scenery. So, when we found an inexpensive round-trip airfare to Boston, Massachusetts and an open week in our schedule, we flew up and rented a car. On the way, we saw a couple of small signs posted in the airport that said if one had recently been in Wuhan, China and was now feeling ill, to do something or other. Report it, or some such, and avoid exposing other people.

Listening to the nightly news during our trip, we kept hearing a little more. At the end of the week, we spent one night in Maine. In that hotel room in Maine, I remember getting a text from my sister, Donna Culp-Hixon. She stays up on the latest news. She told me she was going to order some N-95 face masks, just in case. N-95 masks were the most effective at providing protection. I told her it was a good idea.

On the flight home from Boston, crammed into our cheap seats, somebody coughed several rows back. I made eye contact with Leo and pulled my shirt up over my nose and mouth.

"And so it begins," I thought to myself, recalling that famous line from the Kevin Costner movie *"Robin Hood: Prince of Thieves."*

A day or two later, Leo and I were in a grocery store near our home. Somebody coughed on one of the aisles. I had on sunglasses and a hoodie already, and again pulled up the neckline of my shirt to cover my mouth and nose. Leo snapped a picture of me on his phone and laughingly remarked: "My wife, the nurse."

It was the last time we laughed about COVID-19.

Some time later, Donna and her husband, Dan Hixon, would drive from their home an hour and a half away to bring me some of their N-95 face masks to use in my job as a nurse. The COVID-19 pandemic had exploded onto the world stage. Personal protection equipment (PPE) for health care workers very quickly went into short supply.

Leo Bell Lytle III
and Valerie Lynne Culp-Lytle

Our unit in the East Texas hospital where I worked full-time in labor and delivery as a registered nurse stayed in good shape regarding supplies. I credit our nurse manager, Cindy Holloway. I had mentioned to her that I thought we should deep-stock what supplies we could, because the fledgling COVID-19 situation still far away on the horizon would surely worsen, and medical supply shortages would probably happen. Being a fellow keep-up-with-the-news person, she did order as much as she could.

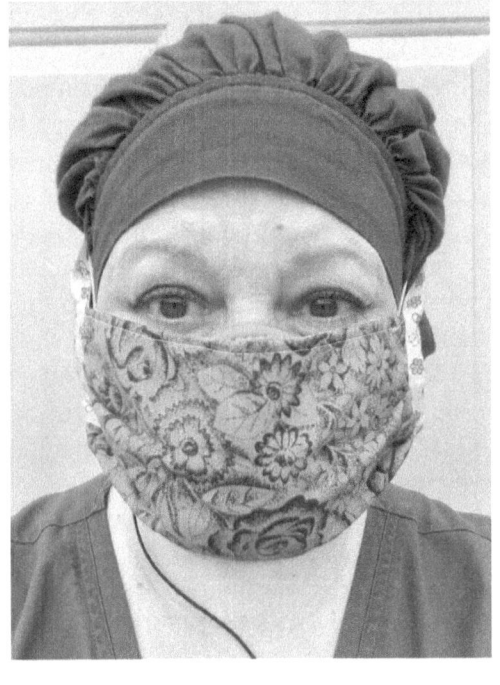

We would be very grateful for her decisive action. But even so, our hospital rationed N-95 face masks early in the ordeal. We were given a few N-95 masks to rotate but had to wear those masks over and over for long periods of time. In normal days we would have discarded them after limited use. I was grateful that I had some N-95 masks from Donna and Dan to keep for an emergency. Like toilet paper, N-95 masks almost achieved currency status during the pandemic.

Our wonderful nurse manager also arranged for our badges to be re-programmed to allow us to use a back staircase to get into our locked unit from a small parking lot. That way we could avoid passing through the emergency room to and from our shifts. This arrangement provided for the safety of pregnant and postpartum women and babies, both not yet born and newborn. The arrangement may have also saved some nurses' lives.

I remember stocking our labor and delivery rooms in those early days of the pandemic, before it fully reached East Texas. As I organized supplies, I was conscious of an oppressive feeling of fear. It felt like a weight on my chest. It caused me to take frequent deep breaths. Keeping up with the news, I could clearly see the catastrophe coming. It was like seeing a "Blue Norther" looming on the prairie and knowing a blizzard is bearing down. It was like hearing the roar of rapids getting louder as one is swept down a river. It was like seeing the sky turn orange as a wildfire devours the countryside. It was like lying in bed and hearing an intruder breaking down the door.

All I could do was pray. Certainly, I turned again and again to 2 Timothy 1:7 KJV: *"For God hath not given us the spirit of fear; but of power, and of love, and of a sound mind."*

A loved one or two suggested that it would be a good time for me to retire. A profile of patients who were at higher risk for death from COVID-19 was starting to emerge. I checked a good number of the boxes: somewhat older and somewhat heavier with a history of asthma and Type II diabetes. My respiratory health had been precarious for most of my life. A simple cold could touch off an asthma episode that might last for weeks. Occasionally my asthma attacks could get so severe that I would have to be treated in an emergency room. I was not lacking for legitimate reasons to leave the field before the battle began.

But I am not a quitter. Nor do I leave my friends in danger and seek safety for myself. As I explained to those who suggested that I stay home and stay safe, to quit before COVID-19 hit our hospital would be like training to be a soldier and then dropping my weapon and running before the first shot was fired. No, I wasn't going to flee. I would stand and serve right where I was and trust the Lord to either keep me safe or take me Home.

But, yes, I was afraid.

For a little while, maybe a few weeks, our hospital inched slowly up the steep incline of a terrifying roller coaster. The slow progress allowed the dread to build. Our hospital crept slowly upward, teetered on the lip of the drop and then plunged into the abyss. COVID-19 had arrived in East Texas with a vengeance.

Patients started dying of COVID-19 in our hospital. Eventually, many or most of us had either a friend, relative or neighbor who had died of COVID-19. The death list just kept on getting longer. One of our much beloved co-workers died directly from COVID-19, although she was not exposed at work. Another co-worker died of a complication attributed to COVID-19. It had become very real.

Labor and delivery didn't see much of COVID-19, praise God Almighty to the highest part of Heaven. The cases we did see were mostly mild ones. I learned that persistent coughing and sneezing or headaches in those days were rarely ever "allergies," as patients would insist. We would test them, and they would be positive. The testing in those early days was awful. We were told to insert the swabs far up the nose. It was scary to do and a painful ordeal to have it done. It was a relief when months later, the testing improved, and new directions required the swab to only be inserted a short distance into the nose.

Testing, schmesting. As the months wore on, I would joke that I could "test" for COVID-19 by talking to a person on the telephone. No kidding, there was a certain quality to the sound of a stopped-up nose that did often signal COVID-19. I remember, too, months into it, being served at a fast-food restaurant somewhere in South Texas. The young woman was stifling coughs behind her face mask. She unconsciously touched her forehead a couple of times as she took our order.

"Do you have a headache?" I asked her.

"Yes, ma'am," she answered.

"You know you have COVID, don't you?" I said to her.

"Yes, ma'am," she again answered. "But there is nobody else to work."

Even now, several years later, my heart rate increases a little bit when I think very long about the dread and fear that saturated those early days, weeks and months of the COVID-19 pandemic.

I also start to feel an echo of the exhaustion. The fear was exhausting. The precautions were exhausting. The social isolation, the shortages and the uncertainty were exhausting. Truly exhausting, too, was the on and off rigamarole of garbing up in Personal Protection Equipment from head to toe every time we had to go in or out of the room of a patient who had tested positive. In labor and delivery, there is usually a LOT of in and out to patient rooms. We wore head covers, safety goggles, two or three masks, a face shield, an isolation gown, shoe covers and two or three pairs of gloves. Lab specimens had to be walked in person to the lab, rather than sent via vacuum tube. There was elaborate hand washing and disinfecting of equipment and a "terminal clean" of the whole room when a positive patient was discharged, which beleaguered environmental safety team members had to do. Even the paperwork had to be quarantined.

I had to drive nearly an hour each way to and from work. My shifts were 12 hours long. But I almost always had more charting to do after the 12-hour shift was finished. Sometimes hours of it. I was an excellent nurse and provided exemplary patient care. But I was also one of those nurses who was usually behind on the paperwork, even when there was not a pandemic.

When I could manage it, I would sleep on a thin pallet on the floor or in the fetal position on a too-short vinyl couch in an empty room. It was better than fighting sleep to drive nearly an hour to get home, only to have to return before daylight the next day. We had a shower in the nurses' dressing room, and I would bring clean clothes. Sleeping wherever I could find was never comfortable, but it was better than falling asleep while driving and gave me a little more time to sleep. I would fall immediately into the unconscious state of the exhausted, and then do it all again the next day. Only the grace of God got me through all of it.

Eventually, it got too tiring to be as afraid as we once were. That was okay, because by that time, the COVID-19 virus was starting to attenuate, or become weaker. We all praised God for it. COVID-19 stopped killing so many people. Instead, more and more people survived it. More and more people had milder and milder cases. Nowadays, people can have COVID-19 and not even know it.

I have had COVID-19 twice so far. The first time, I had it alone when Leo was away on a long ministry trip. It was in early 2022, so the COVID-19 virus had considerably weakened by then, thank God. My breathing was not affected. But I had fever and chills, body aches, sneezing and a pervasive headache. After a rapid onset the afternoon and evening before, it seemed like I was practically unconscious for the next two days. But I was lost in a delirium of fevered sleep punctuated by the thought every few hours that I should try --- I really should try --- to get up and take a couple of swallows of water, maybe take some Tylenol. But I could rarely make myself get up at all. Those tasks required way too much effort and energy.

Sometime during the second full day, my daughter-in-law, Aimee Wilkerson, called me to say she had just left a pot of freshly made kale soup on my front steps. I stumbled out to get it, ate a bowl of the hot soup and felt a little strength return to my body. The thank-you video I sent to her is still on my phone. It is a pitiful thing to watch, my thanking her in my weakened state with tears running down my face. But it was truly heartfelt. The next day I felt stable enough to drive to a drive-through testing site. My results, of course, were positive. I was sick for days, but each day I got better, praise God.

The second time I had COVID-19 was in December 2023. I had attended a ministry event in a closed space with hundreds of people. Several of our group came home with Covid. It was remarkable and wonderful how much less virulent the virus was by that time.

Leo Bell Lytle III
and Valerie Lynne Culp-Lytle

———————

Leo's experiences in 2020, the worst year of the COVID-19 pandemic, were very different from mine. For one thing, in contrast to my reporting to each nursing shift with a heavy feeling of fear during the first few months of the pandemic, Leo was never afraid.

Not only was Leo not afraid. He was also not discouraged, not even when he saw a nicely full calendar of church events evaporate. One by one, pastors would call him and apologetically tell him their churches had suspended in-person services because of COVID-19 and, therefore, would not need him to come preach after all. The cancellations rolled in on waves. It was as though a swarm of locusts had devoured a burgeoning crop in a field. In a twinkling, all that was left were gnawed stalks --- engagements crossed out on the pages of his appointment book, until all were gone.

But COVID-19 would turn out to have a big silver lining for our ministry. Leo pivoted from relying mostly on church engagements for evangelism opportunities to taking it to the streets in the open air. It ultimately caused a profound shift for the better in our ministry. No longer was Leo mostly "preaching to the choir" in churches across the country, with some sharing of crosses along the way. Instead, he was almost exclusively out in the highways and hedges that were teeming with lost people. Far, far more people have come to Jesus on the streets than in the churches.

COVID-19 had one additional silver lining for our ministry. People in general became more convinced of the uncertainty and fragility of life and more mindful of Eternity. Death all around does tend to have that effect.

Nationwide, though, COVID-19 took a terrible toll on churches. At this writing, four years post-pandemic, many churches have still not returned to pre-COVID-19 attendance levels. Lots of people got out of the habit of going to church and haven't made it back yet.

Leo says the following about 2020:

"The last church I preached at before COVID-19 really took hold of the country was Joy Fellowship on March 15, 2020 in Hot Springs, South Dakota. The following day, Monday, March 16, 2020 on the Pine Ridge Indian Reservation was the last time I would share crosses for a while. Bill Martin, the pastor of Joy Fellowship where I had just preached, called to see if the Pine Ridge reservation was still open. He had heard they were closed. So, I went over there, but that was the last time I shared crosses for a while.

CROSS-ing AMERICA
Sharing Jesus Around The Nation

"The next time I shared crosses was May 31, 2020 in Magnolia, Arkansas. The next time I would preach in a church would be July 25, 2020 at Friendship Baptist Church in Buchanan, Tennessee. Friendship Baptist's pastor, Russell Ragsdale, is a friend of ours. So is his wife, Debbie Ragsdale."

For my part, that March 2020 evangelism trip that Leo was on when COVID-19 cases exploded across the nation caused me more anxiety on top of the worry I was already feeling about working as a nurse during the pandemic. I remember watching the news each night after work and comparing new outbreaks with where Leo was at that time. He was heading home from South Dakota. The news got worse every night. It reminded me of watching an adventure movie where the bridges collapse and the

cliffs crumble right after the hero moves from them. The world was going crazy. The world was shutting down. I just wanted Leo home.

He made it home, thank God, and he took all the church cancellations in stride. He started preaching on Facebook Live on Saturday nights and did that for about a month and a half. It was during that time, too, when Bro. Vic asked Leo to make a large rolling cross. Leo made it, and they took turns carrying it as they walked around the loop in Lufkin, Texas the week before Easter.

After that, Leo put the big cross to lots of good use. With permission to use it from Bro. Vic, Leo would travel to a well-populated/well-traveled location and shoulder the big cross. He would carry the cross as he walked for a long time, occasionally pointing upward. In a time when person-to-person contact carried the fear of death, it was Leo's way of continuing to share Jesus and to spread hope even during those very trying times.

At the height of the pandemic, people didn't want to get close enough to another person to carry on a conversation. Leo says one 12-year-old boy on a bicycle followed him in Sand Springs, Oklahoma, and he did lead that boy to the Lord. But most of the big cross activity took place in

Leo Bell Lytle III
and Valerie Lynne Culp-Lytle

silence. Leo would roll the cross for blocks and blocks, sometimes over overpasses. Every now and then he would look up, smile, and point to the sky. It was a powerful reminder that God was still with us, even during a pandemic.

"I carried the big cross around a lot of different places," Leo said. "I carried the big cross in Marshall, Texas; Harrison, Arkansas; Russellville, Arkansas; Benton, Arkansas; Leesville, Louisiana; Yankton, South Dakota; Wichita, Kansas; Salina, Kansas; Mobile, Alabama; Gulfport, Mississippi; Scotlandville, Louisiana; Sioux City, Iowa and Norfolk, Nebraska.

"I don't think I ever got sick with COVID-19," Leo continued. "I worked the whole way in the shop (Leo's custom woodcraft shop). Every chance I could, I went out with the cross."

Looking back, I think Leo may have become sick with COVID-19 at one point in maybe late 2021 or early 2022, but it was over so quickly we didn't get around to testing. One day Leo came back into the house after spending the morning working in his wood shop. He said he didn't feel well and that he had a strong headache. With

that, he took an almost unheard-of daytime nap and slept for four hours. The next day he was back to work as usual. I now think that four-hour nap was probably Leo's version of having COVID-19.

When COVID-19 caught up to my elderly mother, Ida Mae Culp, she became so weak that she spent a night lying on the floor before being discovered. When she was discharged from the hospital, she had to go to a COVID-19 rehabilitation center in another town. My sisters and I would have to stand outside the open window near her bed and talk to her through the window screen because no visitors were allowed inside.

Mama told us that she was talking to staff members and other patients in the COVID-19 rehabilitation center about Jesus. It is inspiring that even bedridden, recovering from COVID-19, my mother was still trying to share the Good News. My late father, David Merle Culp, led many people to the Lord over many years. He was a very active member of the

Gideons International, and Mama was a member of the Gideons International Auxiliary. Daddy often spoke in churches, and had a county jail and then a prison ministry for years. Daddy and Mama also gave Bibles to people they met in campgrounds all over the United States, including Alaska, and across Canada. I am proud of and grateful to God for the legacy of faith and evangelism I have from both my parents. I am grateful, too, that they both lived through COVID-19.

The next few chapters detail some of mine and Leo's experiences of life and ministry in the time of COVID-19. It was a unique moment in modern history. We thank God for allowing us to live to tell the tale. As always, all glory to God.

16

Face Masks, Flames, and Faith

By Leo Lytle
July 2020, Pensacola, Florida

"Watch ye, stand fast in the faith, quit you like men, be strong."
I Corinthians 16: 13 KJV

The year 2020 could be symbolized with face masks and flames. The fresh face of a brand-new decade had quickly been hidden behind mandatory face masks as COVID-19 stalked the nation.

But it got worse. While people were dying in record numbers from the global pandemic, another kind of mayhem infected the cities of America. A series of tragic incidents involving the police set off waves of protests around the nation. These protests reached fever pitch after the deaths of Breonna Taylor in March 2020 in Louisville, Kentucky and then the death of George Floyd in May 2020 in Minneapolis, Minnesota. Both were black people who died at the hands of police officers.

Violence rocked the country. Complex social problems resulted in property being destroyed, law enforcement officers being attacked and businesses being looted. Some innocent people were injured or killed. It was difficult to watch on television and frightening to get close to in real life.

In July 2020, I was down on the Gulf Coast sharing Christ and crosses in Pensacola, Florida. A homeless

man who asked for a cross suggested I go to the "Black Lives Matter" protest they were having every night down by what they called "Graffiti Bridge." I was intrigued by the suggestion and asked if it was a peaceful protest. He said he thought so and gave me directions. At sundown I headed that way.

I soon found my way there. As I approached the railroad overpass, I noticed that the local graffiti artists had found a huge concrete "canvas" on either side of the roadway which they covered with their spray-painted contributions. I drove under the bridge, and there was no doubt I had found the protesters. On this night there were at least 200 people gathered on either side of the grass-covered road where it came out from under the overpass. Amplified music was being played so loudly that it was difficult to discern what was being said or sung.

I noticed a parking area up ahead, maybe 100 yards from where people were gathered. I pulled into an empty space, killed the engine and rolled down my windows to listen and observe. From what I could tell, it seemed to be a peaceful protest. There were handmade signs that said "Black Lives Matter" and a few asking for justice for George Floyd. I thought I heard preaching coming through one of the big speakers and heard Gospel music coming from another.

As I was listening to and observing the activity, I was praying about what God would have me do. My heart's desire was to be used by the LORD in that place to lift up His name.

In just a few short minutes, the Holy Spirit laid on my heart exactly what to do. I would carry the big rolling cross I had inside my red truck's camper shell. I would carry it down the road and under the "Graffiti Bridge," then turn around and come back the same way. The big cross has a "Jesus Is Lord" cross fastened to either side. It would proclaim that message without me saying a word. It sounded like a plan to me. So, I drove my truck over to a poorly lit road about a block from where people were assembled. The big cross is about nine feet long. I let it rest on its side as I gazed for a moment down the dark road that led to the well-lit area.

"This could be dangerous," I found myself thinking.

Leo Bell Lytle III
and Valerie Lynne Culp-Lytle

"No one even knows I'm here," I thought. "Except God!" was my immediate next thought.

I dismissed my fears. It was time to "Cowboy up!"

But because of the reality of the situation, that something could indeed happen, I felt I needed to call Valerie and let her know where I was, what I was about to do and tell her where I had parked the truck. So, I called her, but didn't get her. She was still at work. I left a message on her voicemail.

"Baby," I said into the recording. "I just thought I should call you. I'm in Pensacola, and I'm about to roll the big cross through a 'Black Lives Matter' protest. It looks peaceful. I think everything will be fine. But, just in case, I wanted you to know where I left the truck. It's on the park side of the 'Graffiti Bridge' here in Pensacola. Don't worry. I love you very much. Call you later." Then I prayed for the LORD to use me for His glory.

I gazed one more time down the dark road toward the light and took my first step. Then I took the next step, and then the next step, and the next. They were powerful steps of faith, steps that are vividly etched in my memory.

As I emerged from the darkness into the lighted area, some of the people gathered on my left side started pointing in my direction. A few more feet and every eye seemed to be looking at me. I'm not 100 percent positive, but I think the music stopped as I passed by the first section. Suddenly, people broke out in spontaneous, huge, sustained applause! I raised my free hand upward, pointing to Heaven, and with all my strength called out, "Jesus is the answer!" The applause died down, and the music began to play again as I passed under the bridge.

Then it was time to turn around and go back on the other side. I thanked God, took a deep breath, and crossed back under the bridge to the other side. This side applauded as well. Again, I pointed to Heaven and called out as loudly as I could: "Jesus is the answer!" Slowly, I walked away from the protestors and carried the cross back into the darkness to find my truck.

It was an exhilarating experience. I praise God for His protection through it all. I'll never forget that special moment. How and in what ways God may have used that old cross that night in Pensacola, Florida only He knows. But every time I see the name Pensacola in print, on a highway sign or hear it mentioned in the news or in conversation, it always brings a smile to my face. To God be the glory!

17

Old Shoes, No Socks, No Sunscreen

By Leo Lytle
August 2020, Uvalde, Texas

"Now unto him that is able to do exceeding abundantly above all that we ask or think, according to the power that worketh in us, Unto him be glory in the church by Christ Jesus throughout all ages, world without end. Amen."
Ephesians 3:20-21 KJV

Nearly two years before the small southwest Texas town of Uvalde would be struck by the unimaginable tragedy of a mass school shooting, it was the site of one of our ministry's most memorable experiences.

Of course, I had no idea what the Lord was about to do there in a mighty way. There is no way of knowing what might transpire at any given location where we feel led to stop and share. God has a way of using each place to accomplish things in people's lives that we simply have no way of knowing beforehand. He's God! He's still on His Throne! He is at work in people's lives. Yet, He chooses to use Believers like us all over the world to have a part in accomplishing His will.

I've always preached that it is our responsibility, our duty and our great privilege to represent Him to this lost and hurting world. Like many of you, I've heard it often said, we are "saved to serve." Indeed, we are.

CROSS-ing AMERICA
Sharing Jesus Around The Nation

For our part, He has equipped each of us with certain gifts, talents and abilities. He intends for us to use them to advance the Gospel. Sadly, most Believers today are absorbed in their own busy lives. Little effort is made in making Christ known to those in their own circles of influence. It ought not be that way! When I think of what He went through so that I could be saved and have an abundant and Eternal Life, it inspires me. I **want** to serve Him. Not because I **have** to serve Him, but because I **want** to serve Him!

It's that very personal relationship with Christ that informs my choices in this life. If you're not inspired to serve Him, then perhaps you don't really have a personal relationship with Him. The journey from the head to the heart is only about 18 inches, but it's the difference between Heaven and Hell!

Now back to the special day of August 20, 2020, in Uvalde, Texas.

It was August 20, 2020, and I was running late to leave home. I still needed to check the mail at the post office, go to the bank and tie up a few loose ends in my shop. Valerie was still working as a full-time Labor and Delivery nurse. Her schedule wouldn't permit her to go. It was a seven-day evangelistic trip to Southeast Arizona where I'd be sharing "The Door" message at churches in Bisbee and Douglas. With "The Door" message I put together a four-panel cypress door as I preach and use it to illustrate many spiritual truths. Of course, along the way I would share Christ and crosses as usual. Valerie and I prayed for each other, kissed and said our goodbyes. I hopped in the truck. We waved to each other until we were both out of sight. I was really going to miss her.

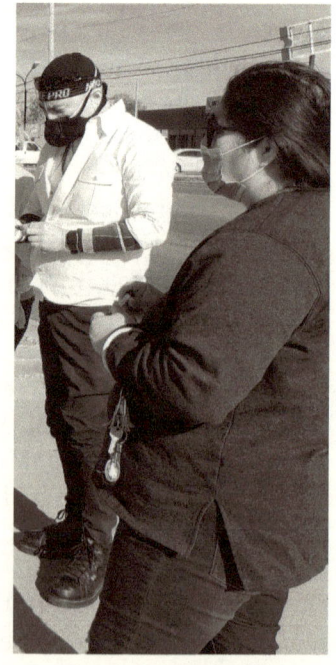

A few hours later, somewhere near San Marcos, Texas I got my first call for a free cross. It was a young lady on her way home from work. On the side of the road, she allowed me to share Jesus with her. A short time later she accepted God's free gift of Eternal Life Jesus Christ!

Just as she was leaving, a worker at a nearby business saw us. He climbed over a fence, then walked over to get a free cross. He, too, was saved right there on the side of the road. Then, a nearly empty school bus pulled over. There were three ladies on the bus. They all said they were Believers. All wanted a free cross and the story behind what I was doing. After my brief explanation, the driver insisted on praying for me before leaving. None of us in that impromptu prayer meeting could know what God would do in Uvalde a few hours later.

It was a hot Texas summer afternoon by the time I drove through San Antonio. Of course, my air conditioner wasn't working. I had the windows cranked down in our 1998 Dodge Ram we call "Old Red." She had certainly seen better days. She would, however, carry us safely from coast to coast and border to border over the next couple of years.

My plan was to stop around 4 or 5 in the afternoon in some town on U.S. Highway 90 as I headed west. Just maybe it might be a little cooler by then, I hoped.

In my haste to get on the road that morning, I had left home without putting on socks and had forgotten my comfortable shoes. I was still wearing my worn-out and ill-fitting work shoes. I stopped at a dollar store and bought a cheap pair of tennis shoes that were at least better than what I was wearing, a couple of pairs of socks and some sunscreen. I'd put them on later when I found a place to share Christ and crosses.

To be honest, I had no idea what town I would stop in that afternoon. At the last minute I'd decided to take a more southerly westward route. It was my first time in that part of Texas. I'd heard of Uvalde and knew it was one of the towns up ahead, but that was the extent of my knowledge about this city that was soon to become a place I'd never forget.

Uvalde was bustling with activity. Businesses of every shape and size lined the main street through town. Of course, I was looking for that special spot. I looked around for a vacant parking lot, an abandoned business or any place where cars could easily enter and exit. On my windshield survey through town, I spotted a couple of possibilities that looked promising. Then my phone rang.

It was from a couple who had been following me through town. They wanted a free cross, so I pulled over in a hotel parking lot to meet them. After my Gospel presentation, both placed their trust in Jesus Christ alone for their salvation!

Driving down a couple more blocks, I saw a grocery store off to my left. It was teeming with cars and people. On my right, directly across from the grocery store, was a large, ragged-looking vacant lot. I knew this was the right place.

I backed the truck up as close to the busy street as seemed safe. I had left enough room to be able to put out my signs and get from one side of the truck to the other. On this trip I was not pulling a trailer. Instead, I used a makeshift platform which was attached to the trailer hitch. It held about 40 crosses. A homemade "FREE CROSSES" sign was attached to it along with my cell phone number. The Vic Bass Ministries team had loaded another 250 crosses in the back of the truck under the camper shell.

Before I could even get my tailgate down and put out my signs, a couple of cars pulled up on either side of the truck. Then, for the next four and a half hours, folks would be driving up on both sides nearly non-stop!

I was sharing my story of how I came to Christ, along with a brief Gospel presentation, with as many people as I could. In fact, so many were stopping I began to ask folks to gather in small groups for me to talk to them.

They waited patiently as I crawled into the back of the truck to bring out more crosses. I had brought nearly 300 crosses for this trip. I thought that would be plenty. I soon realized they might be all given out before I left Uvalde.

During a brief lull, I excitedly called my friend Bro. Vic to tell him what was happening in Uvalde. I remember telling him I had hit the "mother lode" and couldn't tell how many folks had been saved so far, but to please pray! It was Vic Bass Ministries and his team of volunteers who were making the "Jesus Is Lord" crosses at the time, as well as providing prayer support.

The lull ended. People kept coming. I was busy sharing the Gospel and leading folks to Christ until well after dark. Prior to this day, I had never experienced a Holy Spirit-led harvest of souls like this. We would be blessed with more amazing outpourings of the Holy Spirit in the future. Some of those outpourings of the Holy Spirit in the future would result in even more people being saved than on this day. But this was the first time.

It was after 9 that night by the time I loaded up the scant remaining crosses. I turned west onto U.S. Highway 90 and drove away in the dark night toward Del Rio. It felt so good to be off my feet. The cool night air wafted through the open windows of the truck like a soothing balm. After all I had experienced, I needed this special time alone with God.

My heart was full as I reviewed the day. In all my years of preaching, I had never had an experience quite like this. Although I couldn't personally share Christ with everyone who stopped by in Uvalde that afternoon and evening, I had managed, with the LORD'S help, to share Him with most of them. My heart was filled with joy and gratitude to God for what He had allowed me to experience. I praised Him in prayer and song as I made my way to Del Rio. It was a precious time I will never forget.

When I reached Del Rio, I pulled under the neon light of a small motel. It was then that I saw sitting on the passenger seat my new pair of tennis shoes and socks and the can of sunscreen. I never had the chance to put on any of them! I hadn't given those items a second thought while the Holy Spirit was at work. As best I could count, some 25 souls were saved in that parking lot in Uvalde. All Glory to God!

18

Safe Under His Wings

By Leo Lytle
October 2020, Minneapolis, Minnesota

"He shall cover thee with his feathers, and under his wings shalt thou trust: his truth shall be thy shield and buckler."
Psalm 91:4 KJV

Death seemed to be stalking the whole country in 2020. The whole world, actually. COVID-19 was a new virus, extremely contagious and violently virulent. Almost everybody knew people who had gotten sick with COVID-19, and many knew people who had died with it. Fear gripped hearts. Draconian lockdowns devastated businesses, communities, churches, schools and all of American society. To make matters much worse, the country was convulsed with violence. It was a dark time, desperately in need of hope.

Most of us were very alarmed back in 2020 as we watched the riots that had broken out in major cities across the nation. At the root of the violence were complex social issues. But the fiery torch that lit the bonfire of mayhem was the tragic death of George Floyd. George Floyd was a Black man who died while being detained by police officers in Minneapolis, Minnesota. Outrage over his death triggered a tsunami of protests, violence and destruction. It spread in waves to many other places such as New York City, New York; Portland, Oregon; Chicago, Illinois; Seattle, Washington; Kenosha, Wisconsin and dozens of others.

The city of Minneapolis, Minnesota was unquestionably Ground Zero. There, fires, looting and violence destroyed small businesses, private property and even one of the city's police precincts. Residents in or near the carnage locked their doors in fear and did what they could to protect

their own lives and property. Parts of Minneapolis were under siege night after night for weeks. It was frightening and heartbreaking to watch.

I hadn't seen this kind of violence and destruction on such a large scale since the mid-to-late 1960s when I was a teenager. I vividly remember back then it looked like our country was coming apart at the seams. But the instability we all witnessed via television night after night in Minneapolis and elsewhere seemed even worse and more widespread than what I'd seen back in the Sixties.

My heart was deeply touched as I listened to some of the tearful personal stories of those whose lives were impacted by the chaos and violence. I was also touched by the concerns and problems experienced by some of the people who were moved to protest. Peaceful protest is an American right and a function of freedom of speech. But I do not condone violence. I felt the LORD moving me to do something. We all know that Jesus is, of course, the only answer to life's deepest and most complex problems. It made perfect sense to go to some of these hurting cities and share the "Good News."

My friend Vic Bass of Vic Bass Ministries and his team of volunteers generously provided me with 1,600 "Jesus Is Lord" crosses and carefully loaded them on my trailer. On the evening before my departure in October 2020, I met Bro. Vic, some of his team members and other friends of the "Cross Ministry" at the Cross Barn for prayer. I knew I'd be in some unfriendly areas on this journey, but their prayers for protection, safe travel and boldness gave me confidence that the LORD would lead, guide and protect. Something that is also always prayed by these fine men is that each cross find its destination. I was looking forward to helping those 1,600 crosses find each of their destinations. I told the men at the Cross Barn that I was going to call this evangelism trip "Operation Hope."

My sweet wife Valerie was still working full-time as a labor and delivery nurse in Nacogdoches, Texas. She met me in a parking lot as she was driving home from her hospital, and I was heading out. We held one other tightly as we tearfully prayed together.

Leo Bell Lytle III
and Valerie Lynne Culp-Lytle

It's a long way from our home in Pine Valley to Minneapolis, Minnesota: 1,068 miles to be exact. My plan was to take three days to get there and minister in towns and cities along the way. I had my trusty sign on the back of the trailer encouraging folks to call for a cross. As always, I received many calls as I made my way to Minneapolis. Most of the callers told me they were already Believers. But others who allowed me to explain the Gospel found that "sure hope" in Christ as I shared on the side of the road, at a truck stop and a fast-food restaurant.

By the time I reached Joplin, Missouri, a few people had already been saved. After spending a couple of hours in Joplin, several more people had received God's free gift of Eternal Life Jesus Christ at a parking lot near a large retailer. I then drove on through Missouri and into Iowa, where I spent some time sharing Christ and crosses in Des Moines before crossing into Minnesota.

On October 19, 2020, I finally arrived in Minneapolis. The temperature was near freezing with snow flurries as I drove into downtown, looking for the place where George Floyd died.

But then a big problem for "Operation Hope" arose. I was driving in downtown Minneapolis in heavy traffic when suddenly my truck would not shift out of first gear. Once I reached 15 or 20 miles an hour, the engine would race, but go no faster. Now, I've never made any claim to being a mechanic. But a lifetime of driving old cars has left me with a little vehicular

knowledge. Over the years I've had just about everything that can happen to a vehicle mechanically, happen. I knew this was a transmission problem. It seemed a very serious one. My truck was no "spring chicken." It was a 1998 Dodge Ram given to us by our good friends Bobby and Jo Lynn Bays. It had just needed a replacement motor. Valerie and I were very thankful when our home church, Faith Family Church in Burke, Texas, paid to have a used motor installed just before our evangelism began in 2018. Thank you, Jesus!

I've loved watching how God has provided for our needs in this ministry. He has kept us safe as we've traveled. He has always provided the solution in every situation we have faced. I've learned to trust Him, to make Him the priority and not me. So, there I was pulling a trailer full of crosses in the truck that He had provided, to share the "Good News" in a city desperate for hope. I knew one thing for sure: the Lord had this! So, I kept driving slowly in the direction the Holy Spirit was leading me.

One benefit of being forced to drive so slowly was that it enabled me to enjoy the magnificent beauty of the changing foliage. By now, I was traveling through neighborhoods and was able to appreciate the trees. The brilliant colors of the leaves were unlike any I'd ever seen. I was in awe of the artistic handiwork of God.

The location where George Floyd died is in a Minneapolis neighborhood, not far from a busy shopping area that had been heavily damaged during the unrest. The nearby police precinct had been set on fire and destroyed.

As I neared Ground Zero, the streets were still barricaded at least a block in every direction. Graffiti was painted on the sides of every building and even on the streets. As I walked about, I began to acclimate myself to some of what I had seen on television in the prior weeks. The store where George Floyd had been moments before he was apprehended was still open, so I stepped inside. Looking around the store that day was surreal.

The uncertainty of life was vividly apparent. I'm sure George Floyd did not wake up that morning thinking this would be the last day of his life. None of us know when that last day is for us, either. Life is uncertain at best. Tomorrow is certainly not guaranteed. What **IS** certain is that every soul will spend Eternity in either Heaven or Hell, depending on whether each person has asked Jesus Christ to forgive him or her, save his or her soul and has accepted the gift Jesus offers of Eternal Life.

Some of the accounts I've read said that during the time he lived in Houston, Texas, George Floyd had made his decision to accept Christ as his personal Savior. The stories did say, however, that he continued to struggle with addiction and other choices and challenges that impacted both his life and others.

I hope George Floyd was saved. I don't want anyone to end up in Hell. But that choice was his, just as the same choice is ours. Do you know for certain that if you died today you would go to Heaven? Are you trusting in a religion or in a personal relationship with Jesus Christ? Hell is full of people with good intentions who were hoping good deeds and living a good life would somehow help get them into Heaven. They won't!

Leo Bell Lytle III
and Valerie Lynne Culp-Lytle

The Bible couldn't be clearer:

"For by grace are ye saved through faith; and that not of yourselves: it is the gift of God: Not of works, lest any man should boast." (Ephesians 2: 8-9 KJV)

If you want to know how you can begin a personal relationship with Jesus Christ, please turn to the last chapter of this book.

In the store, I purchased a soft drink and spoke with the owner and the cashier about the impact the tragic event had on their business. They said people from all over the world had been in their store as they'd come to visit the tragic site that was now a part of American history. I talked with a couple in the store who identified themselves as Believers. They were interested in getting one of the free crosses. As we walked together for a few blocks to where I had parked, we shared our love for Christ. I gave them a couple of crosses and then walked back for a final look at the sad spot.

The owner of the shop had kindly provided the number to a nearby transmission shop. Now, back in my truck with the address in my hand, I began to contemplate what I was going to do next. I had a trailer loaded with "Jesus Is Lord" crosses and was eager to get started in Minneapolis. But I needed my truck to do it, and it didn't seem up for the task.

As I sat behind the wheel, I prayed for God's direction, then started the engine and put it in "Drive". As I drove toward the stop sign at the next street, the transmission shifted to the next gear. Hope began to stir in my heart. Then, as I drove through the next block, it shifted again as it should. I lifted my hands in praise! Block after block, as the transmission seemed to be back to normal, hope cast uncertainty to the curb. I praised and thanked God every time the gears shifted properly. Forget the transmission shop! I was ready to search for a place to share "Operation Hope" in a city that desperately needed a huge dose of hope.

I spent the rest of the day in Minneapolis/St. Paul, Minnesota. Sharing Christ and crosses, I had a few heart-to-heart discussions about racism, Black Lives Matter, protests and Jesus. I shared about 200 crosses that day and nine people prayed to receive God's free gift of Eternal Life in Jesus Christ. All Glory to God!

As night fell, I drove toward Wisconsin. Praise God, my transmission seemed to be working properly. I called my knowledgeable mechanic friend, Monty Nettles, for advice. Monty is also a member of our home congregation, Faith Family Church in Burke, Texas. He and his wife Veronica (Roni) Nettles are very dear friends of ours. Monty, who had been the one who installed the used motor, said to check my transmission fluid. The next morning, I found the transmission-fluid was indeed low. I noticed there was a small leak, also. For the rest of the trip, I checked it every day and added transmission fluid as needed.

Over the 16-day trip of "Operation Hope," I was blessed to share Christ and crosses not only in the Minneapolis/St. Paul area, but also in Milwaukee and Kenosha, Wisconsin; Chicago, Illinois; Detroit, Michigan and Louisville, Kentucky. I spoke with hundreds of people and gave away all 1,600 crosses.

Scores of folks accepted Jesus Christ as their personal LORD and Savior! Among those who did were college students in St. Paul, a postal worker in Kenosha, EMS workers outside Chicago, a Muslim in Minneapolis, a grandmother in Detroit, a professional Motocross rider in Arkansas, folks in Missouri, a mother and daughter in Milwaukee and many, many more. All Glory to God!

I thanked God and gave Him all the praise that I had no other mechanical troubles the rest of the trip. The LORD kept me going day after day until I was safely home.

19

A Text In Time

By Valerie Culp-Lytle
October 2020, Pine Valley, Texas

"Iron sharpeneth iron; so a man sharpeneth the countenance of his friend."
Proverbs 27:17 KJV

The night was chilly and dark. My heart felt the same way. I could not make myself get out of my car.

It was October 2020. I had just driven nearly an hour to get home after working a 12-hour shift as a labor and delivery nurse. Leo had met me in Nacogdoches, Texas when I finally finished charting. It was the town where I worked in a hospital about 35 miles from our home. We rendezvoused in the parking lot of a business near the hospital, somewhere he could pull in easily with the 12-foot trailer we had at the time attached to our old red truck. We embraced, kissed and prayed for one another.

I took a few pictures. In those photos, Leo looked excited and happy, in a Christian T-shirt and with a fresh haircut. I looked happy, but tired. My hair was swathed in a cloth surgical cap that was slightly too large for my head. The cloth caps, like the layered face masks we had to wear then, were emblems of the time of COVID-19.

COVID-19 had the nation in its deathly grip. Labor and Delivery was not on the front lines of the pandemic battle, but pregnant women could also get the virus. Other parts of our hospital had many cases, and some patients were dying. Early on, when the disease was still new and virulent, it was a truly terrifying time to be a nurse. I worked straight through the first nearly two years of COVID-19 and never got it --- glory, hallelujah, all praise be to God. We had friends who died with it, however. At this time, in October 2020, COVID-19 was still very scary. The ever-present threat posed by the invisible enemy made working in health care even more of a strain than usual. The fear was exhausting.

To make matters worse, the nation seemed to be going up in flames. Protests filled the nightly television news. Mobs ransacked businesses, tore down statues, looted and burned buildings. Racial tensions were high, and several tragedies involving the police had turned deadly. This had led to powder keg conditions in many major cities across the country.

It was straight into the maw of these conditions that Leo was blithely driving that night in October 2020. He was, at the time, on the backside of his sixties, a gray-haired, white man who often wore a red cap that said something about God. I would tell him to please not wear that cap on the street because it could too easily be confused with a political cap to which some people took offense. But Leo is one who will do whatever he thinks best, however he feels led by the Holy Spirit. Really, after all this time, I should know better than to waste my breath.

I sat that night in my little car beside the 12-foot by 20-foot tiny home where we lived for more than four years. It was swathed in darkness, too. I sat there wondering if I had just seen Leo alive for the last time. He was deliberately heading to some of the most troubled cities in the country. His itinerary included cities such as Minneapolis, MN, where several months earlier George Floyd had died on the street in police custody. He was going to cities such as Kenosha, Wisconsin where deadly riots broke out after yet another police tragedy.

Did he have a death wish, I had asked Leo. No, he had calmly answered me. He loves life as much as anybody I have ever known. He said

Leo Bell Lytle III
and Valerie Lynne Culp-Lytle

as much, and I knew it to be true. But the people in those cities need Jesus right now, he had said. Jesus is the only answer. God's call on Leo's life is to spread the Word, to spread the Good News of the forgiveness and salvation only found through Jesus. Leo was going to answer that call, and none of my misgivings were going to sway him. Leo is one who will do whatever he thinks best, however he feels led by the Holy Spirit. Really, after all this time, I should know better than to waste my breath.

I sat there in my little car in the chilled darkness. I was already lonely, thinking of Leo being gone for weeks. My work situation at that moment was such that I could not join him. The worry kept chasing through my mind that it would be so easy for somebody to just shoot him and speed away. An older man in a red cap standing next to a trailer full of crosses, talking about Jesus --- he seemed to me to be a sitting-duck target. Normally, I rarely cry. But that night I sat there in the dark --- tired and lonely and so afraid --- and sobbed. I cried and cried.

It's called ugly crying, the kind with guttural noises and shuddering sobs and a streaming nose. In time, it burns itself out. The shuddering sobs transition to little panting breaths. Eventually, it is time to blow your nose and reassess. It's like venturing outside after a violent storm and walking around the yard, seeing what was damaged and what survived. In that time of transition, my cell phone pinged. Someone was texting me.

It was Sally Pilcher. She's a friend from church past, a sister in Christ. She and her husband, Randy Pilcher, have been good friends to Leo and me for quite a few years. They are both optimistic, fun people. Loyal. Love Jesus. The kind of people you're always happy to see. Folks who stay your friends no matter how much time passes. One thing I always remember about Sally is how she introduces her husband as "my first husband." He is her only husband, and it makes me smile whenever she says that. I don't think Sally has ever texted me before or since that night. But on that night, she reached out and said that she knew Leo had just left for the long ministry trip and asked how I was doing.

Fine, thank you --- well, actually, I was just sitting in my car crying my eyes out. But fine, thank you ... Sally and I texted back and forth. As I had been crying, I had been praying for God to please, please, please keep Leo safe. Please use him to share the Gospel and further the Kingdom, but also please, please, please keep Leo safe. As my crying gradually subsided, I started to feel the beginning of peace come over my heart and mind. Scripture was starting to come to remembrance.

She let me talk it out --- my fear and dread of bad news, of harm coming to Leo on the road, of violence against a man who rubbed somebody the wrong way.

Honestly, I don't remember now what I said exactly, nor what Sally said via text that night. What I do remember --- and what changed everything for me going forward --- is what the Holy Spirit said to me. There was no audible voice. But I felt the Holy Spirit was speaking to me by way of bringing to my mind cherished Scripture detailing the promises of God. I started to recall Bible passages that no matter what happens to Blood-Bought Believers in this life, we have the promise of eternal life. Scripture came to mind about both God's protections and, more importantly, His provisions for eternal life.

A powerful sermon that Leo preaches is based on Daniel 3. That is the account of Shadrach, Meshach and Abednego about to be thrown into the fiery furnace for refusing to bow down to the golden image set up by King Nebuchadnezzar. Christians the world over cherish the words of Daniel 3: 16-18:

(16) "Shadrach, Meshach, and Abednego, answered and said to the king, O Nebuchadnezzar, we are not careful to answer thee in this matter.

(17) "If it be so, or God whom we serve is able to deliver us from the burning fiery furnace, and he will deliver us out of thine hand, O king.

(18) "But if not, be it known unto thee, O king, that we will not serve thy gods, nor worship the golden image which thou has set up."

The rest of the story, of course, is that the three men **are** thrown into the fiery furnace. But they are joined there by a fourth man who had a form like "the son of God." Shadrach, Meshach and Abednego come out of the fiery furnace with no harm and without even one hair on their heads singed. Leo, like many other great preachers, makes an entire, very inspiring sermon out of those three words: "But if not."

All that rushed back into my memory. Finally, I thought --- and said to Sally --- you know what, Leo does NOT have a death wish. He loves life. But if he WERE to be killed in the process of sharing Jesus with the world, it would be the perfect death for him. Leo would literally be delighted to die for the cause of Christ. If the Lord tarries, we are all going to die some-day. How much better it would be to die actively working for Jesus instead of suffering for a long time. Of course, people don't get a choice. Leo and I won't have a choice, either. God holds the times of our life and death in His hands. But this thought of how much Leo would prefer heading to Heaven that way was the finishing touch on the gift of peace the Holy Spirit gave me that night. My heart, mind and spirit were at rest, finally.

I thanked Sally profusely for reaching out to me at the exact moment when I needed to talk to somebody. We agreed that her urge to contact me was also the Holy Spirit at work. We ended the conversation. I was able to get ready for bed, pray WITHOUT begging God again and again and again for Leo's safety and go right to sleep.

Now, all this is not to say that I have never been afraid again. The occasional misgiving pops up here and there. Once in a while, Leo will voice a plan that sets my alarm bells ringing. I do share my concerns with him, once or five times. ... But Leo is one who will do whatever he thinks best, however he feels led by the Holy Spirit. Really, after all this time, I should know better than to waste my breath.

And now, I do know better. I may caution him, but I don't harangue. Never again have I felt that crippling fear about what might happen to Leo by himself or to us together on the road. Instead, I remember that night in my car when the Holy Spirit dried my tears and wrapped me in His peace.

20

Name Above All Names

By Leo Lytle
October 2020, Kenosha, Wisconsin

"For I know the thoughts that I think toward you, saith the Lord, thoughts of peace, and not of evil, to give you an expected end."
Jeremiah 29:11 KJV

Names in the nightly news come and go. For weeks or months and sometimes years, certain names will dominate news cycles relentlessly. Eventually, though, those names will move into the pages of history.

We would all do well to keep in mind that the name that should most interest us is the name above all names: Jesus Christ. The Bible says it like this:

(9)"Wherefore God also hath highly exalted him, and given him a name which is above every name.(10) That at the name of Jesus every knee should bow, of things in heaven, and things in earth, and things under the earth; (11)And that every tongue should confess that Jesus Christ is Lord, to the glory of God the Father." Philippians 2:9-11 KJV.

But those nightly news names do loom large for a season. The year 2020, already tainted with the global pandemic of COVID-19, had several notable names that filled headlines for months.

The George Floyd death-related protests in late May to early June 2020 resulted in major civil unrest and property damage that totaled around $1-2 billion in insured damages, according to Axios.

But the year 2020 just kept going downhill. On August 23, 2020, in Kenosha, Wisconsin, Jacob Blake, a Black man, was shot seven times in the back and side by a white Kenosha police officer. Jacob Blake survived but was left paralyzed from the waist down. The police officer said he felt threatened while trying to arrest Blake for several outstanding warrants, and that he thought Blake was reaching for a weapon. Blake's shooting triggered enormous civil unrest and massive protests. After dark, the protests would often turn violent, destructive and dangerous.

Amid the arson and widespread property destruction, things went from bad to worse in Kenosha when, two days after Jacob Blake was shot, 17-year-old Kyle Rittenhouse shot and killed two protesters in what he said was self-defense on August 25, 2020. He was in Kenosha to help defend private businesses from the destructive turmoil ravaging the city. He would later be acquitted of all charges.

Watching it on television from our home in Texas, I felt led to do what I could to show people that the only answer is Jesus. I wanted to tell them to look to the One whose name is above every name. Accordingly, I began to prayerfully plan a trip to the trouble spots. My wife, Valerie, respected my decision and supported me doing what I felt the Holy Spirit was leading me to do. But she was openly afraid for my safety and pleaded with me to be careful. I said I would be careful, and several weeks later, I left home on a trip I called Operation Hope.

On October 21, 2020, after sharing Christ and crosses in Minneapolis, St. Paul, and Milwaukee I arrived in Kenosha. Early that morning I toured the most devastated parts of the city and witnessed first-hand the rubble from building after building that had been looted and burned. Tall fences had been erected around them to keep people away from crumbling bricks and broken glass. It was so sad to see up close with my own eyes.

The people of Kenosha, like those in Minneapolis and scores of other American cities, were hurting. The future seemed uncertain. They needed hope. They needed a sure hope. That sure hope can only be found in a personal relationship with Jesus Christ!

I was well aware that I was just one person in a city of nearly 100,000 people. What good could I do? Should I have just stayed home back in Texas? I was 66 years old at the time. What hope could I possibly offer to so many? But we can all do something. I believe it's always better to do what one can, than to do nothing at all! I believed God could use me to do something. That's why I went. But I was certainly not alone. I could feel the presence, power and leadership of the Holy Spirit as I pulled into town with my trailer full of free "Jesus Is Lord" crosses!

Leo Bell Lytle III
and Valerie Lynne Culp-Lytle

That outlook that everybody can do something for Jesus is at the heart of the Cross Ministry. As I wrote in the opening chapter of this book, two East Texas men heard a sermon in a revival at Denman Avenue Baptist Church in Lufkin, Texas in which Evangelist Bob Pitman of Muscle Shoals, Alabama exhorted the congregation to explore what each of them might do for the cause of Christ and get busy doing it. They were brothers-in-law Lawrence (Buddy) Jordan and Dale Frost. It was Dale Frost who had saved an email article sent to him and his wife from a friend about a church that headed up an effort to make nearly 1,000 three-foot wooden crosses in 2008 in Frankenmuth, Michigan. The 1,000 wooden crosses were then displayed all over town. This action was in response to a lawsuit filed by an atheist asking that crosses be removed from public view. The two men

and their wives, Susie Jordan and LaVera Frost, discussed it all at length, prayerfully considered what to do and decided they would start making wooden crosses, like what had been done in Frankenmuth. Their initial goal, according to Dale Frost, was to put a cross in every yard in Lufkin and Nacogdoches, Texas.

Lawrence (Buddy) Jordan and Dale Frost started making crosses in February 2015. Eventually, Vic Bass would join Buddy Jordan and Dale Frost and assume leadership of getting the crosses made. By the time Vic Bass passed the supervision of the making of the crosses on to Trinity Baptist Church of Lufkin at the end of 2023/beginning of 2024, volunteers had made well over a million "Jesus Is Lord" crosses.

In turn, during that same time, our ministry, Leo Lytle Ministries, has distributed the crosses in all 50 states and used them as an evangelism tool that has seen people pray to be saved in all 50 states. More than 5,000 people accepted Jesus Christ as their personal Savior during the first seven years of our evangelism ministry, largely aided by the "Jesus Is Lord" crosses. All glory to God!

Back to Kenosha in October 2020 — I began searching for the Spirit-led location to set up, and He led me right to it. It was an intersection where the confluence of five streets met at a pair of traffic lights just a few blocks from the crumbling buildings I'd seen earlier. There, in a triangle-shaped parking lot, I backed in my trailer, scattered crosses around it and put out my signs.

The weather was chilly because of intermittent light rain. Despite the chill and damp, people were stopping for a free cross all day long. I can't begin to count the number of people I met in Kenosha on that day. I do know that more than 20 people prayed to receive Jesus Christ as their personal LORD and Savior. To God be the Glory!

One lady I met that day I could never forget. Her name was Melissa Markoutsis. Melissa had a smile that seemed to light up the gloomy overcast day. She was excited to learn about the ministry. I told her I was calling this trip *Operation Hope* because I knew their city had gone through so much turmoil and unrest. I told her I was there to share the free crosses and ask people if they had a personal relationship with Jesus Christ. She had tears in her eyes and seemed genuinely thankful for the crosses. She told me this meant so much to their community.

Melissa and I have become social media friends since that day. In fact, on my second trip there in 2022, I got to meet her husband Adam and their two beautiful children. She is a champion for Christ in Kenosha and shares encouraging Scripture verses every day on her page. I love how God brings such wonderful people into my life from all over America. Thank you, Jesus!

Late in the day, the rain increased. It was getting colder and darker by the minute. I had been on my feet all day and was more than ready for a good night's rest. My plan was to go on to Chicago in the morning, so I knew I needed sleep. But there was one thing I felt strongly led to do before leaving Kenosha. I wanted to go back to the fences around those ravaged buildings I had seen at the start of the day. I wanted to zip-tie a few of the smaller crosses to the top of the fences. At least I could leave a silent witness behind for all to see as they passed by the rubble and destruction. The small crosses could be a symbol of hope for a hurting community.

So, in the cold and heavy rain that was falling by then, I made my way there and parked the trailer. As I was getting my crosses and zip-ties together, I heard a voice in the darkness across the street. I turned to see a young man who looked about 19 or 20 years old. He asked if he could have a cross.

"Of course," I said, as he crossed the street to meet me. "Would you like a big one or a small one?"

"I live in a small apartment," he said. "I don't have room for a big one. But I can put a small one in my window."

Soon I engaged with him in a Gospel conversation and discovered that he was a Believer and that's why he wanted that small cross.

"I passed by you earlier today," he said. "I saw the crosses and want-ed one, but my ride wouldn't stop. I was really hoping to get one, and then I saw you out here tonight from my window." He thanked me and then suddenly disappeared into the darkness as I made my way to the fence.

I carefully zip-tied seven small crosses about 30 feet apart along the fence as the rain con-tinued to fall. I was certain the city or someone would most likely soon take them down. But for this night at least they glis-tened in the falling rain with the aid of the few dim streetlights that were still working. I stepped back into the middle of the street for a few mo-ments to take it all in and look long enough to imprint it firmly into my memory. It was amazing how easily one could read the words "Jesus Is Lord," even on such a dark and rainy night.

I walked back over to my truck and trailer and was about to open the door when I heard that young man's voice for the second time.

"Hey, Mister!" he called. I looked around but didn't see him.

"Up here," he said. "Look what I did with the cross!"

As I looked up toward the second floor, I saw that small cross I had given him carefully secured in his window. He'd positioned a small light on it. It glowed over the rain-soaked street below. He had a huge smile on his face. I shouted toward the window:

"I like it!"

I don't think I'll ever forget that sight.

As I stood by my truck ready to leave, not knowing if I'd ever return, I looked around one more time. It was then that I realized the light from his little upstairs window was the only sign of life at all in the heavily damaged area. Maybe all the other residents had somewhere else to go, but he didn't. I could only imagine what he might have seen from his window during those terrifying nights when his hometown was imploding before his very eyes.

Hot tears mingled with cold raindrops coursed down my cheeks. My heart hurt so much for that brave young man and for his city. Yet, at the same time I thanked God for leading me there. I was so glad I had come. Kenosha, Wisconsin will always hold a special place in my heart. It was a day and night that I will never forget. As I said earlier, and it's so true, "It's better to do something, than to do nothing at all."

All glory to the One whose name is above all names.

21

God's Plan Was a Van

By Valerie Culp-Lytle
July 2021, Pine Valley, Texas

"But my God shall supply all your need according to his riches in glory by Christ Jesus. Now unto God and our Father be glory for ever and ever. Amen."
Philippians 4:19-20 KJV

———————

God dropped a van into our laps.

Well, not literally. That would be catastrophic. But certainly figuratively.

It was truly an amazing display of God's providence.

Here's how it unfolded. We were originally traveling on our ministry trips in Old Red, the 1998 Dodge Ram that our friends Jo Lynn and Bobby Bays had given us and to which we had added a used camper shell. Old Red served us well for years. But it would have its problems from time to time, and it was not suited to sleeping in safely and comfortably.

When Old Red couldn't be used, Leo would drive our 2011 black Dodge Ram truck, which had also been given to us by a very generous friend. But the black truck had an uncovered bed that was a bit too short to hold the seven-foot-long rolling holder for "The Door." "The Door" is a full-size, four-panel cypress door that Leo uses to preach a message illustrating the body of Christ and several other spiritual concepts. He would wrap the wooden holder for the door in a tarp when we had to travel with it sticking up in the open truck bed. But even heavily wrapped, rain would cause the parts of the door to absorb moisture and swell a little bit. That swelling could be disastrous when Leo needed the separate parts of the door to fit together easily and seamlessly as he preached. I used to joke that when we would carry the obviously heavy, tarp-wrapped bundle that was "The Door" into a cheap motel room late at night, it looked suspiciously like we were handling a dead body.

Weather-tight space was a need in other ways, too. As our ministry grew, we started carrying more and more supplies. We had boxes of new Bibles and Bible study books, Gospel tracts, a bin of blankets and warm clothing for people experiencing homelessness, recycled Sunday School books and previously owned Bibles, a few items for children and more, in addition to our clothes and emergency items. Finally, there were the issues of being set up in locations to share crosses far from any public restroom and also having to sleep most nights in a motel, however inexpensive.

When Leo came back from an evangelism trip to the northeast on April 12, 2021, he said to me, "We need a van."

"That would be nice," I agreed.

We didn't have enough money for even an old van. But we agreed that it sure would be more convenient on so many levels.

A couple of days or so later, Leo got a call from Ginger Bye, wife of Lloyd Bye, then-pastor of Lakeside Baptist Church in Pineville, Louisiana. Lloyd and Ginger are long-time friends of Leo's, and they have since retired. Ginger told Leo that she was a member of the board of directors for a charity in Louisiana that was about to disband. Members wanted to donate what money the charity had to various worthwhile causes. The amount they wanted to give our ministry was around five thousand dollars. We were stunned and very grateful.

Leo started looking for a used van. Within a day or so, he found a 2007 Ford Econoline, low-roof panel van that had been a fleet truck for a local heating and cooling company. The total price was less than six thousand dollars. Our friend Monty Nettles looked it over with his mechanical expertise and pronounced the vehicle sound. We had enough money in

Leo Bell Lytle III
and Valerie Lynne Culp-Lytle

the ministry account to add to the charity donation and buy the van with cash. Just like that. By April 19, 2021 we were the new owners. It had been **ONE WEEK** since Leo had come home and said, "We need a van." God works in amazing ways!

Just five days after that, on April 24, 2021, we were back on the road to share Christ and crosses in Many, Louisiana, but this time in the van.

As the Believers' saying goes: "Where God guides, He provides."

All we had to do was make room in our laps.

22

A Cross To Feel Better

By Valerie Culp-Lytle
August 2021, Pacific Northwest

"Casting all your care upon him: for he careth for you."
I Peter 5:7 KJV

———————

Being told to leave never feels good. We've been told to leave a fair number of times all around the nation. The experience is familiar by now, but it still stings.

The element of rejection is part of the blow. Nobody enjoys feeling unwanted. The other part of it is knowing that we troubled somebody. We really do try not to cause any trouble. We pray about where we should go. We look for long-vacant lots that are in a well-traveled part of town, with enough space for two or three cars to pull in and then pull out --- even better if it is a straight pull-out, with no need to go in reverse. If there is a "No Trespassing" sign of any kind, we don't stop there. Our aim is to find an empty and safe patch of pavement where we can set up and watch the Holy Spirit show up.

Sometimes what we are looking for is somewhere to quietly spend the night in the van. Many nights find us in a modest motel, if conditions are too cold, too hot, too dangerous or too mosquito-y as to preclude bedding down in the back. But when conditions are right, we love to sleep in our van. Leo built a wooden platform across the rear of it that offers storage underneath and supports a queen-size, foam mattress on top. The van is not tall enough for us to stand upright inside, so we bend forward at the waist. There is no electricity, and therefore no air-conditioning or interior light. If a night is warm and dry and seems safe enough to do so, we sometimes sleep with the back door of the van ajar to let in some cooler air. If a night is cold, we bundle up in warm clothes and layers of blankets. My CPAP will run for several hours on a portable battery that we can recharge the next time we are in a motel room. There is no plumbing or water. So ...... a plastic pitcher with a lid, tissue and hand sanitizer. Flashlight by the bed. It works.

Our quest on a night in August 2021 in a city in the Pacific Northwest was to find a place to sleep. Moving at trolling motor-speed, we were winding through the parking lot of a large retailer known for its hospitable policy toward the occasional overnight stay on its property. Goodness knows, we give this particular retailer plenty of business. But individual stores sometimes do not allow an overnight stay. Maybe that store has had a bad experience, the one bad apple spoiling it for everybody. We have learned that it is not a given.

Sure enough, on this warm summer evening, it looked like our reception was going to be chilly. A uniformed employee caught sight of us in the parking lot. We saw him spot us. Our gentle meander around the parking lot continued, as if to say, "Hey man, we are just driving right now. Nobody is trying to spend the night ---- yet. You can chill."

In the side mirror, I could see the guy changing course to intercept us at what he figured would be our next turn. Resigned, I told Leo that it looked like we were about to be told to leave, because the employee was so resolute in reaching us. We stopped and waited for him. Girded our loins for the you-can't-stay-here message that we felt sure was coming.

But the slightly out of breath young man who reached us was smiling. "You are hard to catch!" he said. He looked hot in the reflective safety vest he wore over his uniform shirt. Sweat dampened his brown hair against his face. "I want to get a cross," he said. It seems odd, looking back, why we didn't immediately think of him wanting a cross. I guess we were just on high alert for being told to leave. He went on to tell us his story. We'll call him Ben.

His fiancé was in the hospital with COVID-19, Ben told us. She -- we'll call her Marta -- was seriously diabetic and had been very ill. Just the other day, he said, doctors had to place what he called a "trachy." I assume he meant a tracheotomy or a tracheostomy. That is an opening surgically created through the neck into the trachea (windpipe.) The surgeon will insert a tube that allows air to enter the lungs and can also provide a way to suction out secretions. It is an incredibly invasive procedure usually reserved for life-or-death situations. Sometimes a person gets a tracheostomy because they require long-term mechanical ventilation. Any way one looks at it, a "trachy" does not warrant the cheerful tone Ben used when he said Marta now had one.

Ben and Marta had met at the big retail store where they both worked, where we now wanted to sleep for one night. Ben's job was to retrieve shopping carts from the parking lot and line them back up for the next customers. Marta worked inside. They started dating and eventually got engaged. She was a planner, he said, pride evident in his voice. She had it all figured out. They would go to Las Vegas to get married and then go see Hoover Dam. Together, they had

managed to save most of five paychecks for their wedding and honeymoon. But then she caught COVID-19. She was still in ICU, he told us, but ended cheerfully that her "trachy" was working well.

"I just think I will feel better if I can put one of these crosses in my apartment," he said.

We gave him a cross and asked him the diagnostic questions. Ben told us he was sure that he had already prayed to be saved. We prayed with

Ben, earnestly asking God to protect and bless him and Marta. We asked God to please heal Marta, if it was His will to do so. Eventually, we left Ben. He said it was fine for us to spend the night in the parking lot, and we did.

But Ben and Marta have never left my mind. Here were two people who didn't seem to be asking for a whole lot in life. They both did honest work. They wanted to have somebody to love, enough money to pay their bills and have the occasional treat, such as seeing Hoover Dam. But what Ben didn't verbalize, or possibly didn't realize, was how very dire was Marta's condition.

As a registered nurse, to hear that she was a serious diabetic, had a very bad case of COVID-19, was still in ICU and had been given a "trachy" made me figure it would be a miracle if she ever came out of the hospital alive. It hurt my heart to imagine how sad Ben would be without her, alone again. He would be without Marta to love him and brighten his life after his long hours pushing shopping carts back into the store --- day, night, rain, sun, wind, heat, cold. No Marta to dream with and to make plans with and to save part of their paychecks. No Marta beside him if he ever gets to see Hoover Dam.

God is sovereign. Maybe He spared Marta's life. Maybe Ben and Marta are living their best lives right now, happy and whole. I certainly hope so. For months after meeting Ben, I would pray for him and his fiancé. Sometimes, when I woke in the night, I would send up a quick prayer on their behalf. When I had a moment to reflect on people who needed prayer, their names would swim up in my consciousness. I would lift their names up to the Lord.

God is sovereign. Maybe He spared Marta's life. Maybe He didn't. But either way, Ben was sure that he would be Heaven-bound when his time came. That is what really matters in life. And he has a cross in his apartment now, to help him feel better.

Somehow, when I think of Ben and Marta these days, the first part of The Beatitudes comes to mind:
"Blessed are the poor in spirit: for theirs is the kingdom of heaven.
"Blessed are they that mourn: for they shall be comforted.
"Blessed are the meek: for they shall inherit the earth."
Matthew 5: 3-5 KJV

23

Teamwork, Kingdom Work

By Valerie Culp-Lytle
July, 2024, Eagle Butte, South Dakota
January, 2023, Raymondville and Uvalde, Texas

"Two are better than one; because they have a good reward for their labour.
For if they fall, the one will lift up his fellow: but woe to him that is alone when
he falleth; for he hath not another to help him up."
Ecclesiastes 4: 9-10

Eagle Butte, South Dakota;
Cheyenne River Sioux Tribe Indian Reservation

Leo was preaching full throttle. I was sitting demurely on the front row of seats like a good preacher's wife. Our host preacher came up and touched me on the shoulder. I got up and followed him outside.

"Would you please pray for this woman?" our host preacher asked. "Her brother committed suicide yesterday."

He presented me to a Native American woman, taller than me, with eyes swollen from hours of crying. Then he left and went back inside to the service. It was early evening in Eagle Butte, South Dakota on the Cheyenne River Sioux Tribe Indian Reservation. We had partnered with a fledgling church in Eagle Butte called Glory To God Ministries. Jerome Slides-Off is pastor. At that time, the little church was renting a space for $100 a week that they could use for a couple of services. It had one large room, two restrooms and a small kitchen. Any supplies or materials the church used had to be packed in and packed out. They were not allowed to leave anything in the space, as it could be rented out to other groups on the days the church did not have it reserved.

The woman who teaches the children was doing so in the small, attached kitchen space with the serving window curtain pulled down. There was not even room for a table or chairs in the kitchen. But the dedicated teacher ministered to the children in there while the service would be going on right beside them. She reminded the children to be quiet, and she would teach them in those conditions without complaint.

I don't know what earthly events unfolded to get the grieving woman to the service of this church. It was an extra service on a weeknight. She was not a member of the congregation. I don't know if somebody invited her, or if she saw a posted notice about the service, or if she was instinctively seeking spiritual comfort and knew a church met in that place. But I do know that she showed up crying so hard that she stood outside. I do know it was a Divine Appointment.

She told me her brother had killed himself yesterday. I told her I was sorry for her loss. A fresh flood of tears followed. I opened my arms, and she stepped into them. I held her while she cried. For a long time, we stood that way. Her crying in my embrace. Me holding her, my own eyes wet.

Eventually, the torrent of tears started to subside. I started praying for her, still holding onto her. Eventually we separated. She was calm for the moment. I started sharing the Gospel. Eventually she prayed to be saved. Her cousin had come out of the service by that time. He listened attentively to the Gospel message, too, and prayed to be saved, voluntarily joining in as I was leading his cousin in the sinner's prayer.

I was careful to tell them what I tell everybody: that God reads their hearts when they pray. God alone can judge genuine repentance, sincerity and saving faith. Leo and I serve as guides, based on what the Bible says about salvation. But every individual must make his or her own decision about Jesus.

The bereaved sister and her cousin received the Bibles, Bible study guides and any additional tracts or printed material I could give them. I encouraged them to attend services right there with the small but dedicated congregation of Glory To God Ministries. They eventually left, and I returned to the service.

Leo was finishing up when I slipped back into my seat. We would talk afterward about how wonderful we find our teamwork and praise God for it. While he was preaching inside, I was also sharing the Gospel outside the church walls.

It is the same on the streets around the country. Leo and I will both be sharing the Good News at the same time. If one of us is not talking to someone at any point, we are attentive to what the other one might need, such as a Bible and Bible study book. Other times we run subtle defense for one another. I have made quiet small talk with many a child to give a lost parent the opportunity to listen to Leo present the Gospel to them. Distractions can easily quench the Holy Spirit. We do our best to provide cover for one another.

King Solomon certainly had it right when he wrote in Ecclesiastes 4: "Two are better than one; because they have a good reward for their labour."

Raymondville, Texas

Two **ARE** better than one. But two can still feel a bit overwhelmed if the crowd is big enough. To this date, the single biggest day that Leo and I have experienced in nearly seven years of evangelism took place in January 2023 in Raymondville, Texas. We set up with the trailer full of free crosses and people started pouring in to get them.

For the next six hours or so, Leo and I did not even speak to one another. I joke that our only interaction was when Leo accidentally bumped me in the head with a cross as he lifted it off the trailer. We were both busy sharing the Gospel all that time. Two different people brought us water bottles, but we didn't have time to drink them. Leo was preaching from the trailer, much of the time, speaking to small groups of people. Many people prayed to be saved, some of them in those groups.

But the most memorable person who prayed to be saved that day did so alone. She was a young girl who looked about 10 years old. She was part of a group listening to Leo, but she was the only one in the bunch who bravely stepped forward when Leo gave the invitation. She said she wanted to be saved. Leo asked her mother's permission to lead her through the sinner's prayer. The mother gave her permission.

As Leo leaned over the trailer railing to speak softly to her, the little girl clasped her hands, bowed her head and boldly prayed in front of everyone. She appeared completely unmindful of the milling crowd. It was one of the most precious illustrations of childlike faith that I have ever seen. I was blessed to snap a picture of the moment from a good way away. Cropped closely, it is one of our favorite ministry photos. I got permission from both the young girl and her mother to share her picture in our public ministry photos. The image captures an actual "come to Jesus" moment, in the sweetest possible way.

As night fell and there was a momentary lull that day in Raymondville, Leo and I hurriedly packed up the trailer and left. We had dinner plans with a local pastor and his wife. They had patiently waited hours for us to be free. We tried to park the trailer somewhat out of sight to get through the meal at a Mexican restaurant with the pastoral couple. But Leo's phone rang all during dinner, as people still found the trailer even on a dark side street and called for a free cross.

Finally, to allow Leo to eat, I took a tag team turn and started answering his phone. I would tell people to take one cross and ask them if they had come to the place in their spiritual life where they knew for certain that if they died today, they would go to Heaven. This diagnostic question, of course, comes from Evangelism Explosion, developed by the late Dr. D. James Kennedy, who said he first heard it from some other preacher. It is such a good evangelism tool for getting right to the heart of the matter.

Raymondville, Texas was certainly a place where we marveled at the glory of God. The Holy Spirit was moving in such a mighty way. As best Leo and I could count later that night --- going through our photos of folks holding the big red books that we give new Believers and reminding one another of some who had prayed to be saved but didn't get their picture taken --- we estimated that right around 100 people came to Jesus in that one day. It was one of the most amazing experiences with the LORD that either of us had ever had. All glory to God!

Leaving our hotel the next morning, we joked that we had to witness our way out of there. I led one woman and Leo led two women --- including the hotel manager --- to the LORD as we tried to check out and move on to the next town. Teamwork again. And again, all glory to God.

Uvalde, Texas

Sometimes a team of two needs to call in reinforcements. Sometimes a bigger team is needed.

Such was the case a few days later during that evangelism trip in January 2023 along the Texas border. All those outpourings of blessings in the responsiveness of people had made a serious dent in our supply of crosses. We could see that we were not going to have enough to complete our planned route all the way to El Paso.

Vic Bass Ministries and the Cross Men and Women came to the rescue. They arranged to bring 500 more large crosses to us in Uvalde, Texas. This was our ministry's fourth time visiting Uvalde. The first time was about two years before the tragic school shooting that put the South Texas town in the national spotlight.

What a sweet sight it was to see reinforcements roll in on that January day. Here were 500 more crosses and three more people fresh and ready to help share the Gospel. We had a big day in Uvalde, with many people praying to be saved. It was not as large a tidal wave as we had experienced in Raymondville. But it was still a river of folks pouring through that empty parking lot. Having a team of five people made all the difference and kept the response from feeling overwhelming. Instead, it was purely exhilarating.

Bro. Vic likes to tell the story of that day. He recounts how he looked up at one point as he was sharing the Gospel, to see the other four of us also leading somebody to the Lord at the same time. It was a precious moment. I like to think that the five of us who were there share a special bond forged in that experience. Vic Bass, Wayne Reynolds, Joe Horton, Leo Lytle and Valerie Culp-Lytle --- we were just the most visible members on Team Jesus that day in Uvalde. Standing with us, though not in person, were the other members of the Cross Men and Cross Women, the faithful prayer teams, supportive spouses, our supporting churches and their pastors and wives and so many other faithful Believers all over the nation.

"Teamwork makes the dream work," says the popular slogan.

Go, Team Jesus!

24

His Grace
Is Sufficient

By Leo Lytle
June 2021, Del Rio, Texas

"And he said unto me, My grace is sufficient for thee:
for my strength is made perfect in weakness.
Most gladly therefore will I rather glory in my infirmities,
that the power of Christ may rest upon me."
II Corinthians 12:9 KJV

———————

Add a dash of pain and a spoonful of suffering to most any endeavor, and it will become more memorable.

But that same dash of pain and spoonful of suffering can also provide a backdrop against which the measures of grace and strength the Lord provides for that season become very plain to see. It is beautiful to behold.

A dash of pain and spoonful of suffering seasoned one of the most amazing evangelism trips I enjoyed during the early years of our ministry. It was only seven days long and involved the Texas Hill Country and a brief foray into Arizona. I was to leave for Utopia, Texas on Wednesday, June 23, 2021, where I would be sharing "The Door" message at Utopia Baptist Church.

On Sunday morning, June 27, I would preach at First Baptist Church in Sunizona, Arizona in the morning service, then head down to Douglas Tabernacle in Douglas, Arizona for the evening service. By Tuesday night, June 29, I would be back at our home in beautiful Pine Valley, Texas.

Fifty-four folks would end up praying to be saved over the seven days of this trip.

There were two big reasons why this particular trip was unforgettable to me: one being what happened on June 24 in Del Rio and the other being my physical health during the entirety of the trip. I want to deal with the health issue first.

Before I could embark on the seven-day evangelism trip, I was first committed to preach in Louisiana on June 20, 2021. It was while I was driving home from Louisiana on that Sunday before my evangelism journey was set to begin on Wednesday that I first noticed something was amiss.

I've been really blessed with good health all my life. I'm rarely ill enough to miss work or scheduled activities, praise God. That being said, as I was driving home that Sunday evening, I noticed a slight swelling on the left side of my forehead. It didn't really hurt, but something was certainly wrong.

About an hour from home my sweet wife Valerie called me to say that our daughter Christine had car trouble in Corpus Christi, Texas. Christine had managed to park at a convenience store. I called Christine as I made my way home to get a better understanding of the problem and explore options. The car was not going to make it back, so the plan was to drive the 300 miles, pick Christine up and bring her home. I made a quick pit-stop at our home, hugged and kissed Valerie, then headed toward Corpus Christi.

I share this because during the six hours or so of driving to Corpus Christi and back, my facial swelling began to spread, and I started having a little discomfort. I had been clearing some brush around our property recently and thought that maybe I had gotten into some poison ivy or poison oak.

Christine and I managed to drive her car to a nearby auto repair shop in Corpus Christi and left a note to the owner to see if he could repair it. We got a call Monday morning that the motor was bad and would need to be replaced, but that he didn't do that kind of repair. He was, however, gracious enough to let the car stay there until we could retrieve it.

I worked in my woodcraft shop most of the day on Monday. Whatever was causing the swelling wasn't going away. Someone needed to drive those 300 miles again, load Christine's car onto a trailer and haul it back home. It quickly became apparent that that someone was me. I called down to a U-Haul place in the area and made arrangements for a transport trailer to be ready when I got there. I left Tuesday morning for the six-hour round trip. As I drove, the discomfort worsened with the arrival of a persistent, throbbing headache.

I prayed for relief. At one point while I drove, I laid my hand across my forehead and asked the LORD to heal me if it was HIS will. I mentioned to Him that I knew that He knew that I was leaving the next morning for Utopia, Texas and then on to Arizona. I remembered how the Apostle Paul prayed and asked God three times to remove that "thorn" in his flesh. All the sudden this passage of Scripture came distinctly alive to me as I was also asking God for some relief. The Lord answered Paul's request by not relieving his distress, but by assuring him that, "My grace is sufficient." This would be a great lesson that I, too, would learn on this trip – the "sufficiency of God."

On Wednesday morning, June 23, 2021, I drove over to the cross barn to load up what I hoped would be enough for this trip. Karen Bass-Dutton is Vic Bass' daughter. She was one of two ladies who stenciled "Jesus Is Lord" on the crosses at the time. Karen took one look at me and said: "What happened to you? You need to see a doctor!"

When I appeared to hesitate, Karen brought out the big gun:

"I'm going to call my dad and tell him to not let you leave unless you go to the doctor and have that swelling looked at!" she said.

Karen got her dad on the phone. Bro. Vic told me I had better have that looked at before I left. I promised that I'd have it checked out somewhere the next day, but I was running behind schedule and just couldn't do it right then. So away I went toward Utopia.

My plan was to make it through the initial drive, preach the evening service at Utopia Baptist Church, and then get a good night's sleep. Then, on Thursday morning I would try to find one of those stand-alone medical clinics and see if I could get a shot to bring the swelling down and get some relief. As always while I'm driving, I got a few calls along the way for a free cross. One of the callers met me at a gas station in Hondo, Texas. He and a couple of other cars full of friends were on their way to float a river in the Texas Hill Country and do some camping. As we met, I apologized for my appearance and shared Jesus with about five of them out by the fuel pumps. One of the men and two ladies prayed to accept Jesus right there by my truck. That brightened up my day in a hurry, praise God!

When I pulled into the church parking lot in Utopia there were two nice ladies who were willing to help me unload some crosses and help me get all I needed to bring inside for

"The Door" message. I apologized for my appearance and told them what I thought it was. I was wearing a pair of black framed glasses to disguise, at least a little bit, my swollen forehead and the swelling that was now very apparent above and below my left eye. Unfortunately, while removing crosses from the back of my truck, I accidentally hit the swollen part of my head above my eye with the pointed end of a cross.

"Sir, there is blood streaming down your face!" one of the women told me. I'd punched a small hole in the swollen part of my forehead. They gave me some tissues to wipe off the blood. My appearance was rapidly progressing from unsettling to alarming.

I met their pastor, Jeremy McCarty, shortly afterwards and thanked him for the invitation to share "The Door" at his church, I apologized for how I looked. With God's help, I managed to share the message and then spent the night at the beautiful lodge there in Utopia that they had so kindly provided for me. I called Valerie that night. She was still working as a registered nurse at that time. I didn't get to see her before I left and hadn't said much to her about my problem. But I wanted her advice about anything I could do to get some relief. I told her my plan to see about getting a shot to reduce the swelling in the morning. She wanted me to take a selfie and send it to her. Uh, no. No sense in worrying her. I told her I would do it in the morning because I just wanted to get some rest.

Leo Bell Lytle III
and Valerie Lynne Culp-Lytle

It was hard to get comfortable enough to fall asleep with the swelling and the persistent headache, but eventually I managed to get three or four hours of sleep that Wednesday night. When I looked at myself in the mirror on Thursday morning the swelling around my left eye was getting even worse. I started driving toward my next engagement in Del Rio, I was on the lookout for the nearest medical clinic. It turned out to be the emergency room at the local hospital in Uvalde, Texas.

As the emergency doctor and nurse examined me, I told them I thought maybe it was poison ivy or poison oak, but that it was odd that it didn't itch. The doctor's diagnosis was shingles. He was very concerned about my left eye and did a test to see if it had been damaged. Thankfully it appeared to be ok. He said I should 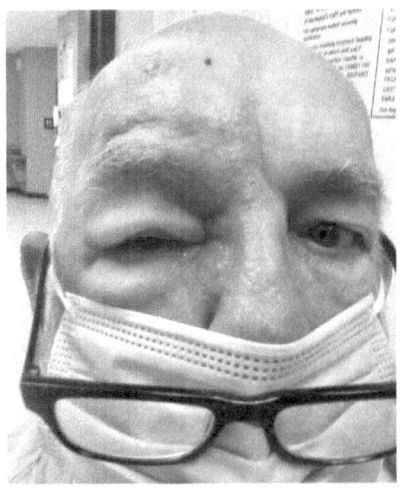 go home and get some rest and prescribed something to help reduce the swelling and the pain. I told him I was an evangelist and on my way to Arizona to preach on Sunday and would not be home until early next week. He gave me the name of an eye specialist in El Paso and urged me to see him if I had any problem with my eye.

So, I left the emergency room and headed over to the main grocery store in Uvalde to get the prescriptions filled and hopefully begin to experience some relief. Less than a year earlier, I had shared Christ and crosses just across the street from the grocery store. In a glorious outpouring of the Holy Spirit at work, more than 20 people were saved.

Medicine in hand now, my next need was to get an oil change because I had just had a rebuilt engine installed. The mechanic had said to change the oil after 500 miles. In fact, the mechanic said he didn't recommend that I take this long of a trip on the newly rebuilt engine, but said it would probably be alright. Just as I was reflecting on the "probably be alright," my engine started losing power. I quickly looked for a place to pull off the road.

At that very moment my phone rang. It was a young lady who saw the sign on my truck for free crosses and wanted one. She pulled behind me as I pulled off the road with my disabled truck.

Now, don't miss this: Here I am, fresh out of the emergency room and the pharmacy. My head hurts like nobody's business. Half of my forehead is swollen. My left eye is nearly swollen shut. Even as I was looking for an oil change place, my newly rebuilt engine had just gone on the blink. As I am pulling off the road for safety, at that very moment, a young lady calls me for a free cross!

There was only one thing to do. I got out of my truck, brought her a cross and shared with her the "Good News". Right there, she prayed to receive God's free gift of Eternal Life Jesus Christ! Praise God!

I got back into my truck, restarted it and gingerly drove to the oil change place. I asked them to please check everything out as thoroughly as possible. While there I witnessed to two other folks who both said they were Believers. When the truck was ready, I hopped in and headed toward Del Rio. Guess what? Whatever had been the problem with the engine earlier was now gone. The engine was running beautifully. I headed west on U.S. Highway 90 toward Del Rio. Glory to God!

What I don't want you to miss is this very important truth. That is, when you dare to live for Christ and seek to put Him first – expect opposition! That opposition is a direct result of Spiritual warfare. You should know that when God is at work, so is Satan. The Devil and his demonic angels are masters of discouragement! They know it only takes a little opposition to discourage most Believers. A little problem here, a little setback there and the next thing you know you're sidetracked from accomplishing what the LORD has put in your heart to do.

Hang tough, my brothers and sisters in Christ! With His strength and His power, we are more than conquerers through Jesus Christ! Just remember what the LORD told the Apostle Paul, "My grace is sufficient." Yes, it is!

Now for the Del Rio part of this story. Before leaving the pharmacy in Uvalde, I took the medicine prescribed by the doctor at the emergency room. I was hoping the swelling would begin to recede and the pain would subside. But I knew it might be several days before I would begin to feel better.

My plan for Del Rio was to visit the now-famous bridge that spans the Rio Grande and the United States' border with Mexico and then find a good location in town to share Christ and crosses. As I drove west on U.S. 90 toward Del Rio, I just wanted to check into a motel and try to get a good night's rest. Although I had never had shingles before this time, I had known people who did, and they all said it was a painful experience. I must say that I am in complete agreement.

As I arrived in Del Rio, I started looking for the bridge. I got a call from a mom and her daughter for a cross. At a bank parking lot, I was able to share Christ with them and both decided to give their hearts to Him right there. They gave me a couple of bottles of water which were much appreciated.

After finding the bridge, I did a Facebook live post and then headed toward a motel in view of getting some rest. But before reaching the motel, I passed the main grocery store and noticed a vacant business across the street from a fast-food restaurant. I thought that would be an ideal location for sharing Christ and crosses. I decided to turn around and have another look. It looked even better the second time. I thought maybe I'd stop there for an hour or so before finding a room. The next thing I knew, I'd pulled in and began setting up. It was like I was on autopilot.

Soon folks began to stop to get a cross. It was nonstop. I met many Believers in that special spot and shared Jesus with folks for many hours. Next thing I knew, it was well after dark. I began to load up everything back in the truck. A kind young couple, who had stopped by earlier, came back to help me and also wanted to treat me to a late supper at a local Mexican restaurant.

As I finally made my way to a motel, I was praising God for all He had done that day. He had allowed me to secure much-needed medical attention, allowed me to lead the young lady to Christ in Uvalde, caused the truck to run beautifully again, and had me cross paths with the mother and daughter who were saved in downtown Del Rio. God had also allowed me to find the perfect spot to share Christ and crosses, had given me the strength to stand for hours sharing Him in Del Rio, and then caused the kind young couple to minister to me with help packing up and a free, hot meal. As best I could count, looking back over the photos I had managed to take and reconstructing how the day had unfolded, 24 people had prayed to be saved that day. It was a day I'll never forget, and I give Him all the Glory!

25

The Real Deal, The Greatest Gift

By Leo Lytle
August 2021, North Pole, Alaska

"For by grace are ye saved through faith;
and that not of yourselves: it is the gift of God:
Not of works, lest any man should boast."
Ephesians 2:8-9 KJV

Santa Claus looms large in the Alaskan town of North Pole. It's fitting that he should, right there on St. Nicholas Drive. At 42 feet tall, the fiberglass Santa sculpture was for 54 years the world's largest Santa Claus. But then the town of Agueda, Portugal put together eight tons of aluminum and iron in 2016 to create a behemoth of a Santa that stands 69 feet tall.

North Pole, Alaska's Santa sculpture may be second tallest in the world now, but it is still by far the largest in the United States, (according to civic information about the town on the Internet). He presides over the landscape right outside the Santa Claus House in North Pole. Tourists from all over the world come to snap a picture with him and to shop. Visitors can sign up to have a North Pole-postmarked letter from Santa sent to children of their choice.

That's how I came to be relaxing in our rented truck on the

afternoon of August 23, 2021 within a stone's throw of Santa in North Pole, Alaska. Valerie was inside the Santa Claus House, busily signing up some of our younger grandchildren to receive one of those North Pole letters from Santa. She was looking at postcards and earrings, too, I felt sure, as I sipped some of the most delicious hot chocolate I have ever tasted. A cool breeze mingled with the light rain. The temperature was in the low fifties. I was sipping while Valerie was shopping. We had earlier spent about three hours doing street ministry in the light rain in Fairbanks. We were both damp and chilled, but rejoicing in the five people who had prayed to be forgiven and saved on the street in Fairbanks. We warmed up in the truck on the way to North Pole.

I was putting together our daily Facebook post and enjoying the hot chocolate when I heard voices coming from the back of the truck. Looking in the driver's side mirror I quickly saw the source of the sound. It turned out to be a group of five young men who had seen the crosses in the back of the truck and the sign saying they were free. I opened my door and met them at the back of the truck. They seemed to all be amazed at what we were doing, so I told them the story behind the crosses. It turned out they were all friends and lived in San Diego, California. They had flown up to Fairbanks for a fishing trip.

Of course, I asked them if they knew for certain that if they were to die today would they go to Heaven? As I looked each one in the eyes, they all agreed that they didn't think so. I then asked if they would be interested in knowing how they could be sure they'd go to Heaven? All five men seemed genuinely interested and wanted to know how they could know for sure.

The witnessing method I use is based on a method outlined by the late Dr. D. James Kennedy. I have modified it, but my method can trace its lineage back to Dr. Kennedy's work. I am a certified teacher-trainer in the "Evangelism Explosion" style of witnessing and have shared it with students for more than 30 years.

Many places in the Bible describe Eternal Life or Heaven as a gift – not something we can earn or deserve. When sharing this great news, I normally offer whoever I'm speaking with a dollar bill to visually illustrate how to receive a free gift. I've found this to be very effective when people stop to get a free cross for two reasons. One reason is that it is a quick gift to offer at a time when I need to be fast. People who stop for a cross had not planned on stopping. They are often on their way to work, school, running an errand, etc. Secondly, it is a visual way to understand how a gift is received. When they accept my gift (the dollar) and take it out of my hand, I say I'd like to ask them three easy questions. First: "What did I give you?" Secondly: "Did you do anything to earn or deserve it?" Lastly: "When did that gift (the dollar) become yours?"

Before I ask the first question ("What did I give you?") I share a very brief personal testimony that goes something like this:

"When I was growing up, I was reared in a good home. I believed that Jesus was the Son of God, that He died on the Cross, rose from the dead, and that He's coming back again. I was a good kid. I was trying to live a good life, hoping that when I died, God would let me into Heaven. But I was really trusting in Jesus about like I'm trusting in George Washington. It's not enough just to know the facts. The Bible says demons believe in God and tremble. They believe alright, but they're not going to Heaven. As Evangelism Explosion puts it, "Faith is not mere intellectual assent." We must make the journey from the head to the heart! At 21 years old, I went from a religion to a personal relationship with Jesus that truly rocked my world."

After I ask the second question, ("Did you do anything to earn or deserve it?") I say:

"I didn't ask you to wash the van or to sing a song. A real gift is given out of love. It's given freely. There are no strings attached. If you try to earn or pay for a gift, then it's no longer a gift. The Bible says that Heaven is a free gift. We can't earn our way to Heaven by our efforts, and we certainly don't deserve it. The Bible says, 'The wages of sin is death.' That's what I deserve. That's what we all deserve. But that same verse also says, "... but the gift of God is Eternal Life through Jesus Christ our LORD." So, you see, Heaven – Eternal Life – is God's gift!

Then comes that third question: "When did that gift (the dollar) become yours?" I say:

"This is where I missed it until I was 21 years old. Yet it is really so very simple." The usual answer to the third question is "When you gave it to me." My response is:

"Think about it for a moment. I reached in my wallet, took out a dollar and held it as close as I could to your hand, hoping that you would accept it. A gift is not yours until you receive it! In fact, I wanted you to have it. I did everything I could for you to have it but one thing. I wasn't going to make you take it. I wanted to see if, of your own free will, you would accept it. You did! That's exactly what Christ did for us on the cross. He said, 'Hey world, I love you! I've done everything I can to make Heaven available to you. I died to pay for your sins and purchased for you a place in Heaven that I offer to you as a gift.'"

But Jesus won't make us accept Him! He wants to see if, of our own free will, we will receive Him. He could have made us like robots and programmed us to do everything He wants us to do. But then how would He know if we ever loved him back?"

Two closing questions come next: "Does this make sense to you?" And, "Would you like to receive God's gift of Eternal Life Jesus Christ?"

Praise God, all five of those men in North Pole prayed to repent and receive God's free gift of Eternal Life Jesus Christ right there behind my truck. Each one asked me to sign and date the dollar bill I had given them. I gladly did. They each took a small cross to carry back to California. By then, Valerie had come out of the Santa Claus House with a little sack of souvenirs and her own cup of that delicious hot chocolate. She positioned us for a group photo in front of the iconic Santa Claus sculpture.

Santa Claus is fun but fake, in this case, a towering mass of fiberglass covered with 18 gallons of red, black and white paint. But these five friends had just accepted the real deal, the gift that will keep on giving throughout all Eternity. It is to be hoped that in all their Christmases to come, these five men won't give Santa a second thought. It's all about Jesus. Through Jesus and Jesus alone, we can have Salvation, the greatest gift of all.

26

Suicide Averted

By Valerie Culp-Lytle
August 2021, Palmer, Alaska

"And the peace of God, which passeth all understanding,
shall keep your hearts and minds through Christ Jesus."
Philippians 4:7 KJV

I t is one of our most cherished stories.

Our first seven years of evangelism yielded many accounts of the goodness of God and instances of His provision and protection. But this one from Palmer, Alaska is one of our favorites. It is the story of a Divine Appointment wrapped up in life and death.

In August 2021, the Cross Men and Cross Women shipped 250 un-assembled "Jesus Is Lord" crosses – large ones – to Anchorage, Alaska. Community Bible Fellowship in Gonzalez, Louisiana (now Wisdom's Call) paid the majority of the shipping. The pastor of Community Bible Fellowship at that time was our friend, Mike Robertson.

Grandview Baptist Church in Anchorage received the unassembled crosses and stored them in their fellowship hall until Leo and I could fly there and assemble them, also in their fellowship hall. We led the first couple of people to the Lord in that

church's parking lot, then packed the remainder of the crosses into the bed of a rented truck and headed out of town.

After doing some street evangelism in Anchorage, we had gone on to share Christ and crosses in Fairbanks and the city of North Pole. Somewhere along the way, I read in a local publication that the Alaska State Fair was going on during that time in Palmer. We were near Palmer, so we thought that might be a great location to capitalize on the increased traffic of local people who would be working at the fair or attending it. We set up in an available spot on the road leading to the fairgrounds.

Quite a few people stopped, and several prayed to be saved. They were all happy to receive a free cross. We were grateful to Cross Men Joe Horton and Ricky Turner for packaging the unassembled crosses so beautifully and shipping them to us. One of the vehicles that stopped contained a man and a woman. I was standing a good distance down the road holding up a cross to try to attract more attention, so I didn't see the man and woman's interaction with Leo. But Leo told me later that the man said he was sure he would go to Heaven, but the woman said she didn't know. She listened to Leo present the Gospel and then prayed to be saved, crying heavily. Afterward, she had a question for Leo.

"Is that your wife?" she asked him, pointing to me way down the road.

"Yes," he said.

"I've got to talk to her," she said.

I saw her coming toward me and met her. She had clearly been crying and would cry some more before she finished telling me her story. She told me she wanted me to know something. She had lost a child, she said, and could not climb out of the whirlpool of grief. That very morning, she told me, she had made the decision that she was going to kill herself. It seemed the only way to get relief from the unrelenting pain and sorrow of her loss. She had decided to do it, she said, but not right then. She would have to do a bit of planning. And that day they had to go work at the state fair.

Leo Bell Lytle III
and Valerie Lynne Culp-Lytle

She and her fiancé saw Leo and the crosses first, she said. And then they passed me, farther down the road, holding up a cross and a hand-made sign that said, "Free Crosses."

"I have to talk to those people," she told her fiance.

They made a U-turn, pulled up into the space where Leo stood with the crosses, and the Holy Spirit took it from there.

I embraced her for a long time as she cried in my arms. I prayed for her, tears rolling down my own cheeks. She left with a brave smile. She was still a woman who had lost a child. But now she was a woman who had a Savior to whom she could turn for comfort and peace. Now she was a woman who could look forward to eternity in Heaven. Now she was a woman who could learn that Jesus can give us a joy that transcends circumstances.

Leo and I were humbled by how the Lord used us that day. I had just spotted that bit of local news about the fair, and we set up there, and the Lord used our presence in THAT place at THAT time to save a woman's life and secure her eternity. Any mention of Palmer, Alaska will always make us smile.

To God be the glory!

27

"There's Those Doughnuts"

By Leo Lytle
September 2023, Kailua, Hawaii

"But my God shall supply all your need
according to his riches in glory by Christ Jesus."
Philippians 4:19 KJV

———————

September 19, 2023 in Honolulu, Hawaii would go down as a special day for our ministry in two ways. First, it would be our 50th state in which to minister. Second, as I Ubered over from the airport to our accommodation, I was blessed to lead my Uber driver to Christ in the parking lot. Now we had led someone to Jesus in all 50 states! Praise God!

Valerie would arrive a few hours behind me on a different flight, so after checking in and dropping off my luggage, I made my way to Waikiki Baptist Church to meet up with Pastor Steve Cowart and his wife Donna from Trinity Baptist Church in Lufkin, Texas. They had arrived a few days earlier and graciously volunteered to assemble 150 "Jesus Is Lord" crosses provided by Vic Bass Ministries. Cross Men volunteers Ricky Turner and Joe Horton had shipped carefully packed, unassembled crosses to Waikiki Baptist Church a few days earlier. Ricky and Joe had packaged them in three bundles of 50 crosses each, tightly shrouded in plastic for their UPS journey across the country and over the Pacific Ocean. Pastor Andrew Large of Waikiki Baptist Church had generously allowed the crosses to be both shipped and assembled there.

When I got to the church, Bro. Steve and Donna had all but about 20 completed, so we visited together while they finished. Valerie and I had learned from our trip to Alaska a couple of years earlier how to coordinate every step so we could efficiently maximize our time and resources. Because Bro. Steve and Donna planned their 40th wedding anniversary around our time in Hawaii, their assembly of the crosses gave Valerie and I an extra day to share Christ and crosses around the island of Oahu.

I love how God uses this team of volunteers to help us every step of the way on our journeys across America. It's exciting to see members of the "Body of Christ" using their gifts, talents and abilities to help advance the Gospel. Glory be to God.

The next morning, we picked up our rental truck in Honolulu and drove over to see Pastor Andrew Large at Waikiki Baptist Church and load the crosses. We bought poster boards and markers to make signs and secured one sign with my cell phone number on it to the back of the truck. Right after that we met our first homeless folks on the island. Both claimed to know Jesus as their Savior. We bought them a hearty meal.

People were seeing our new sign and stopping for free crosses. One lady listened attentively to the Gospel presentation and made life's greatest decision by accepting Jesus as her personal LORD and Savior. Glory! For the next several days, we traveled to nearly every town along the shoreline around the island of Oahu. We stopped often to share Christ and crosses and witnessed to scores of people. God's perfect timing and provision would lead us to be in just the right place at just the right time.

On one of the days during the week we spent in Hawaii, we were in the city of Kailua looking for a place to set up and share. Because the island is relatively small and real estate is so expensive, we had difficulty finding vacant parking lots or shuttered businesses on the main streets. As we searched for a spot, we noticed a Leonard's Bakery truck in a parking lot and decided to pull over and consider our limited options.

Leo Bell Lytle III
and Valerie Lynne Culp-Lytle

Bro. Steve and Donna Cowart had told us about Leonard's Bakery and urged us to try one of their famous doughnuts called malasadas before we left Hawaii. Valerie walked over and bought one for each of us to try. I love a good doughnut.

To my way of thinking, the "gold standard" when it comes to doughnuts is Southern Maid Donuts in my hometown of Shreveport, Louisiana. Fresh doughnuts are served there every day starting at 4 p.m. "Hot, hot, hot!" the sign says. Folks begin lining up before 4 p.m. and go until closing time to get a dozen or more hot, glazed doughnuts. Customers can stand and watch through glass windows as the doughy circles emerge from the cooker and move slowly atop a conveyer belt. They pass under a waterfall of sugary glaze that drenches them thoroughly. They are then scooped up with a wooden dowel rod four at a time. Three neat rows of four doughnuts per row are gently slid off the dowel rod into each box. The iconic boxes are white with green lettering. Each box bears the Southern Maid logo that depicts a standard poodle on two legs pushing a baby carriage loaded with several boxes of doughnuts.

Fun fact: music legend Elvis Presley did the only commercial of his life for Southern Maid Donuts, according to the official website for Southern Maid Donuts. Elvis recorded the company's jingle on November 6, 1954. He was in Shreveport to appear on the Louisiana Hayride. His time at that venue helped him rocket to stardom. Elvis sang: "You can get 'em piping hot after 4 p.m. You can get 'em piping hot. Southern Maid Donuts hit the spot. You can get 'em piping hot after 4 p.m." The website notes that nothing is known about the impact of Elvis' endorsement on sales.

The malasadas were tasty for sure. They are of Portuguese origin, made of rounds of yeasted dough coated with sugar or cinnamon. Some come with filling. The word "malasada" means "badly-baked" or "under-cooked" in reference to the fried outside and fluffy inside. The website Eater.com says that malasadas (sometimes spelled with two Ss: malassadas) were historically prepared for Fat Tuesday with the intention of using all the lard and sugar inside the home before Ash Wednesday. They do not have a traditional hole in the middle like a conventional doughnut. In that way, they are similar to the powdered sugar-coated beignets so famously sold in the French Quarter in New Orleans, Louisiana. Valerie and I did enjoy the malasadas we tried, but our loyalty remains with the hot, hot, hot Southern Maid Donuts!

As we were savoring our malasadas in the parking lot, a man pulled up to talk to us. He said he was a Believer and asked how he could help us. We asked if he knew of a good place where we could set up to share. He said he knew the perfect place. It was the parking lot of his church, located at a busy intersection a few miles away. He called his pastor to be sure it would be okay, and then we followed him to Windward Baptist Church in Kailua. He was right. It was a perfect location on a busy, two-lane highway right by a traffic light. We could hardly wait to scatter the crosses and signs around the truck in anticipation of what God would do.

Even better, it was the beginning of rush hour, and a steady stream of vehicles moved slowly by as Valerie and I held up our signs saying "Free Crosses." We stayed there for a couple of hours, standing in intermittent rain showers, as people pulled in to get a free cross. Six or seven people prayed to be saved during that time. I want to tell you about one of them.

A construction worker driving by in his work truck spotted us as he passed and then turned around and came back. It was raining when he got out of his truck and walked over asking for a cross. At the appropriate time, I asked did he know for certain that if he died today, he would go to Heaven? He said, "No, sir." I then asked if he would be interested in me sharing with him how he could be sure. His reply was, "I would like to know." I shared the simple Gospel message of what Jesus did for us on the cross and asked him, "Does this make sense to you?" He said, "Yes. It makes a lot of sense." Finally, I asked him if he would like to receive God's free Gift of Eternal Life Jesus Christ?" He responded, "Yes!" Even though the rain was more intense by then, he prayed with me and asked Jesus into his heart. Praise God!

As I gave him our follow-up material to help him on this new journey with Christ, he told me why he felt he had to turn around and come back. He shared that the night before, he had talked by telephone with his daughter who lives in Alaska. She is married to a soldier who has been deployed in the military. The new Believer said his daughter had called him crying in a deep state of depression. She told him she had a loaded gun in her hand and was ready to take her life. In her despair she had called him. He said that he and his wife stayed on the phone with her for several hours until she had finally fallen asleep. He told me he was so troubled for her, but felt he had nothing to say to his daughter that might give her hope. Now, though, as he was wiping both the rain and tears from his eyes, he told me he was going to call her as soon as he got home. He was excited to tell her what had just happened to him. Still standing together in the rain, I prayed for him and his daughter. He thanked me, got back in his truck and drove away.

Darkness was overtaking the sky, hastened with the aid of the rain clouds. Valerie and I loaded up to leave. As we drove away, I thought about this man and so many more like him who are struggling in the darkness of this world. So many people are hopeless and mired in deep despair. They do not know where to turn for answers to questions about purpose and meaning in their lives. Certainly, we live in a very troubled world at a very dark time. But there really is hope --- a sure hope. That hope is found only in a personal relationship with Jesus Christ. In Him we find real meaning and real purpose in living. In Him we can face our darkest hours knowing He will never leave or forsake us. In Him and Him alone we have unspeakable joy and peace, no matter the trial we may be facing.

In God's perfect timing, we had stopped at a parking lot and bitten into a couple of pastries. God sent a Believer to us at just the right moment to show us where to go to share. Lives were touched, and souls were saved. Only God can do this.

As that construction worker had driven away, he was beginning a journey like no other. He left with a sure hope as he was beginning his personal relationship with Jesus Christ. If you are lost in this old world searching for hope, why not place your trust in Jesus Christ right now? Turn to the last chapter of this book to learn how to begin a personal relationship with Jesus Christ today. You'll be so glad you did.

28

State Line Lesson Learned

By Valerie Culp-Lytle
January 2022, Texarkana, Texas/Arkansas

"Preach the word; be instant in season, out of season;
reprove, rebuke, exhort with all long suffering and doctrine."
2 Timothy 4:2 KJV

The Lord taught me something very important in Texarkana, first rattle out of the box in the new year. The lesson stung, like the blow of a switch wielded by an irate parent against the bare legs of a wayward child. But the sting made the lesson sink in and leave a lasting impression. It made me a better soldier for the cause of Christ.

We were giving away crosses and witnessing to people on a Thursday afternoon in January 2022. We were in Texarkana, Arkansas/Texas. Texarkana is one of those unique border cities which lies on both sides of a state line, with part of the city belonging to one state and the other part belonging to a different state. In Texarkana's case, the main road through the town is called State Line Boulevard. One side is in Texas, the other in Arkansas. We had enjoyed lunch and a memorable speaker earlier in the day at First Baptist Church Texarkana, on the Texas side. Now we were set up in a vacant lot in a busy section on the Arkansas side of State Line Boulevard. On this day, Leo and I were joined by Wayne and Margie Reynolds, Dr. Kelly Stone and Dennis and Becky Jones.

A steady stream of people swung into the parking lot to get a cross, keeping us busy. We asked as many of them as we could if they were sure of their eternal destination. By the time we finished that day, we would be

143

able to praise God for 11 people praying for Jesus Christ to forgive them of their sins and become his or her personal Savior. But the two men involved in the lesson I learned were not in that number.

A middle-aged man in a ball cap declaring his NFL team preference pulled up in a pickup. I greeted him and must have first asked if he wanted a cross. I may have even given him one or two, as I routinely hold a large and a small cross in my hands when I approach a vehicle. But I don't re-

member that part. What I do remember is how bluntly the man said "No" when I asked him if he died today did he know for sure he would go to Heaven.

"No," he said. "I don't believe you can know."

"Well," I said. "The Bible says you can know. May I tell you how you can know for certain?"

"No," he said again. "We have to get to work. I picked up this man to work for me. People are waiting on us."

"Okay," I said. "May I just give you some printed material that you can look over when you have time?"

"No," he said.

"Alright," I said. "What is your name?"

"Dickey," he said.

"Dickey," I said. I am going to pray for you."

"Pray for this man," Dickey said. "He's the one who needs prayer."

It was then that I noticed for the first time that there was a second man who had walked up silently on my right side. He would be the man Dickey said he had picked up as a day laborer. I smiled at the new man, and he smiled back --- a humble smile, the smile of a man who was braced for judgment. In that one look at him I could see he was not overly tall, but lean and handsome in a slightly weathered way. He looked like he had spent a few too many days in the sun. His still-thick hair was black but streaked with gray. He probably had always been something of a charmer. But now the years and the hard times were starting to take a toll. Sometimes when he thinks about the future, he feels a jolt of fear. Where did the years go, he often wonders, and how did he end up here? At least, that's how I read him, as he stood there so quietly and politely.

"What about you?" I asked in a friendly voice, turning to face him. "If you died today, do you know for certain that you would go to Heaven?"

"No," he answered.

"May I give you some printed material that you can read when you have time?" I asked.

"Yes," he said.

"I'll be right back," I told him.

I turned to jog over to the truck tailgate where we had boxes of Gospel tracts, Bibles and Bible study materials. It was only about 25 yards away from where I was standing beside Dickey's truck. I grabbed up two each of a couple of different tracts that dealt with salvation and a New Testament. Then I ran back to Dickey's truck — only to see it pulling out into the road, being driven away.

"Oh, no," I said, and let my hands full of the tracts and Bible drop to my sides as I watched the truck disappear.

It felt like a blow to the gut. I felt sorrow for the quietly humble man. I felt personal contrition and shame for having failed to have salvation tracts immediately ready. I was ready to talk and explain at a moment's notice. But I wasn't ready for those who had no time to talk, for those who couldn't — or wouldn't — wait for me to cover 25 yards and back before they had to leave. Instantly, the Scripture found in 2 Timothy 4:2 sprang to mind: *"Preach*  *the word; be instant in season, out of season; reprove, rebuke, exhort with all long suffering and doctrine." (KJV)*

I asked the LORD to please forgive me for my failure to be ready. I thanked Him for teaching me a lesson I hope to never forget. I also asked Him to please bless Dickey and the day laborer and to draw them to Himself by the power of His Holy Spirit, so that they might have another opportunity to be saved.

Gospel seeds were planted in that vacant lot in Texarkana. Even in that brief exchange with an abrupt and unsatisfactory ending to the encounter, seeds were planted. Both Dickey and the quiet man with the brave smile heard enough that they could hide it in their hearts and seek more information and counsel from somebody, or even online, later on, farther down the road. Sometimes Leo and I plant the seeds, sometimes we water them, sometimes we are blessed with the privilege of bringing in the harvest. But we are always called to be faithful. That same chapter in 2 Timothy 4, KJV, talks about faithfulness in verse 5:

"But watch thou in all things, endure afflictions, do the work of an evangelist, make full proof of thy ministry."

The adjustment I made going forward was to wear a small cross-body purse large enough to hold some evangelism tracts and two or three small New Testaments. I already wore a little purse that held my phone and some hand sanitizer. Just a touch bigger bag, and I was set. The ongoing additional adjustment I am also making is to memorize more Scripture, to hide more of it in my heart.

I want to be ever more ready to lead people to Jesus, to guide them to ask Him for a future in Heaven. We can all relate to sometimes wondering where the years went. Plenty of people may also wonder how they ended up wherever they are. But among the joys of the Good News of Jesus Christ is that those of us who have put our trust in Him as Lord and Savior need not suffer that jolt of fear when we think about the future. Instead of fear, there is peace. As Isaiah 26:3, KJV, says: *"Thou wilt keep him in perfect peace, whose mind is stayed on thee: because he trusteth in thee."*

29

The Middle
Of Nowhere

By Leo Lytle
August 2021, Glasgow, Montana

*"If we confess our sins, he is faithful and just to forgive us our sins,
and to cleanse us from all unrighteousness."*
1 John 1:9 KJV

G lasgow, Montana is a small town of about 3,200 people located in the northeastern part of the state. It is only 60 miles from the Canadian border. Town lore says it was named by a blindfolded railroad clerk who spun a globe and stopped the globe's spin with his finger. Under his fingertip was Glasgow, Scotland. Thus, the little town in Montana became Glasgow.

If you live in Glasgow and want to visit Walmart, you had better pack a lunch. The nearest one is 130 miles away in Miles City, giving this unique town the distinction of being further away from the near-est Walmart and further away from any metropolitan area in the lower 48 States. A July 2018 article in Conde Nast Traveler says Glasgow is a 4.5-hour drive in any direction from a city. The official nickname for Glasgow is "The Middle of Nowhere."

I left home on August 3, 2021 for what would turn out to

be an exciting 39-day ministry trip. Valerie's work schedule kept her from leaving with me that day, but our plan was for her to fly to Billings, Montana on August 13. She would then join me for the next 11 days in Wyoming, Idaho, Oregon, Washington, and Alaska before flying home. To position myself near Billings, Montana, I drove into Glasgow late in the afternoon of August 11 and spent the night in the van at a local RV park. That next morning, August 12, (our son Adam's 41st birthday) is where this story begins.

I spent the better part of the morning in Glasgow sharing Christ and "Jesus Is Lord" crosses at a location on the main road leading through town. There were only a few folks who stopped, and all but one of them claimed to be a Believer. I did engage in a Gospel conversation with that one, but he told me he was not ready to make a commitment to Jesus Christ. Before leaving town for the long drive to Billings, I stopped for gas. The clerk wanted a few crosses and was interested in hearing how he could know if he would go to Heaven. I shared with him the Good News of the Gospel in between customers, leading right up to the time of commitment.

I've learned a very important lesson through my years of sharing the Gospel, and here it is: When God is at work, so is the Devil! There have been many times when at the very moment in a Gospel conversation where I've asked someone, "Would you like to receive God's free Gift of Eternal Life?" that a distraction of some sort takes place. In this case, the store manager came in and needed help to do inventory at that very moment. The clerk was now obviously distracted. I quickly left him a "Good News For You" Bible study booklet, a New Testament, a Gospel tract, and my cell phone number. I hope I see him in Heaven one day. The Gospel seed was well-planted and well-watered, but the harvest had to be delayed.

I drove for several hours, enjoying the vast and beautiful landscape of Montana on the way to Billings. It's not called the "Big Sky Country" for nothing. I so appreciate and love these moments when I get to experience the majesty of God's creation. Driving through the mountains, seeing herds of antelope and deer, crossing rivers and rock-filled streams fills my heart with wonder and praise.

In the late afternoon, I arrived in Lewistown and wanted to share Jesus there for a couple of hours. After looking around town, the LORD led me to the perfect spot. Within minutes, folks began to stop and the Gospel was being shared. Nine more souls were added to The Kingdom. All Glory to God! Time now to drive on to Billings for the night.

Leo Bell Lytle III
and Valerie Lynne Culp-Lytle

It's nearly 300 miles from Glasgow to Billings. So by the time I got there it was well after dark, and I was well past tired. I was thanking God for all the experiences of the day, and especially thanking Him for those who had made life's greatest decision in accepting Jesus Christ as their personal LORD and Savior. Now it was time to find a place to rest. We had installed in our 2007 Ford Econoline a comfortable foam mattress on top of a custom-built platform under which we carry our luggage, boxes of Bibles, Bible study booklets, Christian key rings, ministry ink pens, special coloring books for children and other supplies.

We also have a place to store "The Door" along with a special stand to hold it upright during my presentation and a six-foot table on which to assemble the door. I share this message all over America in any church that invites us, regardless of size. In fact, it was the opportunity to share "The Door" at Twin Rivers Church in Springfield, Oregon that was part

of the reason for this journey. Pastor Jeremiah Walpert had called me a couple of months earlier about coming to share "The Door" and doing personal evangelism training. Our training includes taking those interested out on the street to share Christ and crosses in their town. I was to be with them on August 29, after the Alaska leg of our trip.

We sleep in the back of the van as often as possible. Usually, we end up in a shopping center parking lot, a highway rest stop, a truck stop parking lot, a church parking lot or an RV park when we need a place to shower or to wash clothes.

So, it's after 9 p.m., and I'm driving through Billings looking for a spot for the night, when I get a call from a woman behind me who wants a free cross. As we talked off the side of the road, I found out that she wanted one for her wife's mother. Although she did not identify herself as a lesbian, she said it was for her wife's mother.

Of course, I thanked her for calling and asked her the same question I ask everyone: "Have you come to the place in your life where you know for certain that if you were to die today you would go to Heaven?" We have found that a good percentage of the people we meet are uncertain or just say no they don't know. I always thank them for their honesty. Valerie says that on the street people are more honest about their spiritual condition. I believe she is correct.

This young lady said no, she didn't think she would go to Heaven. I said to her, as I do with others, that I found out at age 21 that Heaven is a free gift. I couldn't earn it, nor did I deserve it. I said to her, "If you would like to know how you can be sure you'll go to Heaven when you die, I'd be happy to share with you what I discovered at age 21."

I believe it's important when sharing the Gospel to ask permission before doing so. I'm not out to try to win an argument with someone. I want them to be receptive to hearing the Gospel, not to force the Gospel on them. I believe that anything I can talk somebody into, someone else can talk them out of it. I want these Gospel engagements to be Spirit-led, not Leo-led!

After listening to the plain and simple Gospel message, the young lady decided right there on the side of a busy road in Billings, Montana to pray and receive God's forgiveness and accept God's gift of eternal life! Praise God!

I'm sure some will say this young lady must first turn from her lifestyle and then she could be saved. Or perhaps I should have counseled her about the sin of sexual immorality. What follows here is very important if we are going to reach this lost world: Jesus saves us just as we are. Let me say that again. Jesus saves us just like we are at that moment. I'm so very thankful that Jesus saved me just as I was — even with all my flaws, my imperfections, my failures, in short, all my sin. I could never get good enough to merit my salvation, nor can any one of us. I'm just not that good. Neither are you.

By the world's standard, most of us are considered pretty good folks when we compare ourselves with others. But, by God's standard we have all failed. We have come up way short. We are all sinners. The Bible says it better than I can: *"For all have sinned, and come short of the glory of God;"* (Romans 3:23 KJV).

Now, I love fishing, but I have never caught a fish that has already been cleaned. Have you? Of course not! Jesus called us to be "fishers of men." In my many years of personal experience "fishing for men," I've never caught a clean one yet! No one else has either. He takes us — saves us — just like we are, and then He cleans us up and makes us into the man, woman, boy or girl He wants us to be.

It takes the work of the Holy Spirit to convict us, to guide us and to help conform us into the image of Christ. Even so, most of us have a "stronghold" or two in our lives that cause some struggle. The young lady in Billings will need to learn to yield to the Holy Spirit's leadership in her life. Scripture tells us, *"This I say then, Walk in the Spirit, and ye shall not fulfill the lust of the flesh."* (Galatians 5:16 KJV).

After leading the young lady to Christ, I continued my search for a place to sleep. As I drove in and around Billings, I received three more calls for crosses and was blessed to see seven more folks pray to be saved. Hallelujah!

Finally, sometime around 11:30 p.m., I located a large church parking lot on the edge of town where I pulled over for the night. It would be another hour before I called my sweet Valerie back home, messaged Bro. Vic Bass and the prayer team about the day's events, and finished my nightly social media post.

Before I finally drifted off to sleep, I thanked God for an amazing day that had started in "The Middle of Nowhere." It reminded me once again that so many people are lost in this world in the middle of nowhere, too, trapped in the Devil's snares with no hope in sight. They are in a desperate search for purpose and meaning in life, but unable to break away from the chains of sin that have them bound.

If that's you, I've got Good News. I know a chain-breaker. His name is Jesus. He can save you and set you free. Glory, Hallelujah! Please turn to the last chapter of this book and discover how you can be set free from the bondage of sin and begin a personal relationship with Jesus Christ. He'll give you peace, joy, purpose and meaning.

30

Not Beyond
His Reach

By Leo Lytle
August 2021, Belle Fouche, South Dakota

"Behold, the LORD'S hand is not shortened, that it cannot save;
neither his ear heavy, that it cannot hear:"
Isaiah 59:1 KJV

———————

A s confessions go, what I heard in Belle Fouche, South Dakota was a memorable first. It had taken some time to get to that moment, however.

August 8, 2021 was a warm summer evening in Spearfish, South Dakota. I laid down to sleep — or at least tried to — in the back of our van in a parking lot.

We love this state. Although the winter can be brutal with heavy snow and blizzards, it's not unusual to experience triple-digit temperatures during the "Dog Days" of summer. Now, it was nearly midnight with a temperature in the mid 80's. To add a little more discomfort, there wasn't even the hint of a breeze. I had propped the back doors of the van open in hopes an errant breeze might have pity on me.

Earlier that morning I had the privilege of preaching at Joy Christian Fellowship in Hot Springs, South Dakota, where my friend Bro. Bill Martin serves as pastor. A few folks asked if I knew the big Sturgis Motorcycle Rally was in progress and suggested that I consider going there on my way to North Dakota. It seemed like a great idea. I headed that direction after the morning worship service.

I'd heard stories about Sturgis and what goes on there. None of it sounded wholesome or family-friendly. I expected it would be jam-packed with bikers from across America. As I drove, I thought and prayed about how best the LORD could use a guy like me in a place like that.

What seemed like hundreds of bikers steadily thundered past my van and trailer on the interstate as I got closer to the Sturgis exit. Adding to the motorcycle traffic were many tourists who came to take in the experience. It was certainly a sight to see as I made my way through the crowded streets to the heart of town. Thousands of people strolled among the hundreds of motorcycles that were parked side by side covering several city blocks.

I made a couple of passes through the multitudes with my trailer full of free "Jesus Is Lord" crosses. As I slowly "waggled" the trailer through the bumper-to-bumper traffic, heads were turning and fingers were pointing. People were watching. I hoped they would consider the powerful meaning of the cross.

Our usual way of sharing crosses wouldn't fit this unique situation. I parked a few blocks away and decided to use the big nine-foot rolling cross for this opportunity.

With Gospel tracts in one hand and the cross on my shoulder, I was ready to make a go of it. I walked several blocks to reach the heart of Sturgis. Then I walked slowly up and down the streets, rolling the big cross where the motorcycles were parked. "Good News! Jesus is still changing lives! Read all about it!" I said, as I offered the Gospel tracts to anyone who would accept. A few did, but most took a pass on my offer.

Here is a very important truth about sharing the Gospel. Those who reject your witness for Christ are not rejecting you. They are rejecting who you represent: Jesus Christ. So, never take rejection personally. Our responsibility and great privilege is to be a faithful steward of the Gospel message. We can't save anybody. Only Jesus can! The convicting work of the Holy Spirit draws the lost person to see his or her need for forgiveness of sin and eternal salvation. I often say to people that I'm not interested in winning an argument. Anything I can talk you into, someone else can talk you out of it.

After about an hour of walking with the big cross, I decided to just stand with it in an upright position on the busiest corner in town. I shared the same message and offered tracts to all who passed my way. I was able to speak with many passers-by and was thankful to share the Gospel with a photographer who identified himself as a Unitarian and then later to three teenage boys. All four listened to the Gospel message and prayed to receive God's free gift of Eternal Life Jesus Christ. Hallelujah!

Leo Bell Lytle III
and Valerie Lynne Culp-Lytle

As I rolled my way back to the van, I met a Christian cyclist from Ohio who wanted a cross. I helped him strap it to the backrest of his Harley and watched as he drove away. The sun was setting as I strapped the big rolling cross back onto the trailer and headed out of Sturgis. A few miles down the Interstate I took the Spearfish exit.

In Spearfish, I texted my daily report to the Vic Bass Ministries prayer team and posted the nightly social media post. Despite the uncomfortably warm night, I drifted off to sleep.

At dawn's early light, I awoke to the sound of school day traffic. There was a fast food restaurant close by, so I stopped for a sausage biscuit and Diet Coke. Walking toward the entrance, I saw a man pulling at the door. He looked my way and said, "There's a note on the door. Not open until 6:45 am." I thanked him from a distance, got back into the van and headed north.

Very soon I saw the sign for Belle Fouche, South Dakota and realized that I had read about this city being the geographical center of the United States. The geographical center was previously in Lebanon, Kansas until Alaska and Hawaii were granted statehood in 1959. 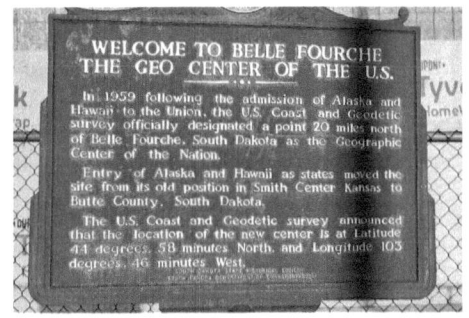 Now Belle Fouche claimed the bragging rights. I don't stop for many landmarks, but my love for geographical oddities was roused as I passed a historical marker in the middle of town. This was a must-stop for me.

I took a few minutes to satisfy my curiosity by carefully reading the engraved plaque and taking a few pictures. As I walked back to the van, an old truck pulled into the parking lot. It looked familiar. When the man got out, I recognized him. He was the man I had seen at the fast food restaurant entrance in Spearfish just a half hour earlier. It quickly became apparent that he wasn't there for a geography lesson.

He walked directly over to me. I was standing by my trailer in front of the crosses. The man asked what I was doing. I was there to share Jesus with people, I told him, and asked if he would like a free cross. He glanced at them and said probably not.

He said his mother was a good person and a Christian before she died. He said he was certain she would have liked one. He explained he was not anything like his mom and wasn't sure if he should take one. When I asked if he were to die today, did he know for certain that he would go to Heaven, he said "No." He said he was certain that a man like him had no chance of going to Heaven. "I wouldn't be so sure of that," I said and asked if I could share with him how I discovered that Heaven/ Eternal Life was a gift. He gave a somewhat reluctant okay. Whether it was to appease me or to satisfy his curiosity, I didn't know. But he gave me the green light to proceed, so I began to share the Gospel.

After sharing what Jesus did on the cross for us, I asked him, "Does this make sense to you?" He said, "Yes." "Would you like to receive God's free gift of Eternal Life Jesus Christ?" I asked. He said he didn't think Jesus would save a guy like him. He began to walk back to his truck. As he did, I said, "You might be surprised." He came back. Then he shared with me that he didn't normally tell people what he did for a living but had decided to tell me his story.

"You know the bikers who come to Sturgis?" he began.

"Yes," I answered. "In fact, I was just there yesterday."

"Well," he said, "I run a bar. To attract the bikers to it, I put on a 'Wet T-Shirt Contest' for them every night."

He paused and then asked, "He wouldn't save a guy like me, would He?" Again, he began to slowly walk back toward his truck.

"He takes us just like we are," I called after him. "He accepted me just as I was."

The bar owner turned around and came back to me as I leaned against the trailer.

"Do you think Jesus would approve of what I'm doing?" he asked.

"Here is what I do know," I said. "If you accept Him into your heart, He will begin to make you into the man He wants you to be!"

He started walking away again and then came back.

"You don't think this is just a coincidence that you and I are here in this parking lot so early in the morning, do you?" I asked.

"No," he said.

"This is what I call a 'Divine Appointment,'" I told him. "I saw you back at Spearfish at the restaurant. Now, a half hour later, here we are together in this parking lot in Belle Fouche. I believe God is giving you an opportunity to respond to Him this morning. He loves you too much to force you to accept Him. You can walk away now, and you **might** have another opportunity to receive Him, but that's your choice."

Leo Bell Lytle III
and Valerie Lynne Culp-Lytle

Again, he slowly walked back to his truck and put his hand on the door handle. I kept still, leaning against the cross trailer. Finally, he walked back to me and said, "Let's do it!"

Right then and there, in the historical marker parking lot in Belle Fouche, South Dakota, in the geographical center of the United States, this jaded bar owner asked Jesus Christ to forgive him and save him. All Glory to God!

No one is beyond the loving reach of Almighty God. Today might be your "Divine Appointment!" If you want to be forgiven and start a personal relationship with Jesus Christ, please turn to the last chapter of this book. You'll be eternally glad that you did.

31

Blind Dog, Good Man

By Valerie Culp-Lytle
August 2022, Kingston, Tennessee

"But seek ye first the kingdom of God, and his righteousness;
and all these things shall be added unto you."
Matthew 6:33 KJV

Here's the thing about our chairs: we rarely sit in them.

The first two chairs we carried in our van were "bag chairs" that had cost about $8 apiece. Flimsy. Eventually, we received a love offering that inspired us to buy a couple of nicer chairs. Sturdy and comfortable, these collapsable chairs have an attached tray large enough to hold a Bible or a plate of food. There's a cup holder, too. We've all heard of ministries that have a private jet, multiple homes and other luxuries. Our ministry has a couple of $45 chairs, and we are grateful for them. Like everything else we have been blessed with in our lives, we want the Lord to use those chairs for His glory and to further His kingdom. He does.

When the chairs were brand new, we found ourselves

in Kingston, Tennessee. It was August 2022. Hot, of course. We were set up in an empty parking lot on a busy street. A young man dressed in black was walking along the sidewalk, about to pass us by. I walked out and intercepted him with, "Would you like a free cross?" He paused, let me talk to him for a few more sentences. But then I realized that only good manners were keeping him upright and focusing on me.

"You're too hot and tired to even listen to me, aren't you?" I asked him.

"Yes, ma'am," he answered.

"Well, come over on this side of the van and sit down in the shade," I said to him. "We just got these new chairs. We haven't really even sat in them yet. You sit down right there and let me get you some cold water."

I sat him in one of the comfortable chairs in the shade of the van and handed him a cold bottle of water and a little snack.

"Sit there until you feel better," I told him. "We can talk later. Right now, just rest. You are safe with us."

The young man had good bone structure, brown hair to which a trace of pink had been added and a small backpack. He reminded me of our own sons. Leo and I have eight sons and daughters in our blended family. This fellow could have fit right in with the youngest three of our sons. I didn't yet know what had happened to him to give him the air of burden that clung to him, but I hoped if one of our sons were ever in similar straits that someone would show kindness to him.

He had lost his job, he told me, and was trying to find a new one. In the meantime, he didn't have a car or a phone, and he was facing eviction within the next few days. Although he looked young to be married, he said that he was, but that he was estranged from his wife. He had a lead on a low-paying job that might be coming open soon, but it would be several days before he would know about it. He would be homeless by then.

The first thing he needed was Jesus.

On my way to earning a paramedic license and later a registered nurse license, one of the basic tenets drilled into me was that as one is noting scene safety and level of consciousness, the medical professional must assess the ABCs first and continually: Airway, Breathing, Circulation. Without those ABCs covered, any other intervention one may attempt is useless. Sharing the Gospel on the street is the same. People come with wheelbarrows full of problems. But if that person is also spiritually lost, then that is their worst problem. Unforgiven sin will send them to Hell. None of the rest of it will matter — not the addiction or the divorce or the eviction or the unemployment. The FIRST thing a lost person needs is to confess that he or she believes that Jesus Christ is the Son of God and ask Jesus to please forgive him or her of their sins and save them. The Holy Spirit will take it from there.

So it was with this young man. Once he had revived somewhat from rest, shade and hydration and had shared his story with me, I introduced him to Leo. Leo introduced him to Jesus. The young man prayed to be saved.

Meanwhile, on the sunny side of the van, I met a man who kept a small dog tucked under his arm while he talked to me. Despite the heat of the day, he kept the little dog close to his body as though to comfort it. "She's blind," he explained. Right away, I liked this man. Who would not like a man showing such com-passion to a little blind dog? I liked him even more when he told me about his ministry, which he shared with some friends. Their focus was helping people who just got out of jail get on their feet.

"What about BEFORE they go to jail?" I asked him.

When the man asked what I meant, I tipped my head toward the other side of the van and low-ered my voice.

"There's a young man sitting on that side who has all kinds of prob-lems," I said. "He hasn't been to jail yet, but it would not take much. He's on a slippery slope."

Before long, the Holy Spirit had ministered to the young man in black as only He can. Not only did the young man now have Eternal Life, he also now had a contact in the city who said he might be able to find the young man a place to live and might know of a job. The man with the blind dog had invited the young man to his church's next service. They had agreed on a place for the ministry man to pick up the young man to take him to church. It was a thing of beauty to behold, all glory to God.

Finally, we asked the young man if he was hungry. Yes ma'am, he certainly was. Leo sent the young man and me to a fried chicken place next to where we were set up. We bought him enough food to fill himself up then and to have enough for leftovers. We did the same for his roommate and his dog. We sent him on his way with two sacks full of food and a big drink full of ice. Of course, we had also given him a Bible and a Bible study workbook.

A bit later in the day the two chairs came into play again. I came around to Leo's side of the van and saw that he had two Mormon missionaries sitting in those brand-new chairs. They were listening respectfully as Leo shared the true Gospel with them. Looking hot in their dress shirts and ties, the young men seemed grateful to be off their feet in the heat and appeared prepared to listen to Leo as long as he wanted to talk. "Yes, Lord," I thought. "Use those chairs!"

———————

"Therefore take no thought, saying, What shall we eat? or,
What shall we drink? or, Wherewithal shall we be clothed?
(For after all these things do the Gentiles seek:)
for your heavenly Father knoweth that ye have need of all these things.
But seek ye first the kingdom of God, and his righteousness;
and all these things shall be added unto you."
Matthew 6: 31-33, KJV

32

Take a Stand

By Leo Lytle
April 2021, Bristol, Virginia

"Whosoever therefore shall confess me before men,
him will I confess also before my Father which is in heaven.
But whosoever shall deny me before men,
him will I also deny before my Father which is in heaven."
Matthew 10: 32-33 KJV

———————

As Christians, we are called to stand for Jesus publicly. Jesus was very clear that when Believers experience hate from the world, they can be assured that the world first hated Him. He was also clear that His followers must not be ashamed of following Him. Luke 9:26 KJV says this:

"For whosoever shall be ashamed of me and of my words, of him shall the Son of man be ashamed, when he shall come in his own glory, and in his Father's and of the holy angels."

In April 2020 I was in Paris, Tennessee sharing Christ and crosses in a very large parking lot at a shopping center. It looked like a great place to reach people, so I went to the largest business in the shopping center and asked for permission to give away free crosses out by the street in front of their store. They said to go right ahead. Many people came for a cross. Seven people prayed to be saved in the time that I was there.

Around the two-hour mark, a man who looked to be about my age (in his sixties) came up to me.

"I bet you want a free cross," I said.

"No," he said. "I'm the owner of this shopping center, and I'm going to have to ask you to leave. I'm a Christian, and I think you're doing a good thing. But I don't want to offend any of my tenants who might not like what you're doing."

I apologized and pointed to the largest business where I had obtained permission to be there.

"Did someone complain?" I asked.

"No, not yet," he said. "But I can't take the risk that they might."

"So, you're telling me that you're a Christian," I said. "You own this shopping center. You believe in what I'm doing here. But you're asking me to leave because one of your tenants might complain, even though none have yet?"

"Yes," he said.

I looked at him sadly and told him I would load up and go. Rather than stand for Christ, the business owner chose to protect himself from potential financial loss.

It's certainly not the first time I've been asked to leave. I try to be very careful about where I set up the trailer and crosses. This was the first time that I witnessed a self-described Believer choose between his faith and his pocketbook. The pocketbook won this one.

As the moral fabric of America continues to unravel, all of us who are followers of Christ will face decisions that will cost us. That's a given. The real question is, will we be willing to pay whatever the cost to advance the Kingdom of Christ?

Encouragingly, I met a woman I'll call Barbara in Bristol, Virginia who made the opposite choice of the shopping center owner in Paris, Tennessee. Barbara chose faith over her pocketbook. Here is her story:

I was on an evangelism trip to the Northeast in April 2021, when I felt led to stop and share Christ and crosses in Bristol, Virginia. I drove around town to look for a good spot and finally located a vacant gravel parking lot with a few small trees and brush on both sides. I put out the signs, scattered crosses around the trailer and was ready for action. A few minutes later, a woman stopped for a cross. As we talked, she allowed me to share God's plan of salvation with her and prayed with me to ask Jesus to be her Lord and Savior!

As I was giving her a Bible and a Bible study booklet designed for new Believers, I heard a woman speaking loudly in my direction. She was walking swiftly across the empty concrete space toward me.

164

Leo Bell Lytle III
and Valerie Lynne Culp-Lytle

"Sir!" she called out. "Sir!" she called again as she got closer.

"Sir, I'm sorry to tell you this, but you're going to have to leave," she said when she reached me. "You're on our property. My boss just called, and she told me to tell you to leave."

"I'm a Christian," Barbara said. "I believe what you are doing is a good thing. But I am sorry to say that you're going to have to leave."

Well, I'd heard those words before. My mind flashed back to Paris, Tennessee.

"Of course," I apologized. I explained that I didn't know the gravel lot was a part of the business she was managing. I told her I would load up and look for another place.

I picked up all the crosses and all the signs and secured them. I was just about to get into the truck to drive away when I suddenly heard Barbara's voice again. Once again, she was walking rapidly toward me across the concrete expanse. Her message was different this time, though.

"Sir!" she called out as she walked. "Sir, don't leave."

"Please stay," she said when she reached me. "I'm a Christian. What you are doing is important. Our town needs this. Don't leave. Please stay."

I said, "But you said your boss told you to tell me to leave."

"She did," Barbara responded. "But I thought about what you were trying to do. We need people who will share the truth. I'm a Christian. The Lord convicted me about this, so I knew I needed to ask you to stay. I don't care if I get fired from my job for doing this. It's what I should do. God will help me and my kids if I get fired."

"Are you sure about this?" I asked.

"Yes!" Barbara said. "Please stay."

As she walked back to her office, I started unloading for the second time while thinking about the courage of this young woman. Within minutes, a young man around 30 years old stopped. In short order, he decided to pray to receive God's free gift of Eternal Life Jesus Christ!

Others stopped by over the next couple of hours, including a 16-year-old boy accompanied by his stepmother. He told me they had stopped at

a convenience store around the corner moments earlier. He said he had found a paper inside the restroom and started reading it. It was a Gospel tract. He said he was just thinking that he wished he had someone to explain to him what the paper was talking about, when he and his stepmother turned the corner. They saw my crosses and signs and decided to stop. Before long, he, too, made life's greatest decision in accepting Jesus Christ as his Savior and Lord!

Finally, I was ready to leave. But there was one last thing I needed to do. I grabbed a cross and walked up to the building where Barbara worked. I gave her the cross and thanked her for her courage in putting her livelihood on the line so that I could continue to reach out to her community with the Gospel. She said again that she was a Christian and it was the right thing to do.

"If I lose my job," Barbara said again, "I know God will provide for me and my kids."

Her decision to stand for Jesus had borne eternal fruit, and I wanted her to know.

"One more thing I wanted to tell you," I said to her.

"When you came out the first time to ask me to leave," I told her, "the lady who was there had just received Christ. Then, when you came back and asked me to stay, two more people prayed to be saved after that: a young man and a 16-year-old boy. Because of your faith and courage, their names have now been written in the Lamb's Book of Life in Heaven."

Barbara's faith and courage that day were remarkable. I share her story often from pulpits around the nation. My aim is to encourage others to truly live out their faith in these unusual days as we seek to show Christ to a confused, lost and hurting world. I'm reminded of a quote from the late Adrian Rogers, a beloved American preacher:

"What we need is not great faith," Adrian Rogers said, "but faith in a great God."

We also need more Barbaras who are brave enough to take a stand in support of that faith.

33
Of Invisibility And Atheists

By Leo Lytle
April 2021, Standish, Maine

"Let your speech be always with grace, seasoned with salt,
that ye may know how ye ought to answer every man."
Colossians 4:6 KJV

A s a child, I used to imagine it would be great fun to be able to go invisible. As an adult, though, I have found it is not nearly as fun as I
dreamed.

It was April 2021. I had spent most of the day in Portland, Maine
as part of a trip I was calling "Operation Grace." It was one of those days
though, when I felt all but invisible. Only a handful of people stopped to
get a cross.

One man who did stop listened to the Gospel presentation. He was
so close to making his personal decision to accept Jesus Christ. But being
close only counts, as they say, in "horseshoes and hand grenades." In the
end, he drove away with a free cross, but **not** with God's free Gift of Eternal
Life Jesus Christ. Of course, not everyone who hears the "Good News" re-
sponds affirmatively to it. It reminds me of King Agrippa's response to the
testimony of Paul. As Paul shared Christ with King Agrippa and the large
group of leaders and officials that day, the king was listening carefully. We
read his response in Acts 26:28: *"Then Agrippa said unto Paul, Almost thou per-
suadest me to be a Christian."* It is, after all, a personal decision that each person must make. Unfortunately, if you choose not to accept Him, then you
have, in fact, chosen to reject Him. The consequences are eternally grave.

167

Days like that remind me that I'm not responsible for the results. God is! People are not, in fact, rejecting me. They are rejecting who I represent. I am, after all, just a vessel. Each person is ultimately accountable for his or her own personal decision about what to do with Jesus. I learned long ago that as Believers, it is our duty, our responsibility and our great privilege to share Jesus. We should be very intentional about it, too.

Later, I tried a second location in Portland on a busy street near a traffic light. Traffic was heavy and slow. Some vehicles came to a stop right in front of me. As they waited for the light to change, I was so close I could look the drivers in the eyes as they passed. Still, only a few stopped. One who did was a local college student who identified himself as agnostic.

He and I had a good 20 minutes together to discuss his skepticism about there being a God. We discussed evolution, the Big Bang, the age of the earth and all sorts of modern scientific theories on life and creation. I love talking with agnostics, atheists, pagans and people involved in cults and world religions. They all have a story to tell. I've found it best to listen carefully and respectfully. They have a reason for why they don't believe or why they doubt the existence of God. There is a reason as to why they have chosen to follow some far-out myth, cult or works-based world religion. You won't learn that reason if you don't listen.

It's been my experience, particularly with atheists, that many have had a bad personal experience or tragedy in their past, one in which they earnestly asked God to intervene. Because He didn't intervene or prevent the tragedy, they take that to be evidence that He does not exist. Others see wars, famines and inequities in society as proof that God does not exist. Of course, many are also quick to point out cases of hypocrisy by those who identify as Christians as a reason for their unbelief.

Without a long lesson in Christian apologetics here, let me just say this: The Bible tells us to "... *be ready always to give an answer to every man that asketh you a reason of the hope that is in you, with meekness and fear.*" (I

Leo Bell Lytle III
and Valerie Lynne Culp-Lytle

Peter 3:15 KJV). Also, Colossians 4:6 KJV says, *"Let your speech be always with grace, seasoned with salt, that ye may know how ye ought to answer every man."* The complexity of life, down to the smallest single cell, proves beyond any reasonable doubt that life has a Designer. Not only **does** life have a Designer, it **must** have a designer. We are most certainly not the products of blind evolutionary chance. The mathematical precision of the universe demands a Designer. And, of course, there is no explanation of how time, space and matter came into existence from nothingness apart from an unimaginably intelligent Designer! Make no mistake about it, my skeptical friends, that Designer is God.

Late that afternoon, I left Portland, Maine, heading to New Hampshire. Driving through the beautiful countryside, I was praying for one more opportunity to engage in a Gospel conversation before reaching New Hampshire. The LORD answered that prayer and gave me that opportunity at Standish, Maine.

Standish is a city of about 10,000 people, situated very near the Maine/New Hampshire border. Within minutes after my arrival, I noticed a vacant corner lot at an intersection with a traffic light. I pulled in there faster than a Texas gunslinger. I quickly put out my free crosses signs, and in short order people began to stop. It was exciting!

Most who stopped identified themselves as Believers. One exception was an 18-year-old man. He and I soon engaged in a Gospel conversation. Standing with me on that vacant corner lot in Standish, Maine he prayed to receive Jesus Christ as his personal LORD and Savior! Glory! I was so happy to see my prayer answered so quickly. After experiencing a less than enthusiastic response earlier, I was thankful that folks were stopping.

As I was finishing a conversation with a couple, I saw a man walking over from his vehicle parked across the street. I waved to him and called, "I'll be with you in a moment." I thought he said to me, "I'm a Christian." I finished my conversation and walked over to meet him.

"So, you're a Christian," I said, after greeting him.

"Oh no," he said. "What I said was, 'I'm not a Christian.' I'm an atheist."

Then he handed me a 10-dollar bill. I was a bit puzzled by his kind gesture, especially coming from an atheist.

"Now, let me get this straight," I said. "You're an atheist. I'm out here sharing Jesus with folks, and you are giving me a 10-dollar donation? I don't understand."

"I've been watching you from across the street for some time," the man said. "What you're doing here is giving people hope. This world needs more hope, and I want to help support what you are doing."

He was probably in his fifties. We talked for a few minutes about God and atheism. Not a deep or heated discussion. In fact it was a very pleasant conversation. I believed what he experienced there had already begun to soften his heart. I thanked him again for his kindness. Then he walked back across the street to his car and drove away. I put the 10-dollar bill in my pocket and was soon engaged in another conversation with a mother and daughter.

I've spoken with several atheists over the years. They normally don't renounce their atheistic views at our first encounter. At best, maybe God used me that day to water a small seed of hope struggling to spring up in his life. Perhaps he'll be more receptive the next time he gets to talk with a Believer. Maybe the next Believer will be able to water that seed of hope, too. Maybe someday there will be a harvest.

Jesus made it crystal clear about the only way to Heaven when He said, *"I am the Way, the Truth, and the Life. No man cometh to the Father, but by me."* (John 14:6 KJV).

I hope the generous atheist thinks about our meeting from time to time. I hope the seed that was planted in Standish, Maine continues to grow. I hope we meet again someday --- in Heaven!

34

God Provides,
Even Parking Places

By Leo Lytle
April 2021, Providence, Rhode Island

"And the LORD, he it is that doth go before thee;
he will be with thee, he will not fail thee, neither forsake thee:
fear not, neither be dismayed."
Deuteronomy 31:8 KJV

I f you're a fan of coffee and doughnuts or enjoy restaurant dining, then Providence, Rhode Island is the place to visit. It's famous for being one of the cities in America with the most coffee and doughnut shops and restaurants per capita. So, if Providence is one's destination, it's best to arrive hungry.

The city was founded by visionary political and religious leader Roger Williams in 1636. He named it in "honor of God's merciful Providence" in helping him and his followers find this special place to start a settlement. He had been exiled from the Massachusetts Bay Colony because of religious persecution. A couple of years later, Williams would start the First Baptist Church, which is the first and oldest Baptist Church in America.

On Monday morning, April 5, 2021, I arrived in Providence on my first trip to the Northeast. I began looking for a place where I could set up to share Christ and crosses. Because it is one of America's oldest cities, established long before the automobile was invented, the city relies on a haphazard street layout from bygone days. It would take a good while before I finally found the perfect place that God had already prepared for me.

CROSS-ing AMERICA
Sharing Jesus Around The Nation

The day before was Easter Sunday. I had worshiped at Northeast Baptist Church a few miles away in Danbury, Connecticut, where I heard a wonderful sermon by Pastor Joe Vassek. He and his wife, Amy, graciously  invited me to join their family for lunch and fellowship after the service. They also gave me a few minutes to share about our unique ministry in their evening service. I spent the afternoon between church services there in Danbury sharing Christ and crosses. Several people responded to the Gospel and prayed to be saved. Thank you, LORD.

Now, in Providence, I was again praying to see people accept Christ. That prayer was certainly answered as 11 people prayed to receive God's free Gift of Eternal Life Jesus Christ. I give Him all the glory and praise for what he arranged by His "providence" in Providence! In addition to those who were saved, I met a few wonderful, committed Believers. One was Gerald Perkins, who owns an exterminating business and has a music ministry in Providence. He was so encouraging to this old Southern boy trying to negotiate my way through the Northeast and New England. We have remained Facebook friends.

One lesson God taught me that day in Providence was how to overcome discouragement. I was full of excitement and anticipation as I drove into the city. However, the difficulty of locating a place to set up was discouraging and increasingly so the longer I searched. Finally, I saw what appeared to be a vacant parking lot at the top of a "T" in the road down from a nearby shopping center. I quickly put out my "Free Crosses" signs and scattered dozens of crosses around the trailer.

Maybe 10 or 15 minutes later, a truck pulled up in the parking lot. A couple of men got out and opened a gate that was a little more than 75 feet from where I was. I realized then that maybe this was not a vacant parking lot after all. I spoke with the men and asked if it was okay for me to share free crosses there. They said I'd have to talk to their boss who would be along shortly. In a few minutes he arrived. I apologized for being there, for mistaking it for a vacant lot and shared with him what I was doing. He

Leo Bell Lytle III
and Valerie Lynne Culp-Lytle

could clearly see the signs and cross-es as he walked over to the trailer. But he told me I would have to leave. I apologized again and quickly load-ed everything back up and drove away. That burst of excitement only minutes ago had vanished.

I guess we all have those mo-ments when our plans, our hopes and our dreams seem all but unreach-able. Some disappointments are very small, such as having to move the trailer to a new location. But some disappointments are catastrophic. We can't understand why God doesn't seem willing to intervene in our con-fusion and despair and grant us our desire. After all, as in this admittedly

minor instance, I was just wanting a place to be able to share Him in this busy city. Surely, He could lead me to the right place, as He had done so many times before. I had, in fact, just about decided that maybe Providence wasn't where I was supposed to be that day. Maybe I should just drive on toward Massachusetts.

But, in my heart I really believed Providence was the place He want-ed me to be right then. So, I kept driving around to look. After a while, I passed a spot that I had dismissed as a possibility earlier because it seemed too small. I didn't think I could maneuver my trailer into it. I had already passed the spot two or three times. But on this pass, I took a long, hard look at it and decided to see if I could back my trailer into what looked like an exceptionally tight spot. The location was on a very busy street. But traffic moved slowly and stopped often because of a traffic light about a half-block away. So, I pulled down a narrow driveway beside a small shopping center. The vacant building associated with the parking lot had a low metal fence around it and had to be entered on the side. I would need to pass that en-trance and then carefully back the trailer through that narrow opening and then up to the street. Now I'm not the best "backer-upper" in Texas by a long shot, but after repeatedly backing up and moving forward in small, incremental adjustments, I managed to get the trailer pulled into the spot and backed up to the street where the action was. I certainly give God the credit for guiding me into that tight spot.

I scattered the crosses around the trailer, put out the "Free Crosses" signs, and soon people stopped. I had an amazing afternoon. Hundreds of vehicles passed by slowly. I watched as some intently gazed at this unusual sight in their city. I was blessed to speak with many residents. Eleven people made life's greatest decision in asking forgiveness and accepting Jesus to be their Savior and LORD. Hallelujah!

Hours later, as I drove toward Massachusetts, I realized that the reason for my earlier discouragement wasn't God's doing – it was my fault. To refer again to Providence founder Roger Williams, "God's merciful Providence" had been within my grasp from the beginning of my search. I had passed right by it at least three times. I was looking for an easier path and didn't have the faith initially to see His "merciful Providence" in Providence, Rhode Island.

Thank God He doesn't give up on us even when we're discouraged and can't seem to find our way. Our plans don't always match up with His plans. But in His loving-kindness, He has a way of nudging us back to the center of His will. I'm so thankful He loves and cares for us like He does.

Our journey with Christ is not always on the easy path. Many times, it is in fact, a quite difficult path. There are times when He gives us the machete to clear a trail that others will soon follow. Having transplanted into Texas, I have great admiration for those who blazed the trail that led to Texas independence back in 1836. As a matter of fact, Texas history records the contributions of a patriot who was a native of Providence, Rhode Island. Albert Martin was his name.

Like many others during the late 1820s and early 1830s, Martin left his home in a northern state to make his way to Texas. He left Rhode Island and opened a business in Gonzales, Texas, where he soon became involved in the fight for Texas independence. He became a captain in the local militia and was one of the "Old Eighteen" who refused to surrender their cannon to the Mexican army advancing on their city. Their famous response is known to every Texan to this day: "Come and Take it."

As the large and well-trained Mexican army under General Santa Anna began their campaign to capture the fortified mission known as the Alamo, Captain Martin and about 30 other men from Gonzales made their way to San Antonio to help. Martin's brother in Gonzales urged him not to go because of the danger, but Martin was not swayed.

Leo Bell Lytle III
and Valerie Lynne Culp-Lytle

Soon after his arrival at the Alamo, the commander there appointed Martin to a special task. Colonel William Barrett Travis sent several missives from the Alamo, but the one he entrusted to Martin would become the most famous among them. Known to history as "The Travis Letter," it was signed "Victory or Death" and dated February 24, 1836. The letter called for all lovers of liberty to help in the fight for Texas Independence.

Martin passed the letter to the next courier and could have decided not to return to the Alamo. The defenders of the Alamo were vastly outnumbered by the Mexican army. Returning meant almost certain death.

But at only 28 years old, Providence, Rhode Island native Martin did return to the Alamo. He joined the small group of reinforcements from Gonzalez, Texas who answered Colonel Travis' plea for help. Known now as "The Immortal 32," Martin was one of only 32 men who came from Gonzalez to help defend the besieged Alamo, crossing enemy lines to do so. There, he bravely fought alongside the others who all gave their lives, as he did, for Texas Independence.

His path was not an easy one. But he didn't quit because it was too hard. Captain Albert Martin, along with all the others, blazed a trail of liberty and freedom that would bless the lives of millions of Texans who came after him.

You and I may never stare death in the face on our journey with Jesus Christ. But our walk with Him can be difficult at times. My parking challenge that day in Providence was exceedingly, laughably miniscule compared to the hideous persecution many Christians endure and have endured throughout the ages.

But the experience does illustrate the need to stay focused and committed no matter the size or scope of the challenge. As we near the time for Jesus' return, the Bible tells us that the days will become increasingly more difficult. Always remember this: God has a plan. He never said our journey with Him would be easy. But He did say He would be with us through it all.

"Teaching them to observe all things whatsoever I have commanded you: and, lo, I am with you alway, even unto the end of the world. Amen." (Matthew 28:20 KJV)

35

He Sweetens the Small Stuff

By Leo Lytle
August 2021, Woodland, Washington

"I have planted, Apollos watered; but God gave the increase."
1 Corinthians 3:6 KJV

———————

There are times when just a small, seemingly insignificant effort on our part can be used by God to make an eternal difference in the life of someone else. It seems all but impossible at times that He could use us, with all our faults and weaknesses. But we know that with God even the impossible can become possible. If we are willing to make even a little effort for the LORD, we may very well be surprised at the results. This story from the Northwest will illustrate what I mean.

It was a late summer evening a few miles south of Tacoma, Washington on August 18, 2021. Valerie and I were driving south on busy Interstate 5 in our van pulling the trailer, still more than half full of free "Jesus Is Lord" crosses. We were heading for Vancouver, Washington. We planned to spend the night in Vancouver and then work our way back north over the next couple of days to Seattle. From there we would fly to Anchorage, Alaska where we had already shipped 250 unassembled crosses to Grandview Baptist Church. We would assemble them at the church for use on the Alaska leg of this evangelistic trip.

My phone rang. The lady who called was really excited. It's certainly not unusual for us to receive calls for crosses while driving. It happens nearly every day on a trip. Sometimes we'll receive multiple calls. My best estimate is between five to 10 percent of the people who pray to be saved on these trips are people who call us. Sometimes we are driving on the same highway. Sometimes people call after seeing us fueling up at a convenience store or sitting behind us in the drive-through line at a fast-food restaurant. We always feel a jolt of enthusiasm and optimism when my phone rings. But this lady seemed especially excited.

"I can't believe it!" she said. "You are the people from Texas we heard about who are giving away free crosses!

"I was just telling my husband," she continued. "'I wish we would see them while they are up here in Washington so we could get one of those free crosses.' And then, all of the sudden, we pull up right behind you here on the interstate! This is unbelievable!"

I asked her how she knew we were in Washington. Many times, people will take a picture of our sign with our phone number and post it on community social media pages. We'll get a call or two from those posts. In fact, I got a call from California a few months back asking where I was located so they could get a cross. At the time I hadn't been to California in nearly three years. I asked him how he got my number. He saw it on some friend's Facebook post of a picture of the back of our trailer. I asked for his mailing address. Vic Bass Ministries graciously mailed a "Jesus Is Lord" cross to him in California free of charge.

This excited lady shared that she, too, had seen a picture of our van and trailer packed full of crosses on Facebook. But how did she know that we would be in Washington, I asked. She said the post she saw was from a friend who lived in Lufkin, Texas. Both of our vehicles took the next exit for Woodland, Washington and onto a big parking lot. I was eager to hear, as radio personality Paul Harvey used to say, "The rest of the story."

Leo Bell Lytle III
and Valerie Lynne Culp-Lytle

As we talked in the parking lot, we quickly learned they were both committed followers of Christ. Then she filled in the blanks concerning that social media post from Texas. The picture she had seen was of our van and trailer parked inside a large fellowship hall/gymnasium at a church in Lufkin, Texas. There were people all around it laying hands on the crosses, the van and the trailer. I knew immediately what she had seen on her friend's post. That picture was taken at Trinity Baptist Church in Lufkin, Texas just a little more than two weeks earlier. We all marveled at our providential meeting on Interstate 5.

There have been many occasions, before we leave on one of these evangelistic trips, that Trinity Baptist Church Pastor Steve Cowart and his members have prayed over the crosses. Vic Bass of Vic Bass Ministries was always there, too, until he and his wife, Sheila, moved to another town in Texas to be nearer their son. Even then, Bro. Vic has joined the dedication by phone. The prayer is that each cross will find its unique destination and that God will provide direction and protection for us. We are so thankful for this invaluable prayer support. What is also special about these times is that Bro. Vic Bass and his wife Shelia are members of Trinity  Baptist Church, along with many of the Cross Men and Cross Women who volunteer their time and effort to make these amazing crosses.

Before each session of dedicatory prayer, we usually share a little about the itinerary of the journey. Our itineraries are, of course, subject to change as we follow the Holy Spirit's leading. Trinity Baptist Church is one of 12 churches who provide us with some financial support for this unique ministry. Of course we are most thankful for each one.

But this Vancouver, Washington story does not end here. While we were talking and taking a few pictures in the parking lot, several people stopped to ask for a free cross. One was a mother with her adult son and grandson. It quickly became apparent that the mother and her son had never accepted Jesus Christ as their personal LORD and Savior. I asked permission to share the Gospel and soon was engaged in a Gospel conversation. They were both more than willing to make life's greatest decision in receiving God's free gift of Eternal Life Jesus Christ. They got it settled right there on the parking lot in Woodland, Washington. All Glory to God!

Now this is what amazes me: In God's amazing timing, at 8:15 on a Friday evening, these two souls who needed His forgiveness and salvation just happened to drive onto the parking lot where we just happened to be. I'd never heard of Woodland, Washington before this night. Then, how they were drawn to these simple wooden crosses in our trailer. And finally, how they became recipients of God's amazing grace!

But you know what else? Without that lady's excited call asking for a free cross on Interstate 5, Valerie and I would have continued down the interstate to Vancouver. But you know what else? Without her friend back in Texas making that social media post, the woman in Washington would not have had crosses on her mind that evening. You know what else? In God's perfect and amazing timing, we were on the same road at the exact same time. You know what else? Without Pastor Steve Cowart organizing the special time of prayer and dedication at Trinity Baptist Church, there would have been no picture to share. I could go on and on, but my point is made.

Mostly though, I think about the decision of her friend to share that picture on her social media. It was a "game-changer." A small and seemingly insignificant decision – right? But because she did that one thing, two more names were added to The Lamb's Book Of Life in Heaven. Glory to God! It's like the words from a popular Christian song a few years back: "Little becomes much, when we place it in the Master's hands!"

Are there circumstances, problems and decisions that you need to place in His hands today? Just do it and see what He will make of it. He just might lead you to set off a whole chain of good things. God gives the increase.

36
Better Together

By Leo Lytle
December 2021, Memphis, Tennessee

"Two are better than one; because they have a good reward for their labour."
Ecclesiastes 4:9 KJV

———————

"Luxury" is not a word that Valerie and I have occasion to use often. We are blessed beyond measure and so grateful to God. But the word "luxury" just doesn't regularly apply to whatever we are doing. However, we experienced real luxury on a five-day evangelistic trip to Tennessee and Illinois in December 2021. It was the luxury of working with a team of other committed Believers. Wow, does it make a difference when we have some help.

This particular trip stands out in our memories not only as being such a good time with great friends, but also as Valerie's first evangelism trip after she retired from being a full-time nurse. In the years prior, Valerie had joined me in our evangelism ministry efforts as often and for as long as she could possibly get off work. But this trip was her first after retiring. She often says now that we hit the ground running, and she wonders how she ever had time to work. This chapter is the recounting of that first trip after her retirement, when God blessed us with trip safety, sweet fellowship with friends and a bountiful harvest of souls.

On December 3, 2021, we met up with our good friends Wayne and Margie Reynolds in Marshall, Texas for the five-day evangelistic trip to Memphis and Buchanan, Tennessee and Cairo, Illinois. Wayne and Margie are music evangelists from Gladewater, Texas. We first met them in

Natchitoches, Louisiana where I was preaching, and they were singing at revival services at Grand Ecore Baptist Church. While there that week, on a couple of afternoons before the services, we invited them to join us on the streets to share Christ and "Jesus Is Lord" crosses there in Natchitoches. As Margie tells the story now, they joined us because they felt obligated. But the experience turned out to be life changing.

In Natchitoches on those afternoons before the revival services, we saw several people make decisions to accept Jesus as their Savior and LORD. Wayne would tell me later that those days lit the fire of evangelism in his life. He and Margie have never looked back. They have become bold soul winners who faithfully share Christ and crosses in the northern part of East Texas and have several people from their church and other friends who join them. No telling how many folks they have led to Christ over the past few years. We love being on the streets with Wayne and Margie whenever our schedules permit.

On this trip, our main target was to be in one of the high-crime neighborhoods in Memphis. The genesis of this journey happened about six months earlier at the annual Bible Conference held at Southside Baptist Church in Mansfield, Louisiana. The late Dr. Gary Orr, then-pastor of Southside Baptist, always assembled a great group of preachers for this event. One of the featured speakers in 2021 was Dr. Lee Brand, who would soon be elected as First Vice-President of the Southern Baptist Convention.

At the time we met, Dr. Brand was serving as a professor at Mid-America Baptist Theological Seminary in Tennessee. The seminary is located in Cordova, near Memphis. He watched our five-minute video about our ministry that we showed at the Bible conference in Mansfield. He asked us to come to Memphis where he could join us with a couple of evangelism students. We set a date of December 4, 2021. In the meantime,

Leo Bell Lytle III
and Valerie Lynne Culp-Lytle

Dr. Brand said he would pray for the right location in one of those blighted neighborhoods. It sounded like a great plan.

So, having picked up Wayne and Margie in Marshall, Texas on December 3, we headed to Memphis together, pulling a trailer loaded with about 500 crosses provided by Vic Bass Ministries. As usually happens, we got several calls along the way because of the sign on the back of our trailer. In Texarkana, a woman gave her heart to Christ. Praise God. Then somewhere near Arkadelphia, Arkansas, we received a call from a couple of women who were also traveling east on Interstate 30. We followed them to the next exit and then to a gravel parking area of what looked like a big truck repair business.

As I was witnessing to those two women, a truck driver pulling into the gravel lot asked us to move so she could park her rig. Wayne moved us out of the way while I continued talking to the two women. Both said they were Believers and were excited to get some free crosses.

I saw Wayne talking with the driver who had asked us to move. So, I got back in the truck with Valerie and Margie. I was able to watch in the rear-view mirror and could see Wayne was sharing Christ with the driver.

After a few minutes, he waved me to come out and brought me up to date on their Gospel conversation. Wayne said the truck driver had told him that she was transgender and was tired of pretending to be what she was not. She wanted to change her life but was having difficulty believing that she could be forgiven.

We talked for a moment about God's amazing Grace. How He takes us just like we are and then makes us into what He wants us to be. We told her the first step was to fully surrender herself to the LORD by asking for His forgiveness and accepting His free Gift of Eternal Life Jesus Christ. Then God could begin to change her life. She understood the misery that sin had brought upon her life and was ready to begin a new life in Christ. Right there in a gravel parking lot off Interstate 30 near Arkadelphia, Arkansas, she prayed with us to accept God's free gift of eternal life Jesus Christ! To God be the Glory!

This encounter reminded me of II Corinthians 5:17 which states, *"Therefore if any man be in Christ, he is a new creature: old things are passed away; behold, all things become new."* When we give our best effort, we are sometimes able to reform ourselves for a little while. But it never seems to last. In time we are back in the same hole from which we were trying to escape. What we really need is not a re-molded or reformed life. We need a transformed life! God alone can transform a life. That transformation begins when we place our hope and trust in Him alone. If you need what that truck driver needed, I want you to know that He is patiently waiting for you to begin your amazing journey with Him. Please turn to the last chapter of this book to learn how you can begin a personal relationship with Jesus Christ right now.

By late afternoon we had made it to Forrest City, Arkansas and decided to spend the last hour of daylight doing street ministry. We had hoped to meet Sharon Andrews in Forrest City. Valerie had led Sharon to Christ on a previous trip to Forrest City about a year and half earlier. Sharon had told us she would bring one of her daughters to meet us. But because we were reaching Forrest City so late, she was not able to wait on us because of her work schedule.

We got busy right away. Several folks were saved, and still more were coming even well after dark. It was an exciting couple of hours before we went to our motel. We would finish our drive to Memphis in the morning.

Cool, rainy weather greeted us the next morning. As we were leaving the motel, Dr. Brand called to say he would not be able to join us. He and his wife were on their way to the emergency room with one of their children. He said he would try to get by and pray with us when he could break away. One of his evangelism students, Emmitt Mckenzie, would meet us there. Emmitt would be a great blessing to our team effort. Dr. Brand gave me the address of the site he had picked out and been praying for, and we were on our way, not knowing what God was about to do.

We pulled the trailer onto a large parking lot on a busy street and immediately began putting out our signs. We heard a few noises that we took to be gunshots in the neighborhood as we were getting organized. We would find out later that there had been a shooting the night before at the corner across the street from our location. To be sure, we were in the right place to share the Gospel.

Leo Bell Lytle III
and Valerie Lynne Culp-Lytle

Dr. Brand arrived, and we all joined him in prayer. He brought with him some sweet handmade signs on poster boards that his children had made for us. We were thankful to have them.

It was turning into an amazing day. The rain had stopped, and the sun was breaking through the cloud cover. People were stopping to get a free cross in a steady stream. Emmitt McKenzie proved to be a dynamite evangelist and soon became a new friend. The five of us: Emmitt, Wayne, Margie, Valerie and I would spend the next few hours going from car to car with a cross, asking each person in the vehicle if they knew

for certain if they died today, would they go to Heaven? Of course, many did tell us that Jesus was already their Savior. But by the time we left, 40 people had prayed to accept Jesus Christ as their personal LORD and Savior. Praise God! It was all so very exciting.

The next morning, we were at Friendship Baptist Church about 150 miles northwest of Memphis in Buchanan, Tennessee. Pastor Russell Ragsdale, who is a friend of mine, had invited me to preach at his church that morning and for the Reynolds Family Band to sing. Valerie, Wayne and Margie each briefly shared stories from our experiences of the last two days with the congregation. Afterward, I brought a short message from Acts chapter one that I call "Why Stand Ye Here Gazing?"

Two additional members of the Reynolds Family Band had met up with us at Friendship Baptist Church in Buchanan that morning and would follow us on to Cario, Illinois that evening: Pat and Roy Doughty. They live in Vidalia, Louisiana. Pat is originally from Ferriday, Louisiana, which is the birthplace of music legend and pianist Jerry Lee Lewis. Pat plays the piano and sings like Jerry Lee Lewis. Valerie says that if Pat were to set up her piano in the Valley of Dry Bones described in Ezekiel 37, those bones would want to get up and dance! With Pat playing and singing, her husband Ray singing, Wayne's excellent acoustic guitar playing and vocals and Margie playing stand-up bass, we all had a wonderful time of worship. (Pat and Ray Doughty had also joined us on the streets of Natchitoches, Louisiana during that earlier revival week. They were there performing as members of the Reynolds Family Band at Grand Ecore Baptist Church. I love how God brings other Believers into our lives at just the right time.)

Once the morning worship service at Friendship Baptist Church was concluded, it was time for fellowship. We enjoyed a nice meal at a restaurant in nearby Paris, Tennessee with Pastor Ragsdale and his sweet wife Debbie, before we headed north through Kentucky and then crossed the Ohio River into Cairo, Illinois. We repeated the morning service in Buchanan that night at Bishop Hubert Pirtle's church in Cairo. It is called the Jesus Is Lord Church. We had a wonderful time of worship and fellowship with his sweet congregation.

When we left Cairo to head home toward Texas, we drove as far as Arkansas before stopping for the night. The front desk clerk at the motel prayed to be saved. A man at a convenience store where we were buying gas also prayed to be saved. He had approached us to ask for a free cross, and the Holy Spirit did the rest. Hallelujah! We made it home safely with praise and thanksgiving in our hearts. It was an awesome evangelistic trip with what we believe were 50 people saved in total. We give all Glory to God!

37

Meeting Needs
In Memphis

By Valerie Culp-Lytle
December 2021, Memphis, Tennessee

"Casting all your care upon him; for he careth for you."
1 Peter 5:7 KJV

———————

It is always exciting when the Lord uses us. We pray for the Lord to please keep us safe, but mainly please use us. It is a real blessing when we have a team on the street. The first weekend of December 2021, we were doing street evangelism in Memphis, Tennessee. Dr. Lee Brand, at the time a professor at Mid-America Baptist Theological Seminary near Memphis, had suggested a parking lot for us. Somebody had been shot near there the night before we arrived. It was a place where folks could use a good dose of the Good News.

On this Saturday in Memphis, Leo and I had music evangelists Margie and Wayne Reynolds with us, and then we had Emmitt Mckenzie, who is a dynamic evangelist. He was one of Dr. Brand's seminary students. So, we had the luxury of five of us working. We were all busy, all the time. I was thinking how Leo is often alone on these trips. It reminds me of that song "I Have Decided To Follow Jesus." The chorus says, "Though none go with me, still I will follow."

The day produced some memorable encounters. One particular couple pulled up into the parking lot. They were experiencing homelessness. We'll call the woman Rhonda. She gave me permission to share her story. Rhonda and her boyfriend (we'll call him Charles) were living in their car. Wayne and Leo talked to them first, and both Rhonda and Charles said they had already prayed to be saved.That is the most important thing. When we meet people, they often pour out a long list of serious problems. I say, "The first thing is, you need to be saved. Then the LORD can work everything out."

Leo called me over to their car to pray for Rhonda and Charles. Rhonda was telling me she hadn't had a bath in seven weeks. She said they were sometimes hungry. She had lost custody of her children. Their old car was on its last leg. Addiction had ruined both her life and Charles' life.

"Lord, we are laying this mess at the foot of the Cross," I prayed. "Please give her answers and resources. We are trusting You to give us some answers."

Emmitt called a drug rehab place in the area. But Rhonda and Charles were not eligible for service there because they didn't have COVID-19 vaccinations nor any financial resources. So Leo told Rhonda and Charles to come back at noon, when we planned to wrap up, and we would put gas in their car. 12 o'clock came and went, with no sign of Rhonda and Charles. Leo said that we needed to leave, because people needed to use the bathroom. I asked for an extension of time. Lord knows I'm no stranger to the struggle to get places on time.

"Let's give them some grace," I said. "Let's wait. Leave me here. Let's give them an hour."

Leo wouldn't leave me there alone, of course. He said he would unhook our truck from the cross trailer. But then Emmitt said he could ferry folks to the restroom.

Rhonda and Charles showed up sometime after that, relieved to find us still there. Sure enough, they had had a flat. They were nearly an hour late. But here is the beauty of what had happened in that hour:

While they were gone, a young woman who said her name was Anna had come up to us — all smiles — and said: "Oh, I love what you are doing.

Leo Bell Lytle III
and Valerie Lynne Culp-Lytle

This is so wonderful. If you could have seen me two years ago! I was an addict, and I was on the street.

"Now I am working for this non-profit that helps addicted people," she concluded.

"Oh, my Lord, Anna," I said. "You are a direct answered prayer."

Anna gave me the contact information of the place where she worked that would take Rhonda and Charles for detox. I called, and the detox place agreed to admit them. They would take Rhonda and Charles just as they were: with no money, no insurance, no COVID-19 vaccination. They would take them as is. All Rhonda and Charles needed to qualify for admission was a sincere desire to be delivered from addiction.

It was going to be Monday before they could get into the program. (This was on a Saturday.) Rachel shared privately that she didn't think Charles was ready, but she insisted that she was committed to getting clean.

"We are talking about laying it down," I said to her. "Whatever your addictions are, you are going to have to give them up. This may be your last chance."

"I'm ready," Rhonda answered.

Laying it down because it might be the last chance was fresh on my mind because Emmitt had told me his amazing testimony. It contains a clear example of seizing the chance to get clean if such an opportunity comes along. Emmitt said he was an alcoholic for 19 years and was also on meth. He had a tremendously bad time when he was on the streets. But when he got his chance to get clean, he gave up alcohol and meth, all by the grace of God. He said he was with a woman at the time who he had planned to marry, but she wouldn't leave the streets.

"We've got to do this," Emmitt said he told her. "This is our chance. We've got to lay it down."

But she wouldn't do it. She said she wasn't ready. So Emmitt told her he was going to end their relationship. He had to leave to get clean. Ten years later at that time, he said, his former fiancé was still on the streets.

The five of us invited Rhonda and Charles to join us for lunch. I asked Emmitt to share his testimony with them. Rhonda listened to every word. We went out into the parking lot to call the facility again.

"Did you hear what Emmitt said?" I asked her. "It may be that you have to leave Charles if he turns out to not be ready to do this. We want the very best for him. But this may be your only chance."

"I'm ready," she answered. "I am going to do whatever it takes."

Leo paid for them to eat their fill and box up enough leftovers to tide them over until they could be admitted to the facility. Wayne bought them a used tire to replace the tire that had gone flat. Leo filled their old car up with gas. We wanted nothing to crop up as an obstacle that would prevent them from turning themselves into the detox facility on Monday. We gave Rhonda our phone number and asked her to let us know how they were doing. We gave each of them a Bible and prayed to thank God for His provision.

Our encounter with Rhonda, Charles and Anna revealed directly answered prayer. I also consider the encounter an instructive example of an important truth: God does give us chances in life to change course. But each individual has to decide whether or not he or she is ready to lay down any hindrances. We never know when a particular chance could be our last.

38
Truth *Versus* Fiction

By Leo Lytle
December 2019, Salt Lake City, Utah

"There is a way which seemeth right unto a man,
But the end thereof are the ways of death."
Proverbs 14:12 KJV

———————

I t was a cold December evening when I arrived in Salt Lake City, Utah. A few minutes more and I would reach my destination in the busy downtown area: the Mormon Tabernacle of the Church of Jesus Christ of Latter-Day Saints. Even though it was a chilly evening the area was bustling with tourists. It was the Christmas season after all, December 2019. Dozens of locals and visitors were on foot taking in the lights and the sights of this "Mecca" of the Mormon world.

After finding a place to park my truck and trailer, I joined the walking throng to the Temple area. In short order, I heard the familiar sound of Christmas songs coming from one of the buildings adjacent to the Tabernacle. It was their information center. Once in-

side, I saw the source of the music: a youth choir performing for the folks mingling about. I stood and listened for a few moments before being approached by a nice young female Mormon missionary who asked if I was enjoying the music and if I had any questions? I answered "yes" to both.

We talked for the better part of half an hour about various questions I had, while the choir continued singing the familiar carols of Christmas. Politely and kindly, I asked her about the founder of the Church of Jesus Christ of Latter-Day Saints, Joseph Smith, and about some of their doctrines and practices. We had a lively, but civil conversation. I could tell some of my questions were troubling her. They weren't difficult questions, but rather they addressed some foundational concerns about the LDS church.

As the choir sang "Jingle Bells," I could see mild distress in her eyes. She seemed unable to find a suitable answer to explain the foundational elements of the LDS church in question.

I sensed this was my opportunity to share the uniqueness of Jesus Christ with her. However, in moments, we were interrupted by another female Mormon missionary. I believe she was the young lady's mentor. The new woman began to quiz me as to who I was and why I was there. She suggested that perhaps I should leave. So, I did.

I walked around the Temple grounds that evening praying for those caught up in this false religion. I hoped and prayed that I would get the chance to share the REAL Good News about Jesus Christ there in the heart of LDS country. That opportunity came the next morning.

Early the next day, I began the important process of finding just the right Spirit-led spot to share the free "Jesus Is Lord" crosses. Being in the right place at the right time with the right message is, of course, vitally important when one is "fishing for souls". When entering a town or city, I start looking for vacant parking lots that are easily accessible on a heavily traveled road or street. Sometimes there will be several to choose from and other times not so much. I've found this to be one of the most critical decisions I make each day when I'm on the road. In fact, if you are among those who pray for us on these journeys, please pray for God's direction in leading us to the right location each day. Thank you in advance for praying.

When there are several locations to choose from, usually the one with the best visibility and access is the right choice. But I've learned to ask the Holy Spirit to lead us to the right spot. That morning, the options were few. But I kept passing by a large parking lot that was adjacent to a business. It didn't appear to belong to that business. So, I stopped and asked permission to set up there.

After arranging crosses on both sides of my trailer and truck and placing my signs as close to the roadway as possible, I was ready. I'm still amazed at how these "free" crosses draw people to stop. Even in the heart of the LDS empire and on one of the busiest streets in Salt Lake City, many people stopped by for a free cross. Some were members of the LDS church. Yet even in Salt Lake City, I spoke with many Believers who stopped to get a free cross and thanked me for sharing the Gospel in their city.

I'm not sure how many people prayed to be saved that day. But I remember at least two of them were members of the LDS church. One was an LDS lady in her early eighties stopping to get a cross to place on her son's grave. I asked her if she were to die today, would she go to Heaven? Her reply was that she didn't know if she would. It was so sad to see this sweet lady, who was a lifelong member of the LDS church, look so confused about what would happen to her upon death. Thankfully, she allowed me to share with her about God's free gift of Eternal Life Jesus Christ! Then she prayed to ask forgiveness for her sins and accept Jesus as her personal LORD and Savior. Glory to God!

That day in Salt Lake City reminded me of the power of even a simple yard cross to plant a seed of faith in someone. There are times when people are not stopping as frequently as I would like, and I begin to wonder if I'm in the place that the Holy Spirit chose or the place that I chose. Yet, I realize that those who pass by and see the crosses are in some way confronted or reminded about the meaning behind the Cross. Through practice, I've learned to be patient and wait on God before moving on too quickly to another location. I have no idea what is going on in the hearts and minds of those who are passing me by. It would be true that afternoon in Salt Lake City, too, when a young man named Youssef pulled up in his car inquiring about a free cross.

As Youssef and I talked, the reason for his stopping became evident. He shared with me that he had passed by earlier on his way to pick up his son from school. When he saw the free crosses, he said he hoped I would still be there after the pickup. Thank God, I was! As we continued our conversation, I discovered he was searching for purpose and meaning in his life and had, up until this point, repeatedly come up empty. Raised in the religion of Islam, he had abandoned it because of what he said he

felt were empty rituals and an impersonal god — Allah. His parents were not happy with him leaving Islam. He said he'd been studying many other religions, hoping to find one that would address his emptiness and provide real hope and meaning.

I believe that the LORD has a unique way of putting people in the path of someone who is genuinely searching for truth. I've seen it many times. As things played out in Youssef's life, it was his Christian grandmother that the LORD had placed in his path. He had just recently visited with her at her home in Arizona where she was bedridden, recovering from a stroke. She had been the one to not only plant the seed of faith in his life, but also water it. In fact, he told me he was thinking of his grandmother as he drove past the crosses. Youssef was heading for a "Divine Appointment."

As we talked that day, I shared with him the uniqueness of Christianity compared to all other world religions. I shared what he had already no doubt learned: that they all require personal effort on our part to have even a remote chance for some sort of existence beyond this life. They provide no security because one is always uncertain that his or her efforts will be enough to satisfy all the requirements of their chosen religion. I explained how very loving and personal God is. God desires to have a relationship with us through Jesus Christ. And, of course, we talked about how God proved His great love for us by paying our huge sin debt with His son's sacrificial death on the cross! Jesus offers us forgiveness and the greatest gift of all: Eternal Life when we repent of our sins and trust Him alone as our Savior and LORD!

After sharing the Gospel with him, I asked Youssef: "Does this make sense to you?"

"Yes!" Youssef said. "It makes perfect sense."

Leo Bell Lytle III
and Valerie Lynne Culp-Lytle

"Would you like to receive God's free gift of Eternal Life Jesus Christ?" I asked.

"Yes!" Youssef said.

Right there on a very busy street in Salt Lake City, Utah, Youssef accepted Jesus as his personal Savior. All Glory to God!

We went over to his car where he introduced me to his son and told his son about his decision to accept Christ as personal Savior. I gave Youssef a copy of the "Good News For You" Bible study booklet that we give to all new Believers; a New Testament with a bookmark at the Gospel of John and encouraged him to find a local Bible-believing church to help him on his journey with Christ. The loving seeds planted and watered by his grandmother's prayers through the years had set the stage for Youssef's "Divine Appointment" and his Gospel harvest.

39

One Added,
Two Squeal Away

By Leo Lytle
May 2019, Cairo, Illinois

"For we wrestle not against flesh and blood, but against principalities,
against powers, against the rulers of the darkness of this world,
against spiritual wickedness in high places."
Ephesians 6:12 KJV

G un.

It was my immediate impression.

Only God knows. It was certainly thicker than a cell phone. I only know that in the more than seven years so far into our ministry, after meeting tens of thousands of people, it was the first and only time so far that my every instinct shouted "Gun!"

But God kept me safe during one of the strangest encounters I have had to date. It was a forcible reminder of how crucial the prayer team led by Bro. Vic Bass is to our ministry.

I may well have looked into the face of evil for a minute. Only God knows. But that minute left an indelible impression on me. It took place in a small town in the heart of America. It was May 2019 in Cairo, Illinois.

CROSS-ing AMERICA
Sharing Jesus Around The Nation

One of my favorite geographical locations in America is the confluence of the Ohio River and the Mississippi River. This is where the great Ohio River empties into the "Mighty Mississippi" and forms the borders between three states: Kentucky, Illinois and Missouri. A visitor can walk to the place where the two rivers come together, running side by side for a stretch with their two different colors of water, touching but not yet fully integrated. It is the spot where the Ohio River ends, emptying itself into the Mississippi River. From there, the Mississippi continues its roll southward, expanded and empowered.

A peninsula protrudes into the spot where the waters meet. The area is known as Fort Defiance Park, named for a fort built to protect a gristmill and sawmill during the Dakota War of 1862. A historical marker there says Fort Defiance Park in Cairo is also the site where earlier in American history, renowned explorers Meriwether Lewis and William Clark landed at the confluence of the rivers on November 14, 1803. They spent five days there training their team, the Corps of Discovery, in the use of navigation instruments. These skills would be critical as they continued their incredible westward journey toward the edge of the continent.

I've had the pleasure of preaching in western Kentucky several times over the last few years. It was on my first trip there in May 2018 that I discovered this unique location. In addition to being able to touch the water at the rivers' meeting point, visitors may also accomplish a fancy feat of driving. When traveling west in extreme northwestern Kentucky, one may cross the bridge over the Ohio River into Illinois at the state of Illinois' extreme southernmost point. In a little over a minute after entering Illinois, one will drive onto another bridge that crosses over the Mississippi River. That bridge will take one into extreme southeastern Missouri. Thus, in less than five minutes one will have been to three states and crossed over two of the largest rivers in America. Pretty cool in my book!

Cairo, Illinois is only a couple of minutes' drive north of this confluence of the Ohio and Mississippi Rivers. It is the southernmost town in the state of Illinois. It was once a thriving town of some 17,000 people in its heyday back in the 1950s. Since then, it has steadily declined. Fewer than 2,000 folks live there today. There is no hospital, no grocery store, and no place to buy gasoline. I saw only one small restaurant on my first trip there. It is a community that has long since seen better days. Several once grand buildings, now abandoned, are scattered throughout what was once a prosperous business district. Now only a dollar store offers residents a place for shopping.

After a short visit to Cairo, I knew I wanted to come back to share Christ and crosses at my next opportunity. Less than a year later, I did. I was scheduled to share "The Door" message at two churches in nearby Clinton, Kentucky on Sunday, May 5, 2019. So, I made plans to spend the Saturday before in Cairo.

I found a good location on the main street. A few minutes later I had my "Free Crosses" signs set up around my trailer, ready for action.

People began stopping. I engaged in several Gospel conversations and met some really nice folks. The police chief of Cairo stopped to get a cross and visited with me. He said he was a Believer. A little later, local Pastor Herbert Pirtle (now Bishop Herbert Pirtle) and I visited for a good while. He would eventually invite me back to Cairo to preach at his church on two different occasions. Valerie and I have since grown to love him and his family and his church family, too.

A young mother stopped by who was dealing with the recent loss of her uncle. She saw the crosses and wanted one to place at his gravesite. As we talked, she spoke about the unexpected loss of her mother a few years earlier. It had taken a toll on her. She admitted, frankly, that she was mad at God because of it.

Since then, she had a child. She said she knew she wanted to raise her little girl in the right way. The recent loss of her uncle had heightened her sense of urgency. The awareness of death and eternity had become very real to her. The death of a close family member or friend has a way of reminding us of our own mortality. She wanted to teach her daughter the truth about God. She said she was uncertain what would happen to her when she died.

It was easy to see that this meeting was a "Divine Appointment." We engaged in a Gospel conversation. In a few minutes, the young woman made life's greatest decision by accepting God's free Gift of Eternal Life Jesus Christ! With tears in her eyes, she prayed for His forgiveness right there on the sidewalk in Cairo, Illinois. Praise God!

As in this instance with the young mother, I can recall scores of times that some event, circumstance or loss has drawn other people to stop when they see the crosses. I'm amazed at how the LORD uses these simple crosses to draw folks to Himself.

Later that afternoon, I had the aforementioned unusual experience with someone who was also drawn to the crosses

A late-model black Mercedes drove toward my location and stopped about 100 feet from me on the side of the street. I wondered if the people inside were stopping for a cross, and, if so, why did they park so far away?

A man who looked to be close to 40 years old stepped from the driver's door. He had very short hair and was wearing a white T-shirt and gray sweatpants. Before he closed the door, he slipped something black in the back waistband of his sweatpants. My first thought was maybe it was a gun. It was much wider than a cell phone. In that fleeting moment, with the flashes of intuition and discernment that the Holy Spirit occasionally gives us, my overwhelming initial impression was a possible gun. But I told myself "surely not" and walked toward him as I normally do to greet people who stop for a free cross.

When we were about 20 feet apart, I said to him, "I bet you want a free cross." Although he was looking directly at me, he didn't say a word. Just then the passenger door of the Mercedes opened. A woman hurriedly got out, leaving the door ajar. She appeared to be quite a bit older than him. As she stepped out, she began yelling at him and running toward us. She screamed at him saying, "You #$@$*# Satanist, you can't have a cross!!! I'm a #$@$*# Catholic, and you can't have no #$@$*# cross!!!"

I was reaching out to shake his hand before she started her obscenity-filled tirade. He kept walking toward me and never turned around to face her. Now we were maybe five feet apart. He was looking at me, and I was looking at him. Over his shoulder I could see her running up toward us. Again, she angrily screamed out her profanity, "Did you hear me?!!! You're a #$@$*# Satanist, and you can't have no #$@$*# cross!!! I'm a #$@$*# Catholic, and you can't have no #$@$*# cross!!!"

He didn't look around to acknowledge her. We were now within arm's reach of one another. The woman ran up behind him and slapped him on the top of his head with all her might. He stopped in his tracks.

Leo Bell Lytle III
and Valerie Lynne Culp-Lytle

He turned around and looked at her. He turned back around and looked at me for a moment. Suddenly, without a word, he turned and walked back to the Mercedes. She did the same. He got in on the driver's side, and she got in on her side. They shut the doors, made a squealing U-turn and roared back in the direction from which they had come.

I thought to myself: "What was that all about? She called him a Satanist. Was he really a Satanist? Was that a gun he slipped inside the waistband of his sweatpants? Did he really want a cross? Was he there to cause trouble? Did he want to shoot me?" I didn't know the answers to any of these questions. But what I did know was God's protection was there for me at that moment!

Amazingly, I was not afraid during the incident. In hindsight, I believe that God had a "hedge of protection" around me that day. Back home in Texas, I knew Bro. Vic Bass had a prayer team of about 40 Believers who were praying for our ministry.

Since the beginning of 2024, the "Jesus Is Lord" crosses are now made by Trinity Baptist Church in Lufkin and the volunteer group known as the Cross Men and Cross Women. But Bro. Vic Bass continues to lead the prayer team from his home in Marble Falls, Texas. He keeps prayer team members up to date via text messages. From the moment Valerie and I leave home until we are safely back home on every trip, I message Bro. Vic every day as to where we are, what we hope to do and where we are going next. I keep him informed of each day's activities and of all those who pray to be saved each day. If a special need arises, we will send an urgent prayer request to Bro. Vic. Just as soon as he gets our message, he passes it on to the prayer team members. Prayer is essential in any evangelistic work. We are so blessed to have this amazing group of prayer warriors standing — and kneeling — with us for the cause of Christ.

I wanted to include this story in our book not to frighten or discourage anyone from sharing his or her faith with others. Quite the opposite. The reason I relate it is to encourage all Believers to witness. Here's why: my unsettling and potentially dangerous experience in Cairo was extremely rare.

From 1985 to 2018, I was a teacher/trainer with Evangelism Explosion III International. For years, I've taken a couple of trainees with me sharing the Gospel over a 13-week period for each training session. In doing so, I've had the privilege of training scores of people with an effective way of sharing Christ. Those Evangelism Explosion experiences combined with my 33 years as a pastor and seven years so far of evangelism have allowed me to talk to tens of thousands of people in all sorts of places and situations. We hardly ever have a bad experience.

Since 2018, Valerie and I have traveled all over America spreading the Good News. We have been safe, by the grace of God. Almost all our interactions with all those people have been pleasant. In all my years of witnessing for Christ, I can count on one hand (with a couple of fingers left over) the number of times I have encountered a hostile person or a difficult situation. It almost never happens.

If you have been born again, then you have a "story" to tell. Please don't allow any fear of possibly difficult or even dangerous encounters deter you from telling your story. This is your testimony of how you came to have a personal relationship with Jesus Christ and how your life has changed because of that relationship. You might not remember the exact day, but you should remember the event. Were you at home when you made that decision? At church? At a church camp or retreat? If you have been born again, you will know where it happened. If you don't know, please turn to the last chapter of this book and read how you can begin a life-changing, personal relationship with Jesus Christ. It happened to me in my "bachelor pad" at the age of 21 in 1975 in Shreveport, Louisiana. He rocked my world then, and He's still rocking it today. Glory to God!

Leo Bell Lytle III
and Valerie Lynne Culp-Lytle

40

God Shed His Grace On Thee

By Leo Lytle
March 2021, Washington, DC

"If my people, which are called by my name, shall humble themselves,
and pray, and seek my face, and turn from their wicked ways;
then will I hear from heaven, and will forgive their sin, and heal their land."
II Chronicles 7:14 KJV

———————

Blessed as we have been, to share Christ and crosses border to border and coast to coast, several times, across this great nation, I felt the need to get to the heart of it all. I needed to go to Washington, D.C.

On March 26, 2021, I left beautiful Pine Valley, Texas on the first day of an 18-day Gospel journey to the Northeast and the New England states. At that time, Valerie was still working full-time as a registered nurse in Labor and Delivery. Her schedule would not permit her to make this trip.

My trailer was loaded with 2,000 "Jesus Is Lord" crosses, graciously provided by Vic Bass Ministries. I planned to share them in towns and cities along the way. I called this journey "Operation Grace." The plan included stops in major cities such as Washington, D.C.; Baltimore, Maryland; Philadelphia, Pennsylvania; New York City, New York and Boston, Massachusetts.

The many safety measures related to COVID-19 were beginning to relax in much of the nation, less so though, in these large cities.. It was nearly three months since the January 6, 2021 protest, and the Capitol Building was still surrounded by metal fencing. National Guard troops and the Capitol Police guarded the Capitol Building. The "People's

House" had become an armed fortress. Anyone not directly involved in the day-to-day business of the American government was "persona non grata." This was the Washington, D.C. I entered on March 30, 2021.

As I drove through the busy streets near the Capitol Building, I was searching for a parking spot that would handle both my truck and trailer. The day before, I had shared Christ and crosses in the Washington, D.C. suburbs of Arlington and Alexandria, Virginia and saw several people accept God's free gift of Eternal Life. Praise God! But today I felt led to do what I had been doing in other places during the restrictive days of COVID-19.

As many other evangelists experienced, I had watched my full calendar of scheduled engagements for 2020 fall apart. As the news about COVID-19 grew worse every day and a global pandemic was declared, my engagements for revivals or opportunities to preach "The Door" evaporated. Cancellations came in thick and fast. Some of the cancellations came with vague promises to reschedule. But many did not. Because the truth was, no one knew when we would see "normal" again.

Pastors did their best to adjust to safety concerns. They innovated with live sermons on various social media platforms, outdoor services and stay in the car and listen via A.M. radio services. A few daring churches kept their doors open right on through the pandemic. But they were very few, as many municipalities made doing so illegal. COVID-19 was extremely hard on churches. At this writing in 2024, many churches around the nation have still not regained their former membership numbers.

For a time, I was also doing a live social media message every Saturday evening from our home or wherever I was on Saturday at 6 p.m. Central Time. I began to carry a large, rolling cross along busy streets sharing Gospel tracts, small New Testaments and leather key rings stamped with

Leo Bell Lytle III
and Valerie Lynne Culp-Lytle

a Christian message made by my friend Louie Orgo, "The Key Ring Guy," out of San Robles, California.

The large, rolling cross had come to be one of my resources because our dear friend Vic Bass of Vic Bass Ministries in Lufkin, Texas had asked me to make a large cross for him to carry around 15-mile Loop 287 in Lufkin on April 8 and 9, 2020. That was the Thursday before Good Friday and then Good Friday. We each took turns carrying the big cross while the other followed behind in my truck. During our maiden voyage, so to speak, carrying the big cross, we saw that it could become an evangelism tool, like the smaller crosses. During that first trip around the loop in Lufkin, one man pulled over to speak with us, asking what this was all about. His name was Leo, too. Bro. Vic and I praised God that after we engaged in a Gospel conversation with the other Leo, he accepted Jesus Christ as his personal LORD and Savior.

Since that time, I have carried that big cross with me on the side of our trailer. Especially during the pandemic, I would take it off the trailer, shoulder it and carry it through towns and cities such as Boston, Massachusetts; Wichita, Kansas; Yankton, South Dakota; Pensacola, Florida; Tulsa, Oklahoma; Gulfport, Mississippi; Mobile, Alabama and dozens of other places. Now, though, I felt led to carry it around the perimeter of the metal fence surrounding "The People's House."

I ended up about two miles away from the Capitol Building before I found a safe place to park. I loaded up with Gospel tracts, New Testaments and Christian key rings and then prayed before hitting the street.

The first thing I noticed was what seemed to me a noticeable indifference exhibited by those I passed on the street and those who passed by me in their vehicles. In other places where I had carried the cross, I would hear occasional car horns, notice people waving, see a thumbs up now and again or even hear an occasional negative comment. But, here in Washington, D.C., after I walked for three hours on the streets and around the entire United States Capitol complex, there was hardly any reaction.

I was stopped by a homeless man on my way to the Capitol Building, just before passing CNN's Washington Bureau. We talked for a few minutes about Jesus, and he was confident that he was a Believer. He asked if I would let him carry the cross on his block. It made him happy to have the cross on his shoulder that day.

It was a warm spring afternoon. The famous cherry trees (a gift from Japan back in 1912) were starting to bloom. They softened the scene somewhat and added beauty to an otherwise grim view as I made it to the Capitol Building.

There was something very wrong about seeing the huge metal fence around "The People's House" and National Guardsmen with weapons in hand. And there was something wrong with the palpable indifference of those I passed by and those who passed by me as I made my way around this historic American treasure. Had America finally gone too far from God? Would She ever come back to Him? Would God ever bless America again?

These questions were on my heart as I made my way around the United States Capitol Building. As I reached the front entrance, I peered through the metal fence. Then I leaned against the cross, bowed my head, closed my eyes and prayed for America harder than I ever have.

Gazing at the Washington Monument and the vast Mall leading down to the Lincoln Memorial, I thought about how far America has strayed from the God-ordained and God-inspired principles upon which we were founded. Our past allegiance to those principles and our collective faith in God had made us the greatest nation the world has ever known. Those days seem very far behind us. What would the Founding Fathers think about America today? More importantly, what does God think of America today?

I spoke to a few Capitol Police officers and National Guardsmen that day. Sadly, they were not much interested in speaking to a man from Texas with a cross on his shoulder. I wondered what good, if any, I had done.

Just as I was about to leave the Capitol area, a Capitol Police officer pulled up beside me and got out of his car.

"Don't think what you did today went unnoticed," the Capitol Police officer said to me. He seemed to know the discouragement that was on my heart.

Leo Bell Lytle III
and Valerie Lynne Culp-Lytle

"I am a Believer," the officer said. "I can assure you what you did here today was noted by many people. Thank you!"

Then, just as quickly as he stopped, he drove away.

A couple of days later, I heard the tragic news that a Capitol Police officer had been killed at the barricade outside the U.S. Capitol. A man had rammed his car into two officers, killing one, and then emerged wielding a knife. I pray he or she was ready to meet God.

Are you ready to meet God? Perhaps you, too, like America, have strayed. You're searching for peace, joy and contentment. But peace, joy and contentment seem elusive, or even unattainable. Maybe you're just looking in the wrong places. If this is you, please consider Christ. What you're searching for can only be found in establishing a personal relationship with Him. Please take a few minutes and read the last chapter of this book to discover how you can begin a personal relationship with Jesus Christ today.

41

Work, for
The Night Cometh

By Leo Lytle
September 2023, Pahrump, Nevada

"I must work the works of him that sent me, while it is day:
the night cometh, when no man can work."
John 9:4 KJV

I'm sure that like me, most of you have never heard of Pahrump, Nevada. But if you have ever listened to the late-night radio show *Coast to Coast* with host Art Bell, then Pahrump might "ring a bell," (pardon the pun). What I didn't know was that Art Bell lived and broadcast *Coast to Coast* for years in Pahrump until his death in 2018.

Pahrump, Nevada is named after the original indigenous name for the valley, which was Pah-Rimpi. It means "Water Rock," which refers to the valley's many artesian wells. It is situated about an hour's drive west of Las Vegas near its border with California. It is only a few miles away from Death Valley National Park. I arrived there on Sunday afternoon, September 10, 2023. I had come that day from Henderson and then Las Vegas, Nevada. Four people had prayed to be saved in Las Vegas. One was a man who had moved from Chicago and the others were a mother with her two adult daughters. We talked in a parking lot where I had pulled over when one of them called for a cross. They made their salvation decisions just in time, because shortly thereafter I was asked to leave by a security guard. I drove on to Pahrump, and, as usual, scouted out a location on the main road where I could share the Gospel. People started stopping to get a cross and five of them prayed to be saved. Glory to God!

I stayed there until dark and then decided to spend the night in the van in a nearby parking lot. As I sat in the front seat of the van texting Bro. Vic Bass and his prayer team members about the day's events, several people approached to get a cross. Among these were four young people who pulled up wanting to know what I was doing. Before long we were engaged in a Gospel conversation. They all decided to receive God's free gift of Eternal Life Jesus Christ right there in the parking lot. It had been a remarkable day, but it was clear that I would need a more secluded place to sleep. I moved the van.

By then it was around 9:15 p.m., and I was trying to finish my text to Bro. Vic. Three young men separated themselves from a group gathered in the parking lot of a nearby fast food restaurant and walked up to me. With my window down, we engaged in a conversation that started in the usual way: Who was I? What was I doing in their town? Were those crosses really free? Could they each have one? Naturally, I steered our talk

toward Jesus. One of the young men said he had already given his life to Christ a couple of years earlier and was confident of his personal relationship with Him. The other two young men decided to accept God's free Gift of Eternal Life in Jesus Christ. There, in a town I had never heard of and had no idea I would be coming to until that day, I led the two young men to bow their heads and hearts to God and place their faith and trust in Jesus Christ alone for their salvation. It just doesn't get any better than that.

It would be around midnight before I put up our nightly social media post to update our friends and followers across America. It had been a long day, beginning with a church service in Henderson, Nevada and ending in this parking lot in Pahrump. As I lay in bed in the back of the van, I remembered all the salvation decisions of the day and rejoiced over each one. In my first full day in Nevada, the Lord had again blessed this unique method of reaching the lost. Fifteen more names had been written in the Lamb's Book of Life.

Leo Bell Lytle III
and Valerie Lynne Culp-Lytle

One more precious soul would be saved in Pahrump before I left the next morning. It belonged to a woman who came up to me as I stopped to buy a sausage biscuit on the way out of town. She would be one of the many people over the next couple of days in Nevada who would respond to the unchanging Gospel message.

Valerie and I are so thankful to have a part in this ministry that is touching hearts and changing lives around the country. We've seen that sharing the Gospel outside the walls of the church bears fruit everywhere it is tried. If we want to truly be "fishers of men," then we must go where the "fish" can be found. The lost and hurting are streaming up and down the highways and byways outside the walls of our churches every day.

Just as a fisherman will move to a different spot if the fish aren't biting where he first casts a line, so must we move to another spot if conditions aren't favorable. If a security guard says to leave a location, then we leave. There are plenty of "fish" in the sea, in the world outside the walls of the churches. The important thing is to keep working for Jesus. The main reason I had driven to Pahrump was because after leaving Las Vegas it was the closest town I could get to before dark. As I kept casting my net long after the sun had gone down in Pahrump, I thought about the Scripture that talks about doing what we can, while we can. It is the Scripture that began this chapter:

"I must work the works of him that sent me, while it is day: the night cometh, when no man can work." John 9:4 KJV

42

NASCAR or Jesus

By Leo Lytle
September 2022 – Princeton, West Virginia

*"But he that received seed into the good ground is he that heareth the word,
and understandeth it; which also beareth fruit, and bringeth forth,
some a hundredfold, some sixty, some thirty."*
Matthew 13:23 KJV

———————

A little after midnight on September 17, 2022, Valerie and I stopped to sleep in a chain store parking lot in Princeton, West Virginia. We were on a Gospel trip to the Northeast and the New England states.

Princeton is a small town of just under 6,000 people nestled in a cozy valley in the Appalachian Mountains. West Virginia is such a beautiful state. We broke out singing John Denver's song "Country Roads" when we saw the state sign welcoming us to West Virginia.

A town of Princeton's size is the perfect place for sharing Christ and crosses. In a few hours, the whole community is aware that free "Jesus Is Lord" crosses are being given away. Locals share the news via social media, and soon people start stopping. It happened just that way in Princeton. We spoke with many people that day. At least 10 of them accepted God's free gift of Eternal Life in Jesus Christ. All Glory to God!

The first person to respond to the Gospel that day happened upon us as we freshened up in the restrooms of the state visitors' center after sleeping in the van the night before.

While waiting for Valerie, I was in the parking lot doing a little re-organizing in the van, emptying the trash basket and straightening up the crosses on our trailer. While doing so, a man who looked to be about 30 years old pulled up beside me asking for a cross. It wasn't long until we were in a Gospel conversation. A few

minutes later he was ready and willing to ask the LORD to forgive him and save his soul. God be Praised!

Afterwards, he was teary-eyed and hugged me. The impact of what had just happened in his life had touched him deeply. Then he told me how he happened to stop.

A little earlier that morning he had noticed our trailer full of crosses in the parking lot. He read the sign on the back of the trailer that says:

FREE CROSSES
936-225-1660
CALL – I'LL PULL OVER

He said he is a big NASCAR fan and was on his way to Bristol, Tennessee to watch the big race they have there every year. After seeing the crosses and reading our sign, he kept driving toward Bristol. But he couldn't stop thinking about it. He wondered what the reason might be for them being free, and why Princeton, West Virginia?

He said he felt strongly that he needed to turn around and go back. He turned around, hoping we would still be there. Thank God, we were. I'm always amazed at the way the Holy Spirit moves on hearts like He does. We call these "Divine Appointments." Of course, every time a person comes to Christ it is certainly a "Divine Appointment." But when we get to hear the unique details of what brought them our way it illustrates the myriad ways the Holy Spirit woos people. It's awesome.

I gave the young man a "Good News For You" book which is designed to help a new Believer along in his or her journey with Christ. I also gave him one of the New Testaments generously supplied for us by Temple Baptist Church in Clarksville, Texas where Bro. Brandon Teague serves as pastor.

While explaining the importance of Bible study, I opened it to the Gospel of John and suggested he get started with reading the Bible there.

Leo Bell Lytle III
and Valerie Lynne Culp-Lytle

I usually place our ministry card there as a book marker and explain that my cell number is on the card and to feel free to call me with any questions.

I also let him pick out a handmade leather Christian key ring provided to us by our good friend in California, Louie Orgo ("The Key Ring Guy"). It's another reminder of his decision to accept Jesus Christ as his personal LORD and Savior. I encouraged him to write today's date down because it is his "Spiritual Birthday."

Finally, I asked him who would be the first person he would tell about the decision he had just made to accept Christ. He said it would be his wife. Now, he, like all of us who have come to Christ, has a story to tell. I hope he continues to share his story the rest of his life. I hope you share your story for the rest of your life, too. How will they hear if we don't share? Let's get busy!

43

What Are They Thinking?

By Leo Lytle
January 2022, Ragley, Louisiana

"And that every tongue should confess that Jesus Christ is Lord,
to the glory of God the Father."
Philippians 2:11

———————————

It was a beautiful, warm and sunny winter's day in southwestern Louisiana as I drove southbound on US 171 toward Lake Charles. I was pulling my trailer that had been carefully loaded with 800 "Jesus Is Lord" crosses by some of the faithful team members of Vic Bass Ministries. On the back of the trailer, I always travel with a cross or two zip-tied onto it and a simple sign that reads:

FREE CROSSES
936-225-1660
CALL - I'LL PULL OVER

On this day, a truck slowly passed me. It was driven by a man with what appeared to be his 9- or 10-year-old son in the passenger seat. As they passed by, the boy turned his head toward my trailer to get one long, last look.

It reminded me of something I frequently think about while driving across America with our trailer full of crosses. It is, after all, an unusual sight. People stare when I stop at a convenience store for fuel. They are watching when we set up to share crosses in a vacant parking lot. They are watching when we stop at a restaurant. And they watch in all the other situations when they see these crosses. What thought is passing through their minds at that moment?

What was that young boy thinking? What was his dad thinking? Was there a conversation between the two as they drove away? Did he ask  his dad what the crosses were all about? Did the father use the moment to share with his son who Jesus is and what He did for us on the cross? Did they both just drive away in silence, never expressing their thoughts? Would that brief exposure to the crosses ever cross their minds again? Would it be an experience that returns to their minds when they see a cross on a church or in some other place? Who made all those crosses? Why?

The answers to many of these questions are perhaps known only to God. But what I do know is what the Bible says plainly: "Jesus is Lord!" In Philippians 2:11 the Bible says, "And {that} every tongue should confess that Jesus Christ {is} Lord to the glory of God the Father." Also, the Bible says that God will accomplish what His word says. Isaiah 55:11 says, "So shall my word be that goeth forth out of my mouth: it shall not return unto me void, but it shall accomplish that which I please, and it shall prosper in the thing whereto I sent it."

My friend Vic Bass and his team have managed to produce more than one million crosses over the last 10 years. That's right – more than a million. At the end of 2023, Bro. Vic and his wife, Sheila, moved to another city in Texas to live closer to their son. Bro. Vic passed the production of the crosses as a sacred trust over to Pastor Steve Cowart and members at Trinity Baptist Church in Lufkin, Texas. Vic Bass Ministries is still actively involved in the prayer ministry behind the effort with more than 40 prayer warriors. Our ministry absolutely depends on these prayers as the foundation for all our efforts.

All the crosses are given away freely and are displayed in people's yards, flowerbeds, businesses, roadsides, and cemeteries — all across America. Valerie and I have had the blessing and privilege of sharing thousands of these in all 50 states, as well as some in Mexico and Canada, over the past seven years through Leo Lytle Ministries.

Before the crosses leave the "Cross Barn" in Lufkin, Texas, where they are made with loving care, they are prayed over by the volunteers who make them. The prayer is always that each cross "finds its destination." Bro. Vic tells the story of how that particular prayer came to be adopted. One time a cross flew off a load being transported near Livingston, Texas. A woman driving behind them stopped and picked it up. She called the number found on the card stapled on the back and told Bro. Vic that he had no idea how much she needed to receive that cross. Only God knows how many millions of people have seen these crosses one way or another across our great nation. Only God knows how many people have had to consider the mighty message emblazoned on each one: "Jesus Is Lord."

Valerie and I, along with others who share these crosses on the streets, are privileged to see the immediate impact the crosses can have in people's lives. But it is, perhaps, just the tip of the iceberg compared to the seeds planted in the hearts of the untold millions of people who see them.

Back to that young boy at the beginning of this story. Although I didn't know what he was thinking that day in Ragley, Louisiana, I DO know what a young boy about the same age was thinking as he saw me driving through Lincoln City, Oregon on September 1, 2021. He saw the crosses and the sign and asked his mom to please call that number. He said he wanted a cross. She called. I gave him a couple of crosses. Then, with his mother's permission, I shared the Gospel message with her son. They both listened carefully. Afterwards, both received God's Gift of Eter-

nal Life in Jesus Christ in a parking lot by the beautiful Pacific Ocean in Lincoln City. Glory to God!

What are they thinking? It is a question that often comes to mind. While I'm standing by these crosses in a parking lot somewhere in America, and it's one of those days where only a few folks stop, I watch hundreds of vehicles pass me. Every now and then I will catch a glimpse of a face and intently staring eyes. And I will wonder once again, "What are they thinking?"

44

A Sure Hope in Hope

By Leo Lytle
July 2023, Hope, Arkansas

"That being justified by His grace, we should be made heirs
according to the hope of eternal life."
Titus 3:7 KJV

On a hot Saturday afternoon in July 2023, I was driving east on Interstate 30 near Hope, Arkansas. My destination was Jessieville First Baptist Church north of Hot Springs. I was scheduled to share "The Door" message on Sunday morning. I was pulling our smaller "Grandgeorge/Friendship Trailer" with a load of 200 crosses. The Grandgeorge/Friendship trailer is so named for two reasons. The first is that a generous love offering from Friendship Baptist Church in Buchanan, Tennessee allowed us to buy the trailer in the first place. The second is that our friend Junior Grandgeorge welded the metal framework onto the trailer that keeps the crosses organized and secure. Junior is the husband of our friend Letha Grandgeorge. They are members of our home congregation, Faith Family Church of Burke, Texas.

Of course, I had our sign on the back of the trailer which states:

FREE CROSSES
936-225-1660
CALL, I'LL PULL OVER

Having that sign always makes for an interesting and exciting trip. We've had hundreds of encounters all across America with folks who have called us on the road. This encounter in Arkansas is one of my favorites.

A few miles before reaching Hope, a late-model white truck passed me in the left lane of the interstate. I noticed a young girl gazing intently as they passed me. After passing me and another couple of vehicles, they switched over to the right lane and began to slow down. We've seen this many times before, so I was expecting a call soon.

At that point, I moved to the left lane and ended up passing them. A few heartbeats after I moved back over into the right lane in front of them, my cell phone rang – just like clockwork. It is like a dance, this back and forth between the lanes that culminates in a phone call. I enjoy it. This call was from the young girl who had been staring so intently. She wanted a free cross. "Of course," I said, and asked them to follow me to the Hope exit.

Her name was Adele. Adele and her stepmother, Mo, and I stood behind the cross trailer to talk. After a short conversation, I asked them both the question we try to ask everyone who comes for a free cross: "Do you know for certain if you were to die today that you would go to Heaven?" Mo was smiling broadly and confidently answered, "Yes!" Then I turned to Adele and asked for her response. She said she had been thinking about that a lot lately and wanted to go to Heaven but didn't know if she would. I asked her and her stepmother for permission to share how she could know for sure. Both said yes. In a few minutes, 11-year-old Adele prayed to receive God's free Gift of Eternal Life Jesus Christ right there behind the "Grandgeorge/Friendship Trailer" at the Hope exit! All Glory to God!

I gave her a Bible and the "Good News For You" Bible study booklet. I also encouraged her to write the date down so she would always remember her "Spiritual Birthday." Adele would be the first of 12 more names written in the "Lamb's Book of Life" that short weekend in Arkansas. Hallelujah!

A few days later, I received a message from Mo, Adele's stepmother, that Adele was going to be baptized by their pastor back in Henderson,

Texas. Mo sent me pictures of the baptism. I was so happy to see how quickly Adele had followed the LORD's example in Believer's baptism! I am so proud of her! What a blessing for Adele to have a stepmother and a father who are both Believers, able and willing to help nurture her journey with Christ.

Just a little more about Hope, Arkansas: former President Bill Clinton is from Hope, Arkansas. Also from Hope is former presidential candidate and former Arkansas Governor Mike Huckabee. Hope is well known for delicious watermelons, too. They celebrate the big "Hope Watermelon

Festival" there every summer. Interestingly though, the town got its name from another young girl way back in 1873: Hope Loughborough. She was the daughter of a railroad executive.

But the young girl I will always associate with Hope, Arkansas is 11-year-old Adele. She took the "Hope" exit and found a "sure hope" in accepting Jesus Christ as her personal LORD and Savior! If you are searching for hope in your own life, please turn to the last chapter of this book and read how you can find it in Jesus Christ.

45

"This and That"

By Leo Lytle
Random short stories from across America

*"But sanctify the Lord God in your hearts: and be ready always to give
an answer to every man that asketh you a reason of the hope
that is in you with meekness and fear."*
1 Peter 3:15 KJV

Y ou don't become a Christian through osmosis, and you certainly don't catch it like a virus because you live or work with other Believers. No, in fact it's a personal decision – a very personal choice that has eternal consequences! It is life's most important decision. If you have made it, you should know where you were when you made it. You may not remember the exact date, but you should certainly remember the location and the circumstances that led you to make this all-important choice. For example, I was in my *"bachelor pad"* in Shreveport, Louisiana back in 1975 at the age of 21 when I became a Christian. That's where my story begins! Do you have a story? If not, go to the last chapter of this book and read how you can be born again and start Chapter One of your story. You'll be eternally glad you did!

Just as a child after birth begins to grow and mature, so do Believers after being born again. The more we grow spiritually, the better equipped and prepared we are to be ready to share our story with others as we go through life. In fact, sharing your story with others will help you grow spiritually along with prayer, Bible study, worship and fellowship. So, it's never too soon to share your story with others! I often ask new Believers who have just accepted Christ this question, "Who will be the first person you will tell about your decision to accept Jesus Christ today?" Now on to the stories.

It was about 1:30 am when we pulled into the hotel parking lot in Hannibal, Missouri. Immediately we noticed someone cleaning up the parking lot and then moments later, as we drove under the large roof awning connected to the entrance, we saw two men up there working. It certainly seemed odd. I parked and went inside to acquire a room for what was left of the night. As I was getting ready to get back in the van, the two men high up on the roof asked for free crosses. Within a few minutes, I shared the Gospel with them. Both men prayed to accept God's free gift of Eternal Life Jesus Christ at least 20 feet above me on top of the roof! Praise God!

Speaking of late-night hotel check-ins, there is this one from Clarksville, Arkansas. I was making my way home from a three-week trip to the New England states in 2022, and was exhausted from not only a long day, but a long trip. The clerk seemed to be in his twenties, and as I discovered later was a Hindu. I felt direction from the Holy Spirit to ask him the question I normally asked: "Have you come to the place in your life where you know for certain if you died today you would go to Heaven?" But I was so tired and needed to sleep. So I did not ask him. Then he saw the crosses on my trailer through the entrance door and asked me what that was about. In short order we entered into a Gospel conversation, and I shared with him the uniqueness of Christianity in our world of religions. He prayed to receive Jesus as his personal LORD and Savior right there in the hotel lobby! Glory!

I met another Indian family at a hotel in Lexington, Tennessee one evening where mom and dad said they were both followers of Christ during our conversation. However, the mom asked if I would speak to their teenage daughter who was not a Believer and was experiencing bouts of depression and anxiety. She took her out to the lobby where the three of us sat down together. After a lengthy discussion I shared the

Leo Bell Lytle III
and Valerie Lynne Culp-Lytle

"Good News" about a new life available to all in Jesus Christ. She said that was what she wanted and gave her heart and life to Him right there in the lobby! Hallelujah!

In January of 2023 a man called for a free cross somewhere close to Victoria, Texas late one night. He said he had seen us with the trailer full of crosses at a big chain store a few miles back and followed us for more than 10 miles before he caught up with us. I pulled over. He began to share about his life and said he knew he needed Christ. He said he figured that seeing us was a sign from God. So he tracked us down hoping we could pray for him. Not only did we pray for him, but he prayed to receive Christ! It was certainly a "Divine Appointment!" All Glory to God!

Another late-night encounter happened in 2023 near Lordsville, New Mexico. We received a call while on Interstate 10 from a young man who wanted a free cross. He suggested we meet at a fast-food restaurant in nearby Lordsville. As I went out to speak with him, his parents also pulled into the parking lot. They were apparently moving as a family to a new part of New Mexico. Then a young woman who was waiting for her ride home from work came over to listen to our conversation. By midnight, four more names were written in the "Lamb's Book of Life!" Thank you, Jesus!

Sometimes we led folks to Christ over the phone. While sitting in the airport in Denver, Colorado a young woman from back home in Texas called me and asked me to help her understand how to have a personal relationship with Christ. After our Gospel conversation, she prayed with me over the phone and placed her trust in Jesus Christ alone for her salvation!

In another late-night phone call in Gonzales, Louisiana, a woman saw our trailer parked in the hotel parking lot with the sign to call for a free cross. She called. We engaged in a Gospel conversation. Before long, she asked Jesus to save her! We mailed her follow-up material to help her on her new journey with Christ.

Sometimes while driving, people don't have the time to pull off the road and talk. Such was the case of a man from New York who wrote down our number while on Interstate 80 in Nebraska. First, he thanked us for what we were doing. He said it had touched his heart and that was the reason for his call. For the next 15 minutes or so, I shared with him the difference between having a religion and having a personal relationship with Jesus Christ. He started his personal relationship with Jesus that very day somewhere near Ogallala, Nebraska!

In an odd encounter in Rutland, Vermont, a young man stopped at an abandoned service station where we were sharing Christ and free "Jesus Is Lord" crosses. As we talked, he told me he thought we were giving away free firewood (first time I had heard that). In a few minutes our discussion turned to Christ. He said it was odd, but just that very week he had received at least two things in the mail about becoming a Christian. I told him that maybe it was not a mistake that he had stopped here. He prayed right there by the "firewood" to accept Christ!

A young lady somewhere on Interstate 12 near Covington, Louisiana took a photo of our sign on the back of our trailer. She sent it to her boyfriend who was in college at Louisiana State University (LSU) in Baton Rouge, Louisiana. Curiosity got the best of him, so he called our number on the sign. He admitted that he had not placed his trust in Christ. I suggested he listen to God's plan of salvation if he was interested, while I continued to drive. We had a great visit together that ended with his decision over the phone to place his trust in Christ. It was a "Divine Appointment" for sure!

Three young men called us late one night near Clarksburg, West Virginia. They wanted to know if the crosses were really free and if so, they all wanted one. We met at a convenience store in Clarksburg, and I shared Christ with them out by the gas pumps. Three more added to the kingdom while we filled our tank! But then, just after they left, a couple pulled up next to us and also wanted a free cross. They, too, accepted Jesus Christ as their personal LORD and Savior! Within a few minutes, the mother of one of the boys called to thank us for leading her son and his friends to Christ. He had come home and shared with his mom what had just happened to him. God never ceases to amaze us at how He works!

In September of 2023, Valerie and I were looking for a place to share Christ and crosses in Vista, California during the rush hour traffic there. While locked in traffic on an overpass, we received a call for a free cross.

Leo Bell Lytle III
and Valerie Lynne Culp-Lytle

The caller suggested we meet in a nearby parking lot. He said he had been an Atheist most of his life, but was for the first time seriously considering the existence of God in recent days. We had a wonderful conversation for what seemed like half an hour. I could see he seemed ready to place his life completely in God's hands. I said that it was no accident that of all the hundreds of cars on the freeway, he ended up directly behind us, staring at a trailer full of crosses. So, I asked him if he would like to receive God's free Gift of Eternal Life Jesus Christ? He said "yes," and he did just that!

Because we are out on the streets, it's not unusual for people to pass by on a bicycle. Of course, some will stop, which gives us an opportunity to share Jesus. I recall a few who prayed to ask Jesus to be their personal LORD and Savior while sitting on their bicycles. Two teenage boys did just that in Cheyenne, Wyoming. So did a man in Princeton, West Virginia. Another man in El Paso, Texas pedaled away with his cross after accepting Christ, as did a young man in Carson City, Nevada. I love to see them riding away with a free cross!

At a restaurant in Idaho Falls, Idaho, Valerie and I parked the van with the trailer full of crosses and went inside for lunch. Just after we ordered, my phone rang. It was a lady out in the parking lot who wanted a free cross. She was with her daughter and son-in-law. Both she and her daughter were Believers. Her son-in-law admitted that he was not a Believer, but would listen as I presented the Gospel. He prayed to be saved right then and there. Praise God!

I went back into the restaurant, where they had just brought out our order. We asked God's blessing on the food and on this new Believer, then took a few bites before my phone rang again. I went back out to meet two college students who wanted a cross. We had a wonderful Gospel conversation, and both decided to accept God's free Gift of Eternal Life Jesus Christ! When I made my way back to the table, Valerie had my food covered with a napkin to try to keep it warm. We finished our meal thanking God for again leading us to just the right place at just the right time.

One more hotel story before putting a wrap on this chapter: This one takes place in Raymondville, Texas. After a long and amazing day of sharing Christ and crosses, about 100 souls were saved! Valerie and I were both so busy sharing the Gospel that we barely had time to speak to each other all day. We had plans to join a local pastor and his wife at a nearby restaurant for supper. We got numerous calls for crosses during the meal (napkin over the food again). A couple more people came to Christ out in the parking lot. Valerie answered some of the phone calls so that I could eat at least some of my meal.

The Raymondville pastor's church treated us to a nice room at a local hotel for which we were very thankful. Then, the next morning, Valerie says we had to, "witness our way out" of the hotel. She was leading one employee to Christ in the hallway while I was leading another one to Him in the parking lot. Finally, the hotel manager also wanted a cross, and she wanted to hear how to be saved. The manager prayed to be saved right by the front desk with tears streaming down her cheeks. We'll never forget all that God did in Raymondville!

There are scores of stories we could recount about seeing people pray to be saved all over America in hotels, restaurants, convenience stores, on the side of highways, in parking lots, at gas pumps and even at laundromats. We give God all the Glory and Praise for allowing us to have a small part in sharing Christ across America. Wherever we go – wherever you go – we all need to be ready to share the Good News. Share Jesus with someone today.

46

Breakdowns

By Leo Lytle

"God is our refuge and strength, a very present help in trouble."
Psalms 46:1 KJV

As mentioned, Valerie and I at the time of this writing, are in our seventh year of evangelism. It has literally been an amazing ride, though, with that said, our "ride" has sometimes had problems along the highways and byways of America. Those of you who have followed us on social media know that we do not drive a new or late-model vehicle. Not even close!

When we started Leo Lytle Ministries in 2018, our first mode of transportation was a 20-year-old, 1998 six-cylinder Dodge Ram truck given to us by our dear friends Bobby and Jo Lynn Bays of Glenwood, Arkansas. It didn't have a working motor when they gave it to us. But Faith Family Church, our home church, located a used one in a wrecking yard and generously had it installed. We drove "Old Red" for our ministry work for the first three and a half years and still use it as a backup today. Old Red has been a faithful friend from coast to coast and border to border. But along the way we've had a few hiccups.

One such hiccup happened on a Saturday in 2018 in Georgia. The water pump went out. I was scheduled to preach the next morning across the state line in Denmark, South Carolina. So, there I was in a rural com-

munity in Georgia with a busted water pump. The prospect of finding someone to fix it on a Saturday afternoon was slim. They had an auto parts store where I was able to buy a new one. I asked the young man who waited on me if he knew of anyone in the area who might be willing to install it, knowing full well that the answer was most likely "No." But, praise God, he said there was a man on the edge of town who was a "shade tree mechanic." He might be willing. The clerk gave me the mechanic's address. I poured in all the water Old Red's radiator would hold and made a beeline to his place.

The nice mechanic said he would do it, but it might be an hour or so before he finished with the car on which he was already working. I gladly waited, and before long he got me back "on the road again." I sang that famous Willie Nelson tune on the way to South Carolina. I love the miraculous way God took care of me and Old Red that day!

On another occasion, Valerie and I were driving in Oklahoma, south of Stillwater near the small town of Perkins. We were pulling a trailer packed with crosses when one of the trailer tires shredded. After pulling over, we saw the other trailer tire was also very, very low. I got the spare tire ready, jacked up the trailer and started to remove the lug nuts. But then I realized my lug nut wrench for the truck didn't fit the ones on the trailer. My bad! So, we unhooked the trailer, left it well off the side of the road and drove about eight miles to the little town of Perkins. I went into a local convenience store/truck stop to buy one of those multi-size lug nut wrenches. They didn't have any. As I shared my dilemma with a couple of folks working behind the counter, the deli cook overheard me and said I could borrow his. I took the cook up on his offer, and away we went back to the trailer. By the time I changed the shredded tire, the other one was all but flat. Nothing to do now but drive very — and I mean very — slowly along the shoulder and hope we could find a tire back once again in Perkins.

Leo Bell Lytle III
and Valerie Lynne Culp-Lytle

I dropped off the borrowed wrench and thanked the deli cook for his kindness. Then we drove ever so slowly, hoping to find a tire shop in such a small town. Thank God, we did. The axle on our trailer was from a mobile home trailer. That size tire is usually hard to find. But in God's perfect provision for us, they had one in stock. In a few minutes – cue it up Willie – we were "On the Road Again!" Glory to God! We made it on to Stillwater, bought another new tire for the trailer and were off again.

I've already touched on the transmission issue in 2020 in Minneapolis and a similar problem I experienced briefly in 2021 in Uvalde, Texas. I won't rehash those here. However, in April 2021 we were on our way to the Pine Ridge Indian Reservation in South Dakota in "Old Red." We left our home in beautiful Pine Valley, Texas in shorts and short-sleeve shirts. Our brief blip of an East Texas winter had long since passed. We were firmly in warm weather mode. But by the time we reached northwestern Kansas, we were cold. Valerie reached up to the dashboard to turn on the heater, but no warm air materialized. It was then that I remembered Old Red's heater was broken. Valerie just laughed when I broke the news to her.

The tail end of a big blizzard had swept over the high plains all the way up into the Dakotas. We learned that transportation officials were planning on closing the interstate westbound toward Colorado. By morning a light snow was falling, and strong winds were blowing as we left our hotel to head north. Temperatures were in the upper 20s, and strong winds drove home the cold.

Now, Valerie is always prepared for nearly any emergency. She has to be when she's riding with me. She is so uncomplaining and cheerful no matter the situation. She kept smiling even as we were wiping breath frost off the windshield to see the road. I love my wife! She had her neck scarf, warm gloves, layered clothing, fuzzy socks, boots on and several blankets. Me – I'll stop at the next store and get an extra pair of socks if necessary. Valerie always tries to convince me to pack a better supply of warm clothes. But I am more of a minimalist packer.

So away we went through the blowing snow and falling temperatures into Nebraska, where the roads were already snow-covered in places. We couldn't go much faster than 35 miles an hour all the way through the state.

We had hoped to spend the night in Valentine in northwestern Nebraska if the road stayed passable. About 60 miles from Valentine, we began to hear a noticeable rattle under Old Red's hood. I took a look to see what the problem was, but I'm not much on mechanical stuff. It just seemed the manly thing to do. I closed the hood and prayed we would make it to Valentine.

God did deliver us safely to Valentine, and we were able to get the rattle rectified. A dealership repaired a loose pulley or some such. As I said, I'm not much on the mechanical stuff. Unfortunately, we would still be without a heater for the remainder of that trip.

The next day, we stood out in the snow for hours in Mission, South Dakota sharing Christ and crosses. Even though the temperature never rose above 20 degrees, folks were stopping. We led several people to Christ there. It was below 20 degrees for several more days. The only time we were able to warm up was at the hotel each night. We praise God again for the very cold but safe and fruitful trip! We enjoyed every minute of it.

One more tale about Old Red takes place much closer to home. In July 2020 I left the Cross Barn on a Saturday morning with about 200 crosses provided by Vic Bass Ministries. I was heading to Monroe, Louisiana for the weekend. For the short trip, I was not pulling a trailer. The crosses were stacked in Old Red's eight-foot bed, enclosed in a camper shell. When going in that direction, I usually pass through Carthage, Texas. Every time I do, I think I need to share Christ and crosses in Carthage someday. That Saturday was no exception as I made my way around the loop in Carthage to US Highway 79 toward Shreveport, Louisiana. As I made the turn, I had only gone 100 yards or so when Old Red commenced snorting and wheezing. I eased over to the shoulder just as the engine stopped. I couldn't get it to fire back up.

Leo Bell Lytle III
and Valerie Lynne Culp-Lytle

I got out and took my obligatory look under the hood as though I might manage to figure out what was wrong. No chance of that happening! Then I paused to evaluate the situation, weigh all the options and, of course, pray. I remember asking God, "What do you want me to do with your truck?" Everything I have is His anyway, including that old truck. In my view it was loaded with the precious cargo of "Jesus Is Lord" crosses. I didn't want to miss the opportunity to share them and Him.

Well, I had my AAA card and knew they would tow me up to seven miles for free. Also, I knew of an auto repair place in Carthage where I had a fuel pump replaced once before. Logically, the solution would be to call AAA and have the rotation wrecker drop the truck off at the repair shop where they could work on it on Monday. Valerie was at work, but I could just call one of our kids or a friend to pick me up. Problem solved, right?

The only problem with my original plan was just that: it was my plan. As I waited on the side of the road for the tow truck, God gave me His plan. It was this: have the wrecker tow me to a vacant parking lot and leave me there. From that location, I would be able to share my precious cargo with folks in Carthage, Texas. That was the way to go! Suddenly, I remembered I'd seen a vacant parking lot on the main street through town where a pizza place used to be. "Perfect spot," I thought.

The tow truck driver did as I asked, although he did question why I wasn't wanting him to take it to a repair shop. When I shared what my cargo was and what I was planning to do, he said he understood and identified himself as a Believer, too. When we arrived at the vacant parking lot, I showed him where I wanted Old Red positioned near the street. The tow truck driver got the first cross. Then I put the signs out to get started with what God had for me to do in Carthage, Texas.

Many people stopped, including a family who would drive me to a hotel later that night. The same family also picked me up the next morning and even treated me to breakfast. Then they gave me a ride back over to Old Red. Over the partial two days in Carthage, at least a dozen people prayed to receive God's free Gift of Eternal Life Jesus Christ right there in that closed restaurant parking lot beside my disabled vehicle. Praise God!!! If I had followed my plan, it might have been a little bit easier on me. But thank God, I learned a long time ago as a young Believer that it is not about me. It's all about Him!

A friend of ours, Douglas "Taco" Gaddy, would make the three-hour round trip to bring me home late Sunday afternoon. I came back later in the week to pick up Old Red when her repair was complete and bring her home again ready for the next adventure. Our God is so, so good!!! I love how the LORD perfectly met all my needs that weekend. It is fun just to watch Him work.

———————————

In May 2021, we didn't put Old Red out to pasture, but we did ease up considerably on her workload. God provided a 2007 Ford Econoline van for us to use for our ministry. We put a foam mattress and a couple of pillows in the back and started driving it all around the nation. It was on one of our trips to the Northwest in September 2021 when we left our van and trailer at an airport parking lot in Seattle, Washington. We flew into Anchorage, Alaska on a late-night flight. We would spend the next week sharing Christ and free "Jesus Is Lord" crosses for the first time in Alaska.

Valerie had to fly back home for work the day before I flew back from Anchorage to Seattle to pick up the van and trailer to continue the trip. It was midnight by the time I got back to the van.

As I drove toward the downtown area of Seattle, I was searching for a shopping center parking lot to spend the night in the van. Heading north on Interstate 5, I noticed my headlights dimming. Then a low-battery message began to flash on the instrument panel.

Now, this was the time when Antifa was causing a lot of trouble in downtown Seattle. Riots, protests and violence were all over the news. I prayed, "LORD, help me find a safe place to pull over for the night. Then I'll deal with the problem in the morning." God provided once again. With my headlights all but gone, I pulled into a shopping center parking lot and went right to sleep.

The next morning, I located an auto parts store nearby. They kindly checked my battery and alternator. It was the alternator. I bought one and began calling auto repair shops about having it installed.

Every place I called was two to three weeks out before they would be able to replace it. That wasn't going to work for me. I had to be in Springfield, Oregon in a few days to preach "The Door" message. I needed someone to fix it that day.

As always, God was working behind the scenes. The last place I called said he had a mechanic friend who liked to help people and gave me his friend's name and number. I called. He said to bring it to his shop. I did. In less than three **HOURS** (not two to three weeks) I was back on the road. All Glory to God!

Just minutes after leaving his garage, I encountered a couple in the parking lot of a fast-food restaurant. We engaged in a Gospel conversation and soon both people prayed to accept God's free gift of Eternal Life Jesus Christ.

I sat in the van thanking God for His amazing timing. I thanked Him for directing me to the one man who could meet my need. I love how He always makes a way when it seems there is no way, (as the song goes).

I'm certain there will be many more "breakdowns" in the future. Like Valere and I, the vehicles we are driving around America have plenty of miles on them. But God will be with us whenever and wherever those breakdowns may happen. He will make a way!

47

God Provides
A New Ride

By Valerie Culp-Lytle
August 2024, Pine Valley, Texas

"O taste and see that the Lord is good:
blessed is the man that trusteth in him."
Psalm 34:8 KJV

T hat moment comes.

It came for our original van. The moment came when we looked at one another and said, "Eventually, we are going to have to get another van."

Our 2007 Ford Econoline van that we bought used with a blessing-out-of-the-blue donation several years earlier had served us well. We took excellent care of it. But we also drove it all over the nation, racking up many thousands of miles. It took us border to border and coast to coast and from state to state to state and then back home to East Texas on countless trips. It was getting close to 300,000 miles. Costly repairs were starting to mount.

One day, driving down the highway in our original van, we shared the look and said the words. Yes, one of these days we would need to get another van. Not a new one. Just a younger one with significantly fewer miles on it.

"The Lord will work it out," we agreed.

We didn't worry about it. We completely trusted that the Lord would work it out when the time was right. Occasionally when someone would ask if we needed anything for our ministry, we would say that eventually we were going to need to replace our van with something with fewer miles on it. In our prayers we would thank God for His blessings, including His provision and protection and, most importantly, that people were praying to be saved. We would ask for His continued guidance and continued blessing. But we didn't pray specifically for a van. We figured the Lord knew better what we needed than we did. We didn't spend any time looking at vans online or peering into windows of vans parked on used car lots. We just stayed focused on sharing the Gospel and trusted God to take care of any needs that might arise.

As the Lord would have it, some of the pillars of the Cross Ministry felt led to spearhead the effort to help get us into a new van. Dale Frost, one of the two original founders of the Cross Ministry in East Texas, started approaching people and businesses about donating money for a newer van. He would show them a notebook with some of the chapters of this book in it and let them read about what the Lord was doing with our ministry. Some of them felt led to give. The other original founder of the Cross Ministry in East Texas, Lawrence "Buddy" Jordan, also worked diligently to gather funds for the van. Additionally, New Hope Baptist Church in Sparkman, Arkansas has been making regular, generous donations dedicated to paying off the new van.

But back to the story of how it all unfolded. Bro. Vic Bass also did what he could to encourage money to be given and gathered for a newer van. Trinity Baptist Church in Lufkin, Texas set up a special fund for earmarked donations. Bro. Vic asked that a notice be put in the Trinity Baptist bulletin about it, and Pastor Steve Cowart announced it to the congregation.

We were on our way. In a few days, Trinity Baptist Church had a check for us, representing the first of the van donations. We opened a bank account named Leo Lytle Ministries Van Fund. Our thought was that we would allow the account to grow gradually over the following months and start casually looking for another van in the new year.

But Mr. Frost was not on board with that timeline. The bank account for a newer van was barely set up when he started calling us regularly to see if we had found one. Not yet, we said. A few days went by, and he called again to see if we had located a van. Not yet, we said. (Left to our own devices, we would probably have waited until the old van was broken down, steaming on the side of the road in the middle of nowhere.)

After a few such phone conversations, Mr. Frost said that he felt an urgency for us to go ahead and secure a newer van. We should do it right away, he said. Not months from now.

Leo Bell Lytle III
and Valerie Lynne Culp-Lytle

Okay, Leo agreed. We would go that day. Within minutes, we headed out. We drove three hours to a business south of Houston that specializes in pre-owned vans, many of them fleet vehicles. While Leo drove, I researched pricing for various mileage categories and read reviews about the best van to get when one wants a "work horse." The main things we wanted were fewer miles and a ceiling tall enough that we could stand upright without stooping. The bending does a number on one's back and neck after a while.

Leo and I agreed that although we were not feeling the same urgency to secure a newer van, we would trust the leading that Dale Frost was experiencing. After all, it was Dale Frost and Buddy Jordan who first felt led to make crosses in East Texas and then eventually joined forces with Bro. Vic. The efforts of those three men, combined with the work of many volunteers and people like Leo and me who use the crosses as evangelism tools, have led to more than 5,000 people praying to be saved over the past seven years. Yes, we were very much at peace with following their leading in the matter of the van.

After battling Houston traffic, we reached the place, explained what we were looking for and found a van that fit everything we wanted in a replacement vehicle. It was a 2017 Ford Transit Van, 10 years newer than our original van and with 95,004 miles on it compared to close to 300,000 miles on the old van. Ford Transit cargo vans are top-ranked as "best for the money." It had a medium-height ceiling inside that was just high enough for both of us to stand upright. We were given the CARFAX profile. Everything looked good. Leo told the salesman

we would go home to pray about it and look at ways and means. Leo said he wanted the price to come down. They agreed to talk by telephone the next morning.

The next day the dealership offered to knock two thousand dollars off the price and put in brand new headlights. We drove the three hours again with a cashier's check representing what we were able to put down

241

on the van. The amount included donations for the van and then the $5,000 that we were contributing ourselves. The remainder of the sales price we financed. Our hope was that the Lord would allow us to pay off the financed amount quickly.

Within the next 48 hours, several thousand more dollars were donated for the van. At this writing, we are very close to having the entire financed amount paid off, thanks to continued donations for the van. Just as we were amazed and grateful at the providence of God that gave us our original van within scant days of Leo voicing our need for it, we are amazed and grateful again. It recalls Genesis 22, when Abraham in worship added an extra word to God's name. Abraham did so at the place where God provided the ram for sacrifice to spare Isaac. "Jehovah Jireh," Abraham said: the Lord who provides/sees to it.

"You can't out-give God," Leo always says.

He's right.

We've said it before. We'll say it again: All glory to God!

48

The Gospel –
Good News For You!

By Leo Lytle

"For God so loved the world, that he gave his only begotten Son,
that whosoever believeth in him should not perish, but have everlasting life."
John 3:16 KJV

Thank you for reading our book "CROSS-ing America." This last chapter is included to help you understand how to have a personal relationship with God through Jesus Christ. Much of this Gospel presentation comes from the late Dr. D. James Kennedy's book "Evangelism Explosion." I am a certified teacher-trainer in "Evangelism Explosion 3 International" and taught this method to students for more than 30 years.

Let's start with this important question...

Have you come to the place in your life where you know for certain that if you died today you would go to Heaven?

Remember, I said for certain! It is vitally important to be honest with yourself here. The last time I checked, the death rate for humans is still 100%. You will die one day just like the rest of us.

While I'm asking questions, here's another one.

Suppose you did die today and stood before God. If He were to ask you, "Why should I let you into my Heaven?" What would you say?

Most people give a wide variety of answers when Valerie and I ask them this question. They say things such as, "I'm a good person." Or, "I try to live by the Golden Rule." Also, they give us answers such as, "I go to church." Or "I've been baptized." Some even say they have been through so much "hell" on earth that God will certainly let them into Heaven. We've been told that people expect admission to Heaven for everything from being faithful in marriage to occasionally mowing the neighbor's yard. But really, what do you have to do to get to Heaven? What are the requirements?

These are strong questions that can help you understand not only your degree of confidence about whether you think you'll go to Heaven when you die, but also what you are trusting in to get you there. Let me share my story.

I grew up in a very religious home. I had wonderful parents and siblings. We attended our local church faithfully. I considered myself a good person and was hopeful that when I died, God would see fit to let me into Heaven. But honestly, I just wasn't sure about it. I didn't give it much thought, either. I was young (21 years old) and thought I still had a lifetime ahead of me to nail it down.

Then one day I was forever changed! A couple of my friends I grew up with in church, Rusty Hamby and his sister, Jeany Hamby, stopped by my house. They invited me to a new Bible study class designed for college and career-age people like me. I was considering attending the new class. To be perfectly candid, I most liked the idea because I thought I might meet some nice girls there. But there was something different about them that I'd not noticed before. So, I asked: "Jeany, what is it about you?" I had grown up with them, and there was clearly something new about them. She smiled and said, "It's Jesus." I responded, "I know Jesus."

But after they left, I began to seriously consider it. Did I **really** know Him? That afternoon in the Fall of 1975, I pondered that question. I thought of all the spiritual experiences I had growing up in church, all of the revival services I had attended. I thought about being baptized at 9 years old. A couple of weeks before I was baptized, my friend and neighbor Duffy, who was 10 or 11 years old, had walked forward to join our church on a Sunday morning. So that evening, I did the same thing. As I had seen Duffy and many others do, I went forward during the invitation to join the church. Two weeks later, Duffy and I were baptized. Honestly, I thought I had done what one was supposed to do to get to Heaven: join the church and get baptized.

As I thought about all my experiences, I concluded that I was a good, religious person. But my goodness wasn't going to get me into Heaven. I realized what I needed was a personal relationship with Jesus Christ.

Leo Bell Lytle III
and Valerie Lynne Culp-Lytle

Then, right there by my couch, I sank to my knees on the shag carpet and prayed to be forgiven of my sins and for Jesus to save me. I accepted God's free gift of Eternal Life Jesus Christ. That rocked my world and forever changed my life!

Here is what I discovered, and I hope you will make the same discovery:

First, Heaven (Eternal Life) is a free gift. It cannot be earned or deserved. The Bible states, (8)*"For by grace are ye saved through faith; and that not of yourselves: it is the gift of God: (9) Not of works, lest any man should boast."* (Ephesians 2:8-9 KJV). In other words, I can't earn my way to Heaven by my efforts. I could never be good enough to earn a place in Heaven. It is God's gift to us!

Secondly, I learned that man is a sinner and cannot possibly save himself. Romans 3:23 KJV says: *"For all have sinned, and come short of the glory of God."* What is sin, after all? Sin is anything we do that God wouldn't have us do. Sin is anything we say that God wouldn't have us say. Sin is even thinking anything that wouldn't be pleasing to God. Sin is also failing to do anything that God would want us to do. Yes, we are all sinners, on multiple fronts in every category!

Thirdly, I learned a little about God's nature. He loves us and intends for us to be with Him forever in Heaven when we die. He does not want to punish us. But on the other hand, He **MUS**T punish sin. In Psalm 5:4-5, KJV, Scripture says: *"For thou art not a God that hath pleasure in wickedness: Neither shall evil dwell with thee. The foolish shall not stand in thy sight: Thou hatest all workers of iniquity."* So, on the one hand, God loves us and on the other hand He must punish sin. It seems like an unsolvable dilemma, but not for God!

Fourthly, He solved the dilemma in the person of Jesus Christ. Jesus is the infinite God-man. He was at the same time 100% God and 100% man. He was God come down to earth in the person of a man. He was God wrapped up in human skin. Jesus said of Himself in John 14:9 KJV: "... *he that hath seen me hath seen the Father* ..." And in John 10:30 KJV, Jesus said: *"I and my Father are one."*

Now what did Jesus do? He died a cruel death on the cross to pay for our sins. By doing so, He purchased for us a place in Heaven that He offers as a free gift. He freely offers Eternal Life to all who will accept Him. The Bible makes it crystal clear: *"For the wages of sin is death, but the gift of God is Eternal Life through Jesus Christ our LORD."* (Romans 6:23 KJV).

Finally, this gift is received by faith. Let me tell you what faith is **not** before I tell you what faith **is**. Faith is more than understanding on an intellectual basis. It is not enough to know who Jesus is and what He did. Faith is not a temporal or worldly faith. Some people want to treat God like a book on a bookshelf: they can take the book down and read it when they want to and then put it back until next time. That is not saving faith. Saving faith is trusting in Jesus Christ alone for salvation. It is not trusting in what you can do to get to Heaven, but rather trusting in Jesus Christ's finished work on the cross. The Bible says: *"... believe on the Lord Jesus Christ, and thou shall be saved ..."* (Acts 16:31 KJV).

Now let me ask you this: Does this make sense to you? If you answered "Yes," would you like to receive God's free Gift of Eternal Life in Jesus Christ? If this is what you want to do, why not get it settled once and for all right now by praying a prayer like the one that follows below?

God reads each person's heart for sincere repentance and a desire to be saved. Romans 10:9-10 KJV says this: *(9) "That if thou shalt confess with thy mouth the Lord Jesus, and shalt believe in thine heart that God hath raised him from the dead, thou shalt be saved. (10) For with the heart man believeth unto righteousness; and with the mouth confession is made unto salvation."*

Here's the prayer:

Lord Jesus, I know I'm a sinner and that I can't save myself. I believe you died on the cross to pay for my sins and purchased for me a place in Heaven. I turn from my sin, and I turn to You. I ask you right now to please forgive me of all my sin. Please come into my heart and save my soul. I accept your free gift of Eternal Life. Thank you for saving me. Help me to follow You from this moment on. Amen!

If you prayed a prayer like this and meant it, I've got good news for you. You have just established a personal relationship with Jesus Christ. The Bible says your name has been written in the Lamb's Book of Life in Heaven! Congratulations!!! Today is your Spiritual Birthday! Write this date down so you can celebrate it even more than your physical birthday. Please contact us and let us know of your decision to accept Jesus Christ as your personal LORD and Savior. We have some material we want to send you absolutely free that will help you as you begin your exciting journey with Christ. Here are five things that will help you get started today:

1. **Prayer.** Prayer is simply talking to God with dignity and respect. You can bring anything to Him in prayer.

2. **Bible study.** A good place for a new Believer like you to start reading is in the Gospel of John in the New Testament. Pray for understanding before you begin reading. As you get started, try to read at least one chapter every day.

3. **Worship.** You can, of course, worship God anywhere. But there is something special about worshiping Him with other Believers. Find a strong Bible-believing/Bible-teaching church as soon as possible.

4. **Fellowship.** Being with other committed Christians will help you on your new journey with Christ. A strong church family is the best source of fellowship that will help you begin to grow spiritually.

5. **Witnessing.** Witnessing is simply telling someone else your story of how you came to have a personal relationship with Jesus Christ. Who will be the first person you'll tell about what just happened to you? Tell your story to those you know who might need Jesus in their lives.

Welcome to God's forever family! If we don't meet in this life, I'll see you in Heaven!

Afterword

This Scripture hangs on a plaque on the front of the barn where the "Jesus Is Lord" crosses are made in East Texas:

"Not unto us, O Lord, not unto us, but unto thy name give glory, for thy mercy, and for thy truth's sake."
Psalm 115:1 KJV

Only God knows what the future holds.

Our lives are in God's hands. We are committed to keeping our feet on the paths where He leads. It is our fervent hope that the Lord will allow us to continue to travel and share the Good News. If He does let us continue serving Him in this way, our additional hope is that we will write another book, or even several more books. We have already begun the second one.

The Holy Spirit keeps on revealing life lessons that illustrate Biblical truths to us as we go along. We keep collecting more good stories from the road. It seems only right that we will stop and stack some more stones by compiling and sharing new stories as a memorial and testament to God's goodness.

We sincerely thank you for reading this book. It has been a joy to write. Please share it with your friends and family so that others may read about some of the things the Lord has done. Please find here the encouragement to take a stand for Jesus in your own life.

CROSS-ing AMERICA
Sharing Jesus Around The Nation

We would dearly love to hear from you. Our mailing address is Leo Lytle Ministries, P.O. Box 158, Diboll, Texas 75941. Leo's email address is (all lowercase): leolytle@yahoo.com. Valerie's email address is valerie.lynne.rn@gmail.com. Our Facebook page is Leo Lytle Ministries. Leo's presentation of "The Door" can also be seen on YouTube. Our website is LeoLytleMinistries.com.

No matter how small, how large or how remote, we'd love to visit your church. We'll need an official invitation from your pastor. Then, if the Lord allows it, we will prayerfully try to plan a trip to your church, sharing the Gospel as we go, there and back. Leo's number is 936-225-1660.

We thank God with all our hearts for all His bountiful blessings. May God please continue to bless His children and this great nation. All glory to God!

Leo Bell Lytle III and Valerie Lynne Culp-Lytle
September 2024, Pine Valley, Texas

Acknowledgements

It is our fervent desire to include everybody in our lists of acknowledgements and thanks. But that is impossible. Long lists of people spanning several years carry the inherent risk of leaving somebody out accidentally. This is **especially** true because we have been and continue to be **SO** enormously blessed by **SO** many brothers and sisters in Christ showing us kindness and helping us. The good news is that God sees all. He knows the names of every single person who has ever done anything in His name and for His sake.

We are going to try to thank some people at least. We will try to list some of the names that may not have already appeared elsewhere in this book. Please know that we appreciate and thank **everyone** for what they have done and are doing for the cause of Christ and to help support our ministry. We sincerely apologize that it is impossible to list everyone who has ever helped us, although we are deeply grateful for each one. Please forgive us for inevitable omissions.

Getting Started:

We thank the people of Frankenmuth, Michigan and Eddie Beyerlein. We thank Dale and LaVera Frost of Nacogdoches, Texas and Lawrence (Buddy) Jordan and Susie Jordan of Lufkin, Texas.

The Prayer Team:

We are deeply grateful for the faithful and thorough prayer support of all the prayer team members coordinated by Bro. Vic Bass of Vic Bass Ministries. Serving anonymously behind the scenes and yet most important to the Kingdom work, prayer team members serve faithfully in all seasons. Prayer undergirds every effort of our ministry and is the most essential element. We also thank additional family members, friends, fellow church members and social media followers all over the nation who lift the Cross Ministry and our ministry in prayer as we all work together to reach the lost with the Good News of the Gospel of Jesus Christ.

The Cross Team:

UPDATE on the eve of this book's publication; September 2025: Trinity Baptist Church Pastor Steve Cowart said the Cross Men have gained a new volunteer: Marvin Wittenburg, a retired pastor.

This list of current Cross Ministry volunteers as of the end of September 2024 was provided by Glenn Walker, a team leader with the Cross Ministry:

Larry Jansen
Bruce Brumley
David Wells
Glen Brown
Joe Horton
John Jones
Keith Best
Keith Graves
Kenny Modisett
Larry Thompkins
Ricky Turner
Roger Parker
Ron Beck
Ron Chamberlain
Ron Smith

Leo Bell Lytle III
and Valerie Lynne Culp-Lytle

Ronnie Eckert
Ronnie Hutchison
Steve Barnes
Walter Keen
Dale Hill
Eddie Brown
Gary Flowers
Jerry Selman
Tommy Stoval

Team Leader Glenn Walker listed the following as former Cross Men:

Eddie Pahal
Jerry Stout
George Jones
Jerome Lair
Randy Pilcher
Bethel Bryant
Preston Butler
Jim Barnett

Team Leader Glenn Walker listed the following as members of the current Paint Crew, as of the end of September 2024:

Dwayne Dupree
Steve Bryce
T.J. Williams
Darryl Harris
Danielle Harris
Janis Compton
Linda Reinhardt
Devin Dupree

Team Leader Glenn Walker listed the following as former Paint Crew members:

Nick Fain
Karen Dutton

Paul Dutton
Mr. and Mrs. Santana
Bonnie Kaemmerling

Theresa Fain also painted when the crosses were being made for a time at Faith Family Church in Burke, Texas.

This list of volunteers was provided by Steve Cowart, pastor of Trinity Baptist Church in Lufkin, Texas. Pastor Cowart said this list was provided to him by Vic Bass of Vic Bass Ministries at the time of the transition from Bro. Vic heading the administration of the Cross Ministry to Trinity Baptist Church in Lufkin, Texas accepting responsibility for the administration of the Cross Ministry at the end of 2023. This list was provided to us in September 2024:

Pastor Steve Cowart
Bro. Vic Bass
Glenn Walker
Ricky Turner
Joe Horton
Steve Barnes
Ron Chamberlin
Ron Beck
Kenny Modisette
T.J. Williams
Stephen Bryce
Keith Graves
Tommy Stovall
John Jones
Gary Flowers
Eddie Brown
Ronnie Eckert
Dwayne Dupree
Steve Hickman
Ron Smith
Ronnie Hutchison
Larry Tompkins
Walter Keen

Leo Bell Lytle III
and Valerie Lynne Culp-Lytle

Roger Parker
Larry Jansen
Keith Best
Glenn Brown

Bro. Vic Bass also said that when he and his team first started making crosses, John Smith, Mike Allbritton and Preston Butler helped with cutting up wood to make the crosses. Bro. Vic also said that Eddie Pahal helped at the beginning and Mr. and Mrs. Santana painted for about four years.

Jim Barnett is a former Cross Man volunteer already listed who remains dedicated to the mission. Now in his 90s, Mr. Barnett keeps up with everything our ministry does, and is an enthusiastic supporter at all times. He performs the special service of keeping a fellow assisted-living facility resident who does not go online up to date with the very latest news from us anytime we are traveling.

Special mention goes to Paul Dutton and the late Karen Bass-Dutton. Karen was Bro. Vic and his wife Sheila's daughter. She was married to Paul Dutton. Both Karen and Paul were very faithful cross painters. They also assembled crosses. Karen fought a courageous battle with cancer that ended when she passed from death into life eternal on December 1, 2023. As Leo told Karen before her death, only God knows the total and ongoing impact and the numbers of lives and eternities forever changed by her efforts in making the crosses. This is also true of Paul's efforts — and the efforts of everyone involved with the Cross Ministry. May God please richly bless each volunteer in all the various roles. We thank all of them for what they do for Jesus.

Additional Cross Ministry Members:

This next list of volunteers was provided by Dale and LaVera Frost of Nacogdoches, Texas. These men and women cut, constructed and painted many "Jesus Is Lord" crosses. List provided September 3, 2024

Robert Goodroe
Jackie Goodroe
Tom Atchison

CROSS-ing AMERICA
Sharing Jesus Around The Nation

Elizabeth Atchison
Ann Hargis
Nick Southers
Erin Hoya
Dale Frost
La Vera Frost
Gene Gilcrease
John Poskey
Buddy Castleberry
Jan Castleberry
Joe Butters
Suzie Butters
Denny Jones
Billy Warren
James Cline
Max Walton
Paul Cook
Kerry Clements
Jim Kitchens
Bob Morehead
Howard Irion
Joe Penna
Pam Penna
Bobby Boudria
Zi Boudria
Tom Hebert
Joann Hebert
Doyle Pittman
Johnny Pittman
John A. Woods
Richard Partin
Gary Miller
Jim Coats
Jimmie Railey
Roger Niemann
Steve Parkey
Jerry Blackmon
Tip Harris

Leo Bell Lytle III
and Valerie Lynne Culp-Lytle

Johnny Rudisill
Dwight Whitman
Tom Hurst
Tim Warkentin
Don Wyatt
Mike Mayfield
Ed McClurg
Roger Sanders
Gerald Green
Sean Dillon
Seth Johnson
John Gayler
John Young
Mariann Young
Coy Read
Joy Noroozian
Jessie Wheeler
John Stanaland
Forrest Stanaland
Frank Whitehead
Shane Jernigan
Joe Donnell
Jeff Harris
Kerri Harris
Austin Harris
Hayley Harris
Ralph Hollingshead
Doug Matson
Jim Mobley
Joann Mobley
Mike Stutchman
Tommie Wells
Danny Williams
Jacob Willoughby
Ray Wooten
John Schoenrock
Tim Lewellen
Jenny Lewellen

Christopher Lewellen
Sydney Lewellen
Joseph Lewellen
Carson Still
Sue Sanders

Our Supporting Churches:

We are exceedingly blessed to have 12 supporting churches at the time of this book's submission to the publisher in November 2024. They are as follows, in alphabetical order: Christway Church in Bentley, Louisiana; Cornerstone Bible Church in Natalia, Texas; Faith Family Church in Burke, Texas; First Baptist Church Sallisaw in Sallisaw, Oklahoma; Friendship Baptist Church in Buchanan, Tennessee; Lakeside Baptist Church in Pineville, Louisiana; New Hope Baptist Church in Sparkman, Arkansas; Pine Valley Congregational Methodist Church in Pine Valley, Texas; Providence Baptist Church in Hudson, Texas; Temple Baptist Church in Clarksville, Texas; Trinity Baptist Church in Lufkin, Texas and Wisdom's Call Fellowship in Gonzales, Louisiana.

Pastors' and Wives' Names for Our Supporting Churches:

The following list includes the pastors' names and their wives' names for our 12 supporting churches on the eve of this book's publication; September 2025. In alphabetical order, they are:

Pastor Delbert Cates and wife Regina Cates for Christway Church in Bentley, Louisiana

Pastor Brian Casper and wife Diana Casper for Country Baptist Church in Natalia, Texas

Pastor Joe Sawyer and wife Virginia Sawyer for Faith Family Church in Burke, Texas.

Pastor Joe Taylor and wife Rebecca Taylor for First Baptist Church Sallisaw in Sallisaw, Oklahoma.

Pastor Russell Ragsdale and wife Debbie Ragsdale for Friendship Baptist Church in Buchanan, Tennessee

Pastor Tim Turnage and wife Stephanie Turnage for Lakeside Baptist Church in Pineville, Louisiana.

Leo Bell Lytle III
and Valerie Lynne Culp-Lytle

Pastor Wayne Daniell and wife Edwina Daniell for New Hope Baptist Church in Sparkman, Arkansas.

Pastor Bobby Whisenant and wife Karen Whisenant for Pine Valley Congregational Methodist Church in Pine Valley, Texas.

Pastor Bryan Lipscomb and wife Regina Lipscomb for Providence Baptist Church in Hudson, Texas.

Pastor Brandon Teague and wife Stephanie Teague for Temple Baptist Church in Clarksville, Texas.

Pastor Steve Cowart and wife Donna Cowart for Trinity Baptist Church in Lufkin, Texas

Pastor Gene Gayle and wife Kimberly Gayle for Wisdom's Call Fellowship in Gonzales, Louisiana.

Bibles:

Special thanks to Lynn and Rebecca Reid of Hudson, Texas for donating Bibles for us to give to new Believers. We also thank Temple Baptist Church in Clarksville, Texas for supplying Bibles.

Our supplier of the "Good News For You" booklets:

Church Growth International in Neosho, Missouri. Our ministry pays full-price for the booklets, but the people at Church Growth International are always patient and timely in shipping boxes to us quickly when we need them. They have told us in the past that our ministry is their number one customer in the nation for these booklets.

Christian Leather Key Ring Maker:
Louie Orgo of Paso Robles, California: "The Key Ring Guy"

Our Ministry Logo Designer:
Pastor Mike Robertson

Our Ministry Shirt Designer and Maker:
Roni Nettles

Our Handmade Sign Maker:
Cecilia Vann

Our van side panel sign designer:
Sherry Griffin at AAA Trophy Shop in Lufkin, Texas

Our local bankers who are so supportive:
Martha Trujillo, Barbara Corley and Vanessa Vargas with the Diboll,
Texas branch of Commercial Bank of Texas
Our local print shop staff members, endlessly patient with us:
Gina Renfro, Shelia Bizzell and Doug Rachunek at Kwik Kopy Printing
in Lufkin, Texas

Our van insurance agent, always so helpful:
Zach Ingram with State Farm Insurance in Lufkin, Texas. Prior to his
retirement, our helpful insurance agent was Steve McComb of Lufkin,
Texas. Both are members of Trinity Baptist Church in Lufkin.

Our Families:
Amid lives so incredibly blessed in so many ways, we also thank God for
our families. From our parents to our siblings and their spouses and our
children and their spouses and their children, we have been shown so
much love and support all these years, in so many ways. The following are
the names of our family members. We love and thank each of them.

Leo's parents: the late Nellie Mae Lytle and the late J. Fred Lytle

Leo's siblings: the late David Lytle, the late Judy Lytle Simmons and
husband Dr. David Simmons; Jane Lytle Gill and husband Kent Gill; Mark
Lytle and wife, the late Jennifer Lytle; Jill Lytle Ballio and husband Robert
Ballio; Jennie Lytle Wright and husband, the late William (Billy) Wright;
and the late Frank Lytle. These siblings and spouses have been a great
source of encouragement and support for our ministry.

Valerie's parents: Ida Mae Culp and the late David Merle Culp.
Mama is a prayer warrior on our behalf.

Valerie's siblings: Donna Culp-Hixon and husband Dan Hixon and
another sister and her husband who wish to remain anonymous. (Honor-
ary) "Nightmare Brother": Ryan Hassell. Ryan is a youth leader at Trinity
Baptist Church in Lufkin, Texas and also ministers faithfully to many elderly people. All of these siblings and spouses have been very supportive
of our ministry.

Leo Bell Lytle III
and Valerie Lynne Culp-Lytle

Our Children: Matt Lytle and his fiance Lacy Long, Adam Lytle and wife Sarah Lytle, Caleb Lytle and wife Peyton Lytle, Gideon Luke Lytle, Darren Samuel Lytle, our oldest daughter who wishes to remain anonymous, David Isaac Wilkerson and wife Aimee Wilkerson; and Christine Wilkerson. Again, our children and their spouses have been very supportive.

Our Grandchildren: Tyler Lytle, Erin Lytle, Shelby Lytle, Landry Lytle, Andrea Lytle, Chandler Lytle, Luke Lytle, Lake Lytle, Christian Jace Lytle, Ava Lytle, Georgia Lytle, Hazel Lytle, Matilda Lytle, Titus Leo-Paul Lytle, Heartley Wilkerson, Dominic Wilkerson, Clementine Wilkerson. Our **great-grandchildren** are Kayden Lane Mcmillian and Presley Ann Mcmillian.

Our Pet-Sitters/Plant-Waterers/House-Watchers:
Aimee, David Isaac and Heartley Wilkerson; Christine Wilkerson, Jacob Schroeder, Benny Little, Roni and Monty Nettles; and our oldest daughter

Technical Support:
Aimee and David Isaac Wilkerson; Christine Wilkerson, Jacob Schroeder and our oldest daughter

Occasional Airport Shuttle:
Aimee Wilkerson; Christine Wilkerson; Julie Luman, Roni and Monty Nettles and our oldest daughter

Ongoing friendship with help in many and varied ways:
(The range of this category includes donating large-print Bible study books from Providence Baptist Church to share on the road, to making gift packs for children from Pine Valley Congregational Methodist Church, to housing and feeding us so graciously during evangelism work at the Four States Fair in Texarkana, Arkansas, to providing the occasional celebratory platter of Laverne Brownies, to checking on our house after weather extremes, to sharing Bible study booklets when we ran out, and so much more):
Joann Bencivenga, Glenda Tobias, Julie Luman, Laverne Stanford, Dr. Kelly Stone and Donna Stone, Roni and Monty Nettles, Pam Bryce, Steve Bryce, T.J. Bryce, Doc and Jan Cathcart, John Ralph and Sandra Pouland, and Glen Brown. Plus so many more.

Writers of Endorsements:
Dr. Lee Brand, The Rev. Jeremiah Walpert, Dr. Richard Kaufman, Dr. Kent Leonard and Donna Leonard, The Rev. Lloyd Bye, The Rev. Dan Flyger and The Rev. Jeffrey Johnson

Publisher:
We thank Northeastern Baptist Press of Bennington, Vermont for pub-lishing our book. We thank Dr. Mark Ballard, president of Northeastern Baptist College, for telling us that if we would write it, Northeastern Baptist Press would publish it. We thank Tripper Stiles for patiently shepherding the book into print-readiness and for the cover design.

About The Authors

Leo and Valerie Lytle make their home in Pine Valley, Texas. Pine Valley is a small East Texas community outside of the city limits of Diboll, Texas, which is about two hours' drive north of Houston, Texas. Married since July 21, 2007, they have a blended family of eight children: six sons and two daughters. So far, they are blessed with 17 grandchildren and two great-grandchilden.

Leo owns and operates Lytle's Custom Woodcraft. He pastored for 33 years before becoming an evangelist and starting Leo Lytle Ministries in 2018. Leo preaches around the country at church services, revivals, Bible conferences, youth and children's camps and other special events.

Valerie is a former newspaper columnist, editor, and feature writer who still enjoys writing. She maintains an active license as a registered nurse in hopes of participating in medical mission trips. Valerie retired from nursing in December 2021 after working nearly 20 years as a full-time labor and delivery nurse. She also speaks in churches.

This is Leo and Valerie's first book. They are in the planning stages for several additional books, Lord willing.

Biographical information for each of them is as follows:

Leo Bell Lytle III

Leo Bell Lytle III was born in Shreveport, Louisiana. He was the seventh of eight children born to Nellie Mae Lytle and Joseph Fred Lytle of Shreveport, Louisiana. Leo was born again in 1975 at the age of 21. Here are some of his points of interest:

- Born in Shreveport, Louisiana in 1954 and reared in Louisiana
- Born again in 1975
- Formed the contemporary Christian group *"A New Day"* and recorded album in Dallas, Texas in 1976

- 1976-1980 Attended *East Texas Baptist College* in Marshall, Texas; *Louisiana State University-S* in Shreveport, Louisiana and *Northwestern State University* in Natchitoches, Louisiana
- Surrendered to the Gospel ministry in 1982 at *Pinecroft Baptist Church* in Shreveport, Louisiana under Pastor Joe Aulds
- Graduated from *The New Orleans Baptist Theological Seminary* in 1985
- 1984 to 2018 Served as music minister, youth minister, associate pastor and pastor of churches in Mississippi, Louisiana and Texas
- 1990s Founded *"Christians For Responsible Government"* a conservative Christian action organization
- 1990s Founder, editor and publisher of *"The Watchman"* a monthly statewide conservative Christian newspaper in Louisiana
- 1992 to 1994 Host of *"Viewpoint Radio Talk Show"* in Alexandria, Louisiana
- 1986 to present, served as Teacher/Trainer in *Evangelism Explosion III International*
- 1999 to present, owner/operator of *Lytle's Custom Woodcraft*
- 2018 to present, established and operates *Leo Lytle Ministries*

Leo Bell Lytle III
and Valerie Lynne Culp-Lytle

Valerie Lynne Culp-Lytle

Valerie Lynne Culp-Lytle was born in Lufkin, Texas. She was the first of three children born to Ida Mae Culp and David Culp. Valerie accepted Jesus Christ as her personal Savior in December 1972 at the age of 12. Here are some of her points of interest:

- Born in Lufkin, Texas. Grew up in various East Texas towns.
- Saved in 1972 at the age of 12
- Graduated in 1978 from **Hudson High School**.
- Graduated from **The University of Texas at Austin** in 1983 with a Bachelor of Journalism degree
- Worked in various levels from part-time/full-time/part-time off and on as columnist/editor/feature writer at **The Lufkin Daily News** from 1976 to 1980; 1983 to 2003.
- Became Licensed Paramedic after completing the Emergency Medical Technician Program at **Angelina College** in 2000
- Earned Associate of Applied Science Degree in Emergency Medical Services from **Angelina College** in Lufkin, Texas in 2002
- Earned Associate of Applied Science Degree in Nursing from **Angelina College** in Lufkin, Texas in 2002
- Worked full-time as a labor and delivery registered nurse from June 2002 to December 2021, first at **The University of Texas Medical Branch John Sealy** and then at **Nacogdoches Memorial Hospital**.
- Retired from nursing in December 2021, in part to be able to more fully participate in the Kingdom work of **Leo Lytle Ministries**.
- Hopes to complete a master's degree in Christian Apologetics from Liberty University

www.ingramcontent.com/pod-product-compliance
Lightning Source LLC
Chambersburg PA
CBHW030403130626
46549CB00004B/1614